Don Werner

Global
Assignments

J. Stewart Black
Hal B. Gregersen
Mark E. Mendenhall

Global Assignments

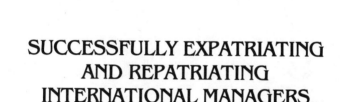

SUCCESSFULLY EXPATRIATING
AND REPATRIATING
INTERNATIONAL MANAGERS

Jossey-Bass Publishers · San Francisco

For sales outside the United States contact Maxwell Macmillan International Publishing Group, 866 Third Avenue, New York, New York 10022.

Manufactured in the United States of America

The paper used in this book is acid-free and meets the State of California requirements for recycled paper (50 percent recycled waste, including 10 percent postconsumer waste), which are the strictest guidelines for recycled paper currently in use in the United States.

10% POST CONSUMER WASTE

Library of Congress Cataloging-in-Publication Data

Black, J. Stewart, date.
   Global assignments : successfully expatriating and repatriating international managers / J. Stewart Black, Hal B. Gregersen, Mark E. Mendenhall. — 1st ed.
      p.   cm.—(The Jossey-Bass management series)
   Includes bibliographical references and index.
   ISBN 1-55542-473-2 (alk. paper)
   1. Executives—Employment—Foreign countries.   2. Employment in foreign countries.   3. Cross-cultural orientation.   I. Gregersen, Hal B., date.   II. Mendenhall, Mark E., date.   III. Title.
IV. Series.
HD38.2.B595   1992
650.14'024658—dc20   92-13928
                                                                         CIP

FIRST EDITION
HB Printing   10 9 8 7 6 5 4 3 2 1   *Code 9271*

The
Jossey-Bass
Management
Series

Contents

Part Three: During the Assignment

Part Four: After the Assignment

Preface

The rapid globalization of business and its impact on firms are beyond dispute. The debate in corporate boardrooms now focuses on how firms should respond to the demand of being globally integrated but also responsive to the needs of different local markets. If multinational firms are to prosper now and in the future, they must develop people who can successfully formulate and implement strategies, invent and utilize technologies, and create and coordinate information in a global context. In this book, we argue that global assignments are critical to the development of global leaders and the deployment of people who can successfully manage worldwide coordination and control functions as well as cross-border information exchanges.

We took on the challenge of writing *Global Assignments* for two reasons. The first reason is the relatively high frequency and high cost of failures associated with global assignments. Such failures as premature return, poor performance, and repatriation turnover are common and can cost even a moderately sized multinational corporation tens of millions of dollars per year. The personal costs, in terms of damaged careers, failed marriages, and substance abuse, are perhaps even more tragic. The second reason why we wrote this book is that strategically designed global assignment systems (selection, training, cross-cultural adjustment, performance appraisal, reward and compensation, commitment, and repatriation) can significantly enhance the global competitiveness of firms and be an essential experience for the growth and development of future leaders.

All three of us have lived overseas with our families. We have experienced and seen firsthand significant losses and profits to organizations and individuals, the results of poorly or well-designed global assignment systems. These experiences gave us real understanding of the issues and intense motivation to provide a systematic guide for constructing effective systems. Such systems should provide critical links in the development of global executives for the future, facilitate the ability of firms to integrate worldwide operations and remain responsive to differences in local markets, and make the global assignment an experience of growth and enjoyment for individuals and their families.

Audience

Firms have been utilizing international assignments for years. What has been missing is a systematic understanding of whom to select; how to train people; how to determine the factors that affect their adjustment, performance, or commitment; and how to keep and utilize people once they return home. There has been an increase in scholarly research on the topic recently, but much of it has remained tucked away in academic journals, unknown to the executives who could benefit most from this knowledge.

Therefore, we wrote this book primarily for executives who must deal with the global economy and the strategic role of people in achieving international competitiveness. The audience includes chief executive officers (CEOs), line managers, and especially human resource management executives. The contents of this book are designed to give executives a sophisticated but practical understanding of the strategic roles of global assignments, as well as the dynamics of the full cycle of these assignments. The book is organized so that virtually each chapter examines a specific problem concerning global assignments, explains the underlying principles for understanding the problem, provides a framework for analyzing the issue, and presents recommendations that executives can follow in redesigning or enhancing current systems.

Overview of the Contents

The book covers every major aspect of global assignments. Chapter One sets out the strategic roles that global assignments can play and discusses how those roles must be adjusted to the firm's particular stage of globalization. Chapter Two provides a general explanation of the process of cross-cultural adjustment, which is critical for people to work and live effectively in foreign cultures. Chapter Three examines the issue of selecting people for global assignments and addresses both whom should be selected and how they should be chosen. Chapter Four tackles the challenge of effectively training people so that they perform effectively while overseas. Specifically, the chapter provides a framework so that firms will not over- or underinvest in the training needs of people sent on foreign assignments. Chapter Five describes the specific factors that affect successful cross-cultural adjustment and points out ways for firms to facilitate the process. Chapter Six offers pioneering insights into the dynamics of global assignees' dual allegiance—to the parent firm and to the local foreign operation—and discusses how firms can foster "dual citizens," or employees with high allegiance to both organizations. Chapter Seven examines the difficulties of effectively appraising employees while they are on foreign assignments and provides a model of how this critical task can be performed effectively. Chapter Eight explores the high compensation costs for expatriate employees and outlines a means of significantly reducing those costs while improving employees' motivation to accept and perform well in global assignments. Chapter Nine discusses the process of coming home and the factors that affect repatriation adjustment and job performance, and it outlines specific steps that firms can take to facilitate adjustment and job performance after repatriation. Chapter Ten explains the factors that determine whether high-performing repatriated managers will stay with the firm or leave. In particular, this chapter provides recommendations for keeping and utilizing high-performance managers and executives after global assignments. Chapter Eleven summarizes and integrates the critical elements of the full cycle of the global assignment. It also provides descriptions of firms using "best practices" concerning selection, training, appraisal, compensation, and repatriation.

Acknowledgments

We owe thanks to many people and organizations. First we must acknowledge the support and understanding of our wives—Janet Black, Ann Gregersen, and Janet Mendenhall—for their willingness to live in Japan, Finland, and Switzerland. We are also grateful to the many men and women who shared with us their experiences of working and living in foreign countries. We thank the schools of business at Brigham Young University; the University of California, Irvine; the University of Tennessee, Chattanooga; and Dartmouth College. We are grateful as well to Gary Oddou, Lyman Porter, Greg Stephens, and other colleagues who have collaborated with us and supported our work over the years.

July 1992   J. Stewart Black
                                    Hanover, New Hampshire

                                    Hal B. Gregersen
                                    Hanover, New Hampshire

                                    Mark E. Mendenhall
                                    Chattanooga, Tennessee

The Authors

J. Stewart Black is associate professor of business administration in the Amos Tuck School of Business Administration at Dartmouth College. He received his B.A. degree (1983) with honors in behavioral science and English, and his M.S. degree (1984) with distinction in organizational behavior from Brigham Young University, and his Ph.D. degree (1988) in administration from the University of California, Irvine. Black's main research activities focus on strategic human resource management and international assignments. He has been a consultant for many Japanese and American multinational firms, on issues concerning international human resource management, cross-cultural negotiations, and participative decision-making systems. He has lived in Japan on different occasions, for a total of over four years, and speaks Japanese fluently. He received a University of California Regent's Fellowship, coauthored a paper that received the Best Paper Award from the International Management Division of the Academy of Management, and is a member of the Beta Gamma Sigma Honor Society.

Black has published over thirty articles in academic and practitioner journals, including *Academy of Management Journal, Academy of Management Review, Journal of International Business Studies, Sloan Management Review, Human Resource Management*, and *Personnel*. He is also serving a three-year term as the newsletter editor for the International Management Division of the Academy of Management.

Black and his wife Janet have three children—Jared, Nathaniel, and Kendra.

Hal B. Gregersen is a visiting assistant professor of business administration in the Amos Tuck School of Business Administration at Dartmouth College. He received his B.A. degree (1981) in management from the University of Utah, his M.S. degree (1983) with distinction in organizational behavior from Brigham Young University, and his Ph.D. degree (1989) in administration from the University of California, Irvine. He completed a Fulbright Fellowship for research and teaching at the Turku School of Economics and Business Administration, Turku, Finland. Gregersen's primary research projects have focused on general strategic human resource management issues and on topics such as the conflicts of commitment and loyalty that expatriates face during global assignments. He has published a variety of articles on expatriates and commitment in academic and practitioner journals, including *Academy of Management Journal, Journal of Applied Psychology, Personnel Psychology, Journal of International Business Studies*, and *Sloan Management Review*. He also regularly consults with firms in the United States, Canada, and Finland, and his projects include workshops, executive seminars, and organizational diagnostics on managing strategic change, developing global executives, implementing effective international human resource policies, and empowering employees in worldwide operations.

In addition to researching and consulting on global assignments, Gregersen has experienced the challenges of living overseas for three years in Finland, where he learned to speak Finnish. He and his wife Ann have traveled widely with their children—Matthew, Ryan, and Amber.

Mark E. Mendenhall holds the J. Burton Frierson Chair of Excellence in Business Leadership at the University of Tennessee, Chattanooga. He received his B.S. degree (1980) in psychology and his Ph.D. degree (1983) in social psychology, both from Brigham Young University. Mendenhall's main research activities have been in the area of human resource management, especially cross-cultural adjustment of expatriate managers, and Japanese organizational behavior. His research interests stem from his experiences of growing up in a multicultural community outside Hamilton, New Zealand, and completing a two-year assignment in Japan.

He is coauthor (with G. Oddou) of *Readings and Cases in International Human Resource Management* (1991) and (with D. Ricks and B. J. Punnett) of *International Management* (1993). Besides being a weekly columnist for the *Chattanooga Times*, Mendenhall is a consultant who conducts workshops and seminars on cross-cultural adjustment, Japanese management systems, and leadership development. Active in the Academy of Management, he is currently serving on the executive board of the International Division and will become president of that division in 1993. He also serves on the editorial boards of *Journal of International Business Studies* and *Human Resource Planning*.

Mendenhall has traveled widely and has lived overseas for almost one-fourth of his life, in New Zealand, Japan, and Switzerland. He and his wife Janet have three children—Anthony, Nicole, and Alexis.

Global
Assignments

Part One

Strategic
Global Assignments

Chapter 1

◯

The Strategic Roles
of Global Assignments

Why are some firms able to compete successfully in the world marketplace, while others lose or fail to gain global competitive advantage? Some say that technological innovation is the key. Others say that strategy is the key. Still others say that structure is the key.

Our thesis is that people are the key. People invent and utilize technology, people formulate and implement strategy, and people design and build organization structures.

In today's global marketplace, to get the right people with the right skills inventing and utilizing technology, formulating and implementing strategy, and designing and building organization structures at the right place and at the right time, movement is needed—movement of people across national borders. In this chapter, we explain why people and their effective movement and management across borders can play strategic roles in global competitiveness. In subsequent chapters, we will integrate the best practices, thinking, and scientific evidence to provide a sophisticated but feasible guide for effectively using those strategic roles.

Strategic Roles of Global Assignments

U.S. firms tend not to use global assignments for strategic purposes (this is perhaps less true of European and Japanese multinational firms). Global assignments are critical, however, both to strategy formulation and to implementation. There are key strategic roles that global assignments can play: in succession planning and managerial development, in coordination and control, and in information sharing and exchange.

Succession Planning and Global Assignments

A recent survey[1] found that the primary strategic concern of CEOs was management development. CEOs saw the development of managerial talent as a critical aspect of the formulation and implementation of corporate strategy. Greater managerial talent at the middle levels of organizations is needed to effectively implement strategic plans developed by top management. Greater managerial talent is also needed at the top to formulate the strategy of the future more effectively. In today's business environment, neither strategy formulation nor implementation can be effectively conducted without careful consideration of the global context.

Developments in the global marketplace present breathtaking opportunities and threats to managers in the 1990s and beyond. Consider the following factors, for example:

- The democratization of Eastern Europe
- The unification of Germany
- Emerging trading blocs (the U.S.–Canada, Western Europe)
- Invasion of foreign firms into domestic markets
- Liberalization of financial markets (Great Britain, Japan)
- Protectionist moves of some governments

To formulate or implement strategic plans for the twenty-first century effectively, managers and executives will need the ability to focus on the unique needs of local foreign customers, suppliers, labor pools, government policies, and technology and, at the same time, on general trends in the world marketplace. At the individual level, this requires tremendous environmental scanning abilities, just to pick up the information. It requires vast knowledge and processing abilities, to categorize and interpret raw data effectively. It requires managers who can understand and effectively work with people from different cultural, religious, and ethnic backgrounds and the ability to manage teams composed of cross-cultural members. Managers who fail to develop these skills, and organizations that fail to develop these managers, risk being irrelevant in the 1990s and beyond. Global assignments can be a very effective means of developing the skills and knowledge that future leaders will need. For example, General Electric (GE) estimates that 25 percent of its managers will need global assignments in order to gain the knowledge and experience necessary to understand the global markets, customers, suppliers, and competitors the company will face in the 1990s and beyond. Because Colgate-Palmolive, in the mid 1980s, had a hard time finding high-quality people for top posts with international responsibilities, it began a program of systematically providing opportunities for high-potential managers to work in a variety of global markets, in order to develop the leadership skills required for its top international and corporate positions. These are just two examples of the increasing number of companies where people are seen as the key to the effective formulation and implementation of corporate strategy in today's global marketplace, and where global assignments serve a strategic role in the successful development of people and necessary skills.

Coordination and Control Systems and Global Assignments

Global assignments can also play a strategic role in the coordination and control of international corporations. In today's global business environment, the effective coordination and control of units throughout the world is complicated by three factors. First, transportation and communications technology have shrunk the world, in one sense, but also expanded it. We can now phone virtually any spot in the world in a matter of minutes or seconds, and we can get anywhere in the world in a matter of hours. Because communications and transportation were more difficult and time-consuming in the past, not every place in the world was part of normal business operations; the whole world has always been out there, but it has not always been relevant, accessible, or included. Today it is. Consider N. V. Philips, headquartered in the Netherlands. It now operates in sixty different countries, on every continent in the world. It has subsidiaries from Austria to Zimbabwe, from New York to New Zealand, ranging in size from five to five thousand employees. The coordination and control aspects of this worldwide network are staggering.

The second factor is the breadth and depth of cultural diversity, and all its implications for customers, suppliers, workers, and governmental relations. For example, what might be construed as a bribe in one country or culture is considered normal business practice in another; low costs may be a key in one market, while technology and quality may be essential to another. Consider Vacuum General, Inc., a medium-sized manufacturer of pressure-control devices. It bought Tylan Corp., a manufacturer of mass gas-flow systems, for its subsidiaries in Germany, France, and the United Kingdom. This merger gave Vacuum General a new name— Tylan General—and access to the European semiconductor-equipment market. Each European unit had been run autonomously, however, and each focused on different things. Top management found it extremely difficult to coordinate many aspects of purchasing, marketing, and manufacturing across its U.S. and new European units. As David Ferran, CEO of Tylan General has commented, "Sometimes we talk with the manager [of the foreign subsidiary] and think that they bought in. Then we learn later that it isn't happening. Maybe it is poor communication, or maybe they don't want to understand."[2]

The third factor is the greater geographical dispersion of operations around the world and the resulting greater potential for conflicting demands from governments of the various countries involved. For example, one country may demand the transfer of a particular technology, while the home-country government restricts that particular transfer; the subsidiary in one country may produce technical specialists who are needed in a subsidiary in another country, but the immigration of those specialists may be prohibited because of their nationality. Consider the case of Nike in China. In the mid 1980s, Nike had set up a production agreement with a

Chinese manufacturing operation to produce running shoes, primarily for export sales. Although China offered substantial savings in terms of labor expenses, local Chinese management and workers lacked the technological know-how to produce the quantity and quality of shoes that Nike desired. Nike's most efficient and advanced operations were in Korea, but when Nike tried to send technical specialists from Korea to China, to help the Chinese operation improve its production methods, the Korean workers were denied even temporary visas, primarily because of the political relationship between North Korea and China and the political tension between North Korea and South Korea. Eventually, in an effort to transfer at least some technological know-how to the Chinese operation, Nike officials made tapes of the training and instruction that they had hoped the Korean workers would provide in person.

Geographical distance, cultural diversity, and conflicting governmental demands push firms toward fragmented strategy and operations and increase the importance and difficulty of effective coordination and control. Policies and manuals can sometimes facilitate coordination and control, but they are subject to translation, interpretation, and execution differences often caused by local conditions (culture, government policies, economy, and so on). Furthermore, as subsidiaries grow and mature, such resources as capital, technology, and expertise may not provide sufficient leverage for home-office control.[3] Like maturing children, subsidiaries may want more freedom, and, they may resist direction and control from the parent company. Global assignments are an effective means of placing individuals with shared objectives and interpretations in key positions around the world, to serve as critical sources and means of coordination and control.

Information Systems and Global Assignments

Geographical distance, cultural diversity, complex local and global demand or supply conditions, dispersed innovations, and so on, create a tremendous need for sharing and exchanging information among the various units of an international firm. Information can flow primarily into the foreign subsidiary, out of it, in both directions, or in neither direction.[4] Except in a totally insulated and isolated subsidiary, the flow of information is an important strategic function. Such mechanisms as newsletters and intracompany conferences are ways of facilitating a certain level of information sharing and exchange. Nevertheless, in their ability to facilitate the gathering and exchange of complex information, global assignments are unique in at least two respects.

First, global assignments, because of their length (typically two to five years), provide the requisite time to gather and convey complex information. Whether the exchange involves the transfer of technology from one subsidiary to another or the communication of local customer and supplier relationships to the parent, global assignments provide the time necessary to gather, communicate, interpret, understand, and utilize complex information. One important but often neglected aspect of this information exchange concerns what takes place after the global assignment. Placing Mr. Smith in the firm's Brazilian operation can facilitate the exchange of information between corporate headquarters and the local operation during his global ssignment; and, after Mr. Smith returns home, what he learned about such elements as the Brazilian market, local competitors, and international competitors operating in Brazil can be transferred to corporate headquarters and incorporated into future strategic planning and decision making.

Second, the relationships that are developed between people during international assignments can facilitate communication even after the people are not working in the same organizational unit or location. The relationship developed between Mr. Smith and Mr. Ferrer makes it easier in the future for Mr. Ferrer, in Brazil, to tell Mr. Smith, in New York, about an emerging technology being developed by a domestic Brazilian competitor, or about a change in the Brazilian government's policy, which could affect all the firm's Latin American operations.

In summary, international assignments can be a critical means of achieving strategic objectives. They are vital to the development of the global managers who will be needed in the succession plans of international firms. They are extremely valuable in the coordination and control of a firm's worldwide operations, and they are effective in the exchange of information, both during and after the time abroad.

Changing the Myopic View of Global Assignments

Despite the strategic role that international transfers can play, many executives have a rather narrow and myopic view of how they can be used and of who should be involved in them. Most U.S. firms make global assignments primarily on the basis of the needs of a given position and the inability to fill it with a host-country employee.[5] Succession planning and managerial development are often irrelevant criteria in the day-to-day reality of the decision makers responsible for global assignments. Succession planning becomes replacement planning, and what is urgent drives out what is important.[6]

Even when executives do begin to focus on the strategic role that global assignments can play in terms of managerial development, coordination and control, and information exchange, that focus is typically directed toward the assignment of home-country nationals to foreign subsidiaries. Two factors combine to create a focus on the strategic role that global assignments can play for host-country managers.

First, many foreign governments are pressuring the multinational firms that operate within their borders to "localize" management—that is, to develop and promote local managers to positions of responsibility. Second, many firms have discovered that local managers—who are generally born, raised, and educated in the local country and spend most of their careers in the local subsidiary— often have a tendency to be oversensitive to local conditions, to view nonlocals as alien, and to misunderstand or even fight corporate directives, plans, and strategy. Host-country managers who do not understand the parent firm, its global strategy, or how other foreign subsidiaries are related to one another often become liabilities rather than assets. This factor has led firms to think about and utilize global assignments and foreign nationals for the three strategic purposes mentioned earlier. For example, Kodak has a program whereby high-potential host-country managers are identified and then sent on global assignments to important operations in the United States. Such assignments are designed to serve all three strategic purposes. The overseas assignments facilitate strategic succession planning and managerial development by providing these managers with experience outside the home country, to broaden their perspective, enhance their knowledge base, heighten their interpersonal and communication skills, and improve their ability to assume higher positions back home. The assignments enhance the coordination and control functions of the corporation by socializing the individuals into the Kodak culture and philosophy. They also facilitate the sharing of information between the foreign managers and domestic U.S. managers. It is not necessary, however, for a host-country national to be sent on a global assignment only to the country of the parent firm. Ford Motor Company increasingly transfers foreign nationals to "third countries"—that is, countries that are foreign both to the individual and to the parent firm. Officials at Ford believe that such global assignments can develop managers with the necessary leadership skills for the future, facilitate coordination and control functions between the parent and subsidiaries and among subsidiaries, and enhance the sharing and exchange of information throughout Ford's worldwide network.

In short, although global assignments are most often utilized to "fight fires," they can also be utilized for strategic objectives. Moreover, while it is important that global assignments be utilized for strategic roles where home-country employees are concerned, it is perhaps equally important to do the same for host-country employees.

Costs of Poorly Managed Global Assignments

At this point, some readers may be convinced of the strategic role of global assignments, and others may not be. Whether global assignments are used to "fight fires" or develop future leaders, it is important to describe the wide-ranging and severe costs that the improper design and execution of global assignments can create. These costs can be roughly divided into four categories: failed assignments, "brownouts," turnover after repatriation, and downward-spiraling vicious cycles.

Failed Assignments

The proportion of U.S. expatriates who fail in their global assignments (that is, who ask or are asked to return prematurely) is approximately 20 percent.[7] This means that approximately one in five U.S. expatriates sent overseas will fail. The failure rates for European and Japanese firms is less than half this rate. (The factors that explain U.S. expatriates' failures, as well as the difference between the failure rates of U.S. and European or Japanese firms, are examined in more detail in Chapter Five.)

Direct Moving Costs. The first and most direct costs of failed assignments are those associated with physical replacement. It costs significant sums of money to ship an expatriate and his or her family (85 percent of U.S. expatriates are married[8]) and belongings overseas. A typical transfer to London from the United States might cost $30,000 to $35,000.[9] It would cost another $30,000 to bring the expatriate and family home, and another $30,000 to $35,000 to send a replacement. Thus, the direct shipping costs alone can be over $100,000 for a failed assignment.

Downtime Costs. During the expatriate's predeparture preparations, there is a period in which the individual is receiving a full salary but is not performing his or her duties fully. There is also a time, during the first few months of the global assignment, when the expatriate is adjusting to the new culture, the environment, and the job. This is natural. The problem in the case of failed assignments is twofold. First, unlike expatriates who recover, adjust to, and perform well in overseas positions, those who fail provide no long-term return on downtime. Second, once an expatriate is overseas, the base salary, foreign-service premium, housing allowance, education allowance, cost-of-living differential, tax-adjustment allowance, and so on, usually at least double the total compensation package, and this doubles the cost of the adjustment downtime, for which there is no long-term return in the case of a failed global assignment.

Indirect Damage. In addition to these more measurable economic costs, there are significant indirect, difficult-to-measure costs to both the organization and the individual. In the case of the organization, a failed global assignment can result in damage to several important constituencies, including local national employees, host-government officials, and local suppliers, customers, and community members. If these damages occur, it will probably be harder for the replacement, even the most capable one, to repair them and effectively carry out other duties and tasks. Despite the difficulty of quantifying these costs, they are sometimes the most significant ones. In the case of the individual, it is unlikely that a failed global assignment will help his or her career or self-esteem. In fact, many expatriates we have interviewed over the years said that they stayed in their global assignments only because they feared the negative consequences of leaving early.

"Brownouts"

"Brownouts" are managers who do not return prematurely but are nevertheless ineffective in the performance and execution of their responsibilities. Some have estimated that between 30 percent and 50 percent of all U.S. expatriates fall into this category.[10]

Perhaps the best way to illustrate some of the costs associated with poor performance during the international assignment is through a recent experience at General Electric.[11] In the mid 1980s, GE went through a massive strategic restructuring. As part of that restructuring, medical technology became one of GE's core business areas. GE's stated goal was for all strategic business units (SBUs) to be in first or second place among their worldwide competitors.

In an effort to increase its global strategic position in medical technology (especially imaging technology), GE took control of Cie Générale de Radiologie (CGR) in 1988. CGR was a French medical equipment manufacturer owned by the state and run much like a government ministry. GE got CGR and $800 million in cash from state-controlled Thomson S.A. in return for GE's RCA consumer electronics business. The acquisition of CGR was viewed by many as a brilliant strategic move, and GE projected a $25 million profit for the first full year of operations. Things did not go as the strategic planners had projected, however.

One of the first things GE did was to organize a training seminar for the French managers. GE left T-shirts with the slogan "Go for One" for each of the participants. Although the French managers wore them, many were not happy about it. One manager stated, "It was like Hitler was back, forcing us to wear uniforms. It was humiliating."

Soon after the takeover, GE also sent U.S. specialists to France, to fix CGR's accounting system. Unfortunately, these specialists knew very little about French accounting or reporting requirements, and they tried to impose a GE system that was inappropriate for French reporting requirements and for the way CGR had traditionally kept records. This problem (and the working out of an agreeable compromise) took several months and resulted in substantial direct and indirect costs.

GE then tried to coordinate and integrate CGR into its Milwaukee-based medical equipment unit. Because CGR had racked up a $25 million loss, instead of the projected $25 million profit, an executive from Milwaukee was sent to fix things at CGR. Several cost-cutting measures, including massive layoffs and the closing of roughly half of the twelve CGR plants, shocked the French workforce. The profit-hungry culture of GE continued to clash with the state-run uncompetitive culture of CGR.

GE's efforts to integrate CGR into the GE culture, by putting up English-language posters everywhere and flying GE flags, met with considerable resistance from the French employees. One union leader commented, "They came in here bragging, 'We are GE, we're the best and we've got the methods.'" The reaction was so strong that a significant number of French managers and engineers left GE-CGR, and the total workforce shrank from 6,500 to 5,000. Although GE officials had estimated that GE-CGR would produce a profit in 1990, the expected loss for 1990 was another $25 million.

In this case example, we do not mean to point an accusing finger at GE; most experts view GE as a well-run multinational corporation. The example does illustrate the costs of poorly designed or poorly executed global assignments, however. Managers on global assignments who do not perform well often do not provide an adequate return on investment, and they may initiate programs or projects that cost time and money and damage relationships that are difficult to repair. They may even drive out high-potential local managers who will be needed in the future.

Turnover After Repatriation

Repatriation is perhaps the least carefully considered aspect of global assignments. Unfortunately for U.S. firms, the proportion of managers who quit and leave within one year after repatriation is approximately 20 percent.[12] On the average, firms spend $150,000 to $250,000 on all expenses (salary, allowances, and so on) for each manager overseas each year. Thus, for the average four-year assignment, the firm invests close to $1 million in each manager. This investment is especially important if the assignment is part of succession planning and the managerial development agenda. On the average, U.S. firms face a 20 percent chance that they will receive no long-term return on this substantial investment. They may even have to duplicate these investments in order to develop replacements. The factors that contribute to repatriation adjustment and turnover problems are explored in detail in Chapter Nine; the important point here is the tremendous expense that the poor management of repatriation can produce.

Downard-Spiraling Vicious Cycles

All these costs can combine to create circumstances that set off a downward-spiraling vicious cycle, which may erode or even destroy a firm's global competitive advantage. Failed global assignments, rumors of "brownouts," and repatriation turnover problems can lead the best and the brightest throughout an organization's worldwide operations to view global assignments as the kiss of death for their careers. This reputation makes it difficult to recruit and send top-quality candidates, which in turn increases the likelihood of more failures. This downward-spiraling quality of candidates and performance can feed on itself, gaining momentum with every turn. The firm may stop sending anyone on assignment outside the home country, which in turn can lead to more difficult coordination and control, as well as to problems with information exchange. Perhaps most important, this vicious cycle may lead to a shortage of leaders who have vital international understanding and experience, which in turn can lead to poor strategic planning and implementation and to an ever-worsening global competitive position.

Many managers and executives may feel that such a scenario is unlikely, but this type of cycle is easier to start than might be expected, and it is much more difficult to stop or reverse than one might estimate. Therefore, to fulfill the strategic roles that global assignments can play, or simply to avoid the staggering costs that poorly managed assignments can produce, the organization must provide a framework of effective people management and international assignments.

Framework for People Management and Global Assignments

Before we explore how global assignments and the people in them can be successfully managed, it will be useful to provide a basic framework for discussion and recommendations. From our perspective, the effective movement and management of people in global assignments is most logically framed in terms of the generic issue of people management. Although the term *people management* is often used as if everyone had the same idea of what it means, we all have very different ideas of what is actually involved. Here, we will briefly discuss our conceptualization of the term.

Five Dimensions of People Management

We view people management not as a function of a specific department (such as personnel or human resources) but as a set of activities that any manager in any functional area of a firm must master. To simplify, let us say that there are five generic functions of managing people.[13]

Getting the Right People (Staffing). First, a manager must identify, recruit, and place individuals in appropriate positions within the organization. Sometimes this process involves people who are already in the company, and sometimes it involves hiring individuals from outside. This first aspect of people management also includes activities associated with determining the types and numbers of individuals who will be needed in the future for certain positions and examining the existing pool of people who could meet those needs. At the corporate level, this raises such questions as, "Are managers with the necessary skills and experience in strategic positions throughout the firm's global operations?"

Most U.S. multinationals select individuals for overseas assignments on the basis of these employees' records in the United States. Although this is one important criterion, it does not guarantee success overseas. Research has demonstrated that it is important to examine several other factors in selecting individuals for international work.[14] (Chapter Two details the problems that firms face in selecting candidates for global assignments and discusses common practices, their consequences, the principles that explain why some practices are more effective than others, and how firms can successfully structure staffing and selection practices for global assignments.)

Helping People Do the Right Thing (Training). Next, the jobs that managers are expected to do and the standards by which performance will be judged must be determined, and the necessary training must be provided. This point raises the question of whether a firm's managers, who must deal with employees, customers, suppliers, or competitors from different cultures and countries, are adequately trained to understand and work successfully with these various groups. The vast majority of U.S. multinational firms fail to adequately prepare individuals to work with individuals from other cultures. In fact, approximately 70 percent of Americans who must work overseas receive no training or preparation at all for their international work.[15] (Chapter Three details common practices and consequences in U.S. corporations, the dynamics that explain why training is or is not effective, and how effective training programs for global assignments can be designed and implemented.)

Determining How People Are Doing (Appraising). Once an employee has been trained, his or her performance must be measured. Measuring the job performance of managers who have been sent overseas is tricky, however. For example, if such traditional U.S. variables as profit, sales, and market share are utilized as quantitative measures, should factors that apply to the local business environment, such as movements in exchange rates, be incorporated into the performance evaluation as well? Most firms have little idea of which specific factors facilitate or inhibit cross-cultural adjustment, organizational commitment, or job performance during an overseas assignment. (Chapters Four, Five, and Six detail the important factors and the underlying processes that affect these outcomes, and these chapters also describe effective means of enhancing and measuring adjustment, commitment, and job performance.)

Encouraging the Right Things That People Do (Rewarding). In addition to measuring an individual's job performance, the organization must provide rewards for specific performance behavior, as well as general compensation and benefits. This aspect of people management raises such questions as, "Should all managers receive equal benefits and bonuses, regardless of the countries in which they are working?" Most firms complain about the high costs of global assignments, and many firms have cut the total number of expatriates to reduce costs. In the absence of understanding or analysis of the reward systems for global managers, this is unlikely to reduce costs per expatriate or improve the performance of individual managers. (Chapter Seven details common practices and consequences in the area of compensation and rewards and discusses the dynamics that motivate global managers and how reward systems can be structured to enhance motivation and performance during global assignments.)

Doing Things Right for People (Developing). Finally, over the long term, a sequence of positions, opportunities, responsibilities, and so forth, will be needed in order to develop the maximum potential of managers. This aspect of management raises such questions as, "How should managers sent on international assignments be utilized once they return?" There is strong evidence that U.S. firms in general do very little planning for the systematic development of global managers.[16] Specifically, most U.S. firms do little planning for the return and integration of global managers who have been overseas for some time. Many of these managers are dissatisfied with their jobs and responsibilities upon returning to the United States; one in five leaves the firm within a year after repatriation. (Chapters Nine and Ten detail the factors and processes that affect repatriation adjustment, commitment, and turnover and describe how firms can manage this aspect of global assignments more effectively. Chapter Eleven pulls all the separate aspects of successfully managing people and global assignments into a comprehensive system and places it in the context of what the business environment is likely to be as we look into the year 2000.)

People Management in the Global Context

The framework for the remaining chapters suggests that all five aspects of people management during global transfers are the same for any firm, regardless of its particular stage or degree of globalization. This is both true and false, of course.

It is true that, regardless of a firm's particular stage or degree of globalization, a global manager still needs to be hired, trained, evaluated, rewarded, and developed. There are slight differences, however, depending on whether the candidate is a home-country or foreign-country national. Table 1.1 provides a brief overview of different management questions for each of the five functions of people management.

Patterns of Globalization

Although the five aspects of people management apply to all firms engaged in transferring people across national borders, important differences do emerge as a function of the stage or pattern of a firm's globalization.[17] When we use the term *globalization,* we have in mind not one fixed point at which a firm is globalized but rather a series of stages or patterns of globalization. Although Table 1.1 does provide a general set of questions that practically any firm with international operations would encounter, specific questions, problems, and solutions concerning people management in global assignments vary according to the nature of a given firm's pattern of globalization. Therefore, we now offer a brief description of four basic stages of globalization.[18]

Export Firms. Export-oriented firms have most of their value-chain activities in one or a very few countries and have little coordination among global organizational units.[19] Firms of this type, such as

Table 1.1. Global Employee–People Management Matrix: Functions of People Management.

	Staffing	Training	Appraising	Rewarding	Developing
Global Managers	What characteristics should be utilized in selecting expatriates? What level of expatriates should be utilized? Why are employees likely to accept/reject expatriate assignments? Under what conditions should a third-country versus a home-country national be utilized as an expatriate? How can a larger pool of potential international managers be created?	What training should be given to an expatriate before an international assignment? How can the cost effectiveness of training be calculated?	How can expatriate performance be monitored in light of exogenous factors, such as exchange-rate fluctuations? What is the appropriate mix of quantitative and qualitative measures of expatriate job performance? To what extent should locals be involved in evaluating expatriate job performance?	To what extent should an expatriate compensation package be utilized, to entice employees to accept overseas assignments versus equalizing cost-of-living expenses? How should different tax laws for expatriates from different home countries be factored into compensation?	To what extent should international assignments be used to develop managers with international understanding and expertise? How can employees with international experience be effectively reincorporated into the parent firm?
Local Managers	What is the skill level in the local pool of managers? How can desired locals be recruited? What about our company is attractive/unattractive to various groups of desired local managers? What local laws have an impact on hiring practices?	Can the parent company's training methods be effectively applied to local employees?	Who should appraise local employees? What appraisal methods should be utilized? How explicit should job tasks and responsibilities be? What local laws have an impact on informing managers of their performance?	What rewards do local managers value? How often should rewards be administered? What local laws have an impact on the administration of financial/nonfinancial rewards and punishments?	How many development/promotion opportunities do local managers expect? How can key high-potential local employees be identified and developed?

L.L. Bean, are primarily concerned with exporting products and then marketing, selling, and distributing them in several countries. Consequently, the focus of international people-management activities is often the staffing, training, appraising, rewarding, and developing of local nationals involved in these downstream activities. There is a generally low use of international managers in export-oriented firms; instead, home-based managers with geographical or product responsibilities visit the various international countries and sites. When international managers are used at all, they are usually placed in positions of general management and have rather broad geographical responsibilities. Figure 1.1 offers a graphic illustration of the typical pattern of deploying international managers at the export stage of globalization. It also shows the patterns for the other three stages.

Multidomestic Corporations (MDCs). Such multidomestic firms as Castrol and Quaker State are most common in industries where competition in one country (or in one small group of countries) is basically independent of competition in others. Because competition for each geographically distinct unit within the firm is focused on the country and the market of the unit's location, a high degree of specialization and adaptation of the unit's value-chain activities is required. Therefore, the culture- and country-specific knowledge that local nationals have is important for the appropriate specialization of the particular unit's activities. It is only natural that the use of international managers, while higher than in the case of export firms, is still relatively low in MDCs (see Figure 1.1). Moreover, the international managers tend to be of two types—executives or technical specialists. The executives are often from a cadre of "career internationalists," or managers who have made and spent most of their careers outside the firm's home office and home country. The technical specialists are generally on assignment for a relatively short time (one to two years) and are sent overseas for specific reasons (for example, transferring a particular technology or solving a particular problem). The multidomestic orientation generally does not lead to the formation of systematic policies and practices for expatriate selection, training, or repatriation because only a small percentage of employees ever serve in overseas assignments,

Figure 1.1. Patterns of Expatriate Deployment
as a Function of Globalization Patterns.

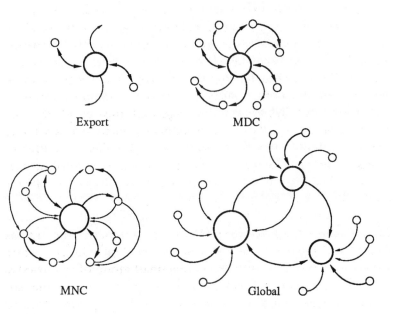

Export   MDC

MNC   Global

and these employees are generally "out of sight, out of mind" where policymakers at the home office are concerned.[20] Instead, the focus of MDCs with respect to international management is on compensation practices and policies, in order to ensure a sufficient number of reasonably capable international managers. International strategy formulation and implementation are primarily restricted to each individual country. For the country-centered strategic plan to be effective, it must incorporate the important and unique aspects of the country, culture, and market where the unit competes. Consequently, even though only a few international managers are utilized in MDCs, it is still crucial for them to understand and adjust to the local situation and culture.

Coordinated Multinational Corporations (MNCs). Like multidomestic corporations, coordinated MNCs (simply referred to as MNCs) also have geographically dispersed operations and units. In contrast to multidomestic firms, however, such MNCs as Xerox and Kodak have extensive coordination between units in different geographical locations (see Figure 1.1). Many MNCs utilize cultural coordination by establishing commonly held corporate values. They tend to utilize more international managers, utilize both home-country and third-country international managers, and place international managers in a variety of organizational levels within foreign operations.[21]

In addition to engaging in the common practice of sending home- or parent-country nationals on overseas assignments in foreign countries, MNCs that utilize informal and cultural coordination mechanisms often also have foreign nationals serving in overseas assignments at the home or parent office. Bringing foreign nationals into the home or parent country and office can help socialize foreign nationals to the philosophy or culture of the parent firm, as well as cross-fertilize the home operation with the ideas of foreign nationals and their own home-country operations. Because the international movement of employees provides a powerful informal means of controlling and coordinating activities across countries, MNCs with this orientation are more likely to have developed, over time, systematic policies and practices for expatriate selection, training, and repatriation. In particular, the two-way directionality of informal coordination raises some very important issues with respect to repatriation. Because expatriate employees gain important experience, which prepares them to understand various international markets, competitors, and operations, it places them in a unique position to contribute effectively to international strategy formulation and implementation at corporate and regional headquarters. Therefore, effective repatriation policies must be created and put into place so that the typical high turnover after repatriation does not occur,[22] and so that returned international managers stay and provide the critical coordination function from overseas operations back to the headquarters.

Global Firms. Firms at the global stage of internationalization, such as Boeing and Airbus, are generally within industries where a firm's position in one country is substantially influenced by its competitive position in another. The objective for a firm with a global orientation (what Bartlett and Ghoshal have called a "transnational" firm[23]) is to coordinate value-chain activities on a global scale and thereby capture comparative advantages and links among countries. If transnational or global corporations were free from governmental restrictions, they would tend not even to think of employees as home-country managers or local nationals; they would simply try to place individuals with comparative advantages and needed skills in the locales of corresponding and appropriate value-chain functions (see Figure 1.1). These value-chain activities in turn could be concentrated in specific countries with comparative advantages relative to other countries. For example, if research and development (R&D) were in France, scientists and related people who had the knowledge and skills to contribute to R&D would be moved to France, regardless of nationality. Nevertheless, a "border-less world," in terms of the movement of people, does not yet exist. Nations have visa laws, domestic employment policies, tax structures, and so on, that prohibit the free and uninhibited movement of people across borders. Thus, in practice, global corporations are restricted in the movement of international staff people. Because global firms often place such linked activities as design and production in the home country of the parent firm, however, global corporations often do not need to utilize the same overall number of parent-country expatriate employees as MNCs do. In fact, if one examines such global industries as commercial aircraft, firms like Boeing find that their need for international managers is relatively low by comparison to the need in similarly sized MNCs.

Table 1.2 illustrates some of the relevant people-management questions for each of these four patterns of globalization. The nature of the questions shifts according to the stage of globalization; later chapters will examine these differences in greater detail.

The Issue of "Fit"

No matter which globalization pattern a firm is in, its international assignment policies and practices must fit the environment and must be congruent with each other. The balance of international assignment policies and practices with the marketplace creates an *external fit*. The balance and congruence among the five aspects of people management within a firm (staffing, training, appraising,

Table 1.2. Matrix of the International Management of People.

	FUNCTION OF PEOPLE MANAGEMENT				
	Staffing	*Training*	*Appraising*	*Rewarding*	*Developing*
Export	What is the local pool of marketing/sales talent like? What qualifications are needed to manage a diverse and decentralized international marketing operation? (low use of expatriates)	To what extent are marketing and sales training practices appropriate for a given locale?	What adaptions have to be made to monitor individual performance? How frequently should home-office personnel be sent to observe local operations?	What adaptations in compensation need to be made to reward/punish marketing and sales employees?	What positions and experiences will enable managers to assume more international responsibilities as the firm globalizes?
Multi-domestic	What is the local general management and especially specialized management labor pool like? What type of expatriates adjust best to overseas assignments? (moderate use of home-national expatriates/GMs and specialists)	How much training should expatriates be given after they arrive in a foreign country?	How formal should the appraisal system be for local employees? How much of the expatriate's performance should be evaluated by locals?	What forms of compensation/punishment are motivating in the local culture? How much of the expatriate's pay should be a function of local performance?	How can locals be developed to assume ever-higher positions and responsibilities?

INTERNATIONALIZATION PATTERN

Coordinated MNC	What qualifications are needed in future general managers? (moderate to high use of home- and third-country expatriates)	What training should be provided to help reintegrate returning expatriates?	How standardized should performance appraisal systems be?	To what extent should compensation be equalized across countries and home- and third-country expatriates? To what extent should individual versus corporate performance be used in determining pay?	How can foreign assignments be utilized to provide targeted managers with important international experience?
Global	Which countries have comparative human resource advantages? Which people have complementary skills for certain value-chain activities? What legal restrictions keep us from moving people to their appropriate value-chain activity? (moderate to low use of expatriates)	What forms of training can be effectively utilized to build necessary skills for important value-chain activities and develop a global corporate culture?	What common set of criteria can be applied to performance, relative to certain tasks associated with a particular value-chain activity?	What common set of rewards, pay scales, and benefits can be applied to a particular set of tasks and performance levels, relative to a given group of value-chain activities?	What development experiences are needed to prepare managers for global competition?

rewarding, and developing) constitutes *internal fit.* Two examples will illustrate this point.

WestCoast Bankcorp. Recently a large West Coast bank (the name of the firm has been disguised) was trying to reduce its total expenditures on international assignments. The bank was at a coordinated MNC stage of globalization. The bank had operations in over twenty countries and sought to closely coordinate such value-chain activities as lending, foreign exchange, and retail banking among its various subsidiaries. The bank also sought to compete by offering low interest rates and fees for the services it provided.

The bank found that its international managers were usually two to three times more expensive to employ than comparable employees in the home country and were several times more expensive to employ than local nationals. These high costs for expatriates were consistent with what most other U.S. firms experienced. West-Coast Bankcorp tried to lower its costs by reducing its aggregate expatriate costs. This goal was achieved over just a few years, through reducing the total number of global managers by half and thereby reducing overall costs for expatriates. The bank also tried to reduce the average cost per expatriate by reducing or cutting various aspects of the standard expatriate package (reducing allowances, locating global managers in low-tax countries, cutting predeparture training, and so on).

The critical implication of this particular cost-reduction program concerns the issue of *external fit.* The key question is whether the effort to lower total costs was carried out in a manner that inhibited or facilitated the firm's competitive advantage in that particular pattern of globalization. Although cutting the total number of global managers reduced the aggregate costs, coordination and control between the parent and subsidiaries, as well as among subsidiaries, became much more difficult. The effort to lower the cost per global manager by reducing predeparture training also reduced the ability of these managers to function effectively. Because relatively fewer global managers were now being placed in top positions within the foreign subsidiaries, their understanding of both the home office and the local operation was critical to their ability to facilitate effective coordination. Lack of resources for cross-cultural training reduced their ability to quickly understand the local situation and therefore also reduced their ability to facilitate coordination. The external fit between the training practices and the environment, and between the overall cutback and the stage of globalization, was incongruent.

International Hotel. Let us now consider the issue of *internal fit.* International Hotel is a large U.S.-based hotel corporation that tried to maintain its competitive advantage through differentiation, by offering services to its guests (for example, business centers equipped with fax machines, computers, copiers, secretaries, and so on) that far exceeded those of its competitors. The exact services provided varied considerably from country to country, however, as a function of its multidomestic pattern of globalization. International managers were encouraged to formulate their own location-specific approaches to the "high-quality service" strategy and were monitored on the basis of their action plans. Reasonable levels of predeparture and postarrival training were provided, which facilitated the managers' ability to quickly gain an in-depth understanding of the values and needs of local markets and design services to meet those needs.

Unfortunately, much of an international manager's performance bonus in this organization was based on overall corporate results, and so while the training led managers to want to focus on understanding local markets, the appraisal and compensation policies had the opposite effect. The managers knew that if they could reduce costs (in some cases, by eliminating certain costly services), profits would increase, and so would their bonuses. Consequently, the internal fit among the training, rewarding, and appraising functions was poor and did not facilitate or encourage expatriate managers' ability to differentiate their hotels in the local markets where they were competing.

Implication: Generic Prescriptions Can Increase Costs

What is the bottom-line implication of all this? It is simply this: *generic recommendations for effective movement and management of people around the world can be a waste of time, energy, and money.* If a firm is to move and manage people effectively in an international business environment, policies and practices must be formulated and implemented within the context of the firm's stage of globalization. Let us consider two examples.

Cultural Sensitivity: When Do You Really Need It?

Academics and consultants have argued that cultural sensitivity is critical to the success of any expatriate working in a foreign country.[24] This is not an easy characteristic to measure, however, nor is it easy to use in selecting managers for international assignments. It takes time, energy and money. Are the benefits always worth the costs? Maybe not: certain stages of globalization require more cultural sensitivity than others do. For example, in a firm at the multidomestic stage of globalization, the importance and nature of the role of cultural knowledge or sensitivity is quite high. Cultural knowledge is the *basis on which* specific changes, enhancements, or characteristics of products or services are chosen. If the market and its relevant cultural values are misunderstood, it is unlikely that a product that meets needs in a unique and desirable way, relative to competing products, can be developed. If one does not know that the pronunciation of the words *four* and *death* is the same in Japanese, one may make the mistake (one firm actually did) of packaging premium golf balls in groups of four for the Japanese market and then wondering why the balls are not selling.

Full-Blown Systems: When Are They Critical?

Academics and consultants have also emphasized the need to have comprehensive global assignment systems (valid selection criteria, rigorous pre- and postarrival cross-cultural training, close contact during the overseas assignment between the expatriate and corporate headquarters, systematic and comprehensive repatriation programs and planning systems, and so on). If one examines firms in each of the four phases of globalization, however, it seems that the suggestions and recommendations of academics increase in importance as firms approach the coordinated MNC level, with mature foreign subsidiaries. This stage requires not only high levels of coordination and control but also generally informal rather than formal mechanisms of coordination. It is in this particular combination that the following characteristics are seen:

1. The highest numbers of international managers are needed and utilized.
2. It is most important to reduce the indirect costs associated with poor expatriate adjustment and performance.
3. It is critical to maximize innovation and effective coordination with respect to information moving from the parent to foreign operations, among foreign operations, and from foreign operations back to the parent.
4. Effective and systematic selection, training, adjustment, and repatriation policies and practices are the vital means by which all of this is achieved.

In the past, however, many academics and consultants assumed that such policies and practices were equally critical in all firms, regardless of pattern of globalization.

Again, this is not to say that expatriate policies and practices are not important at some stages of globalization; in fact, at the beginning of this chapter, we described the severe costs that may be entailed when an international assignment is poorly managed, and such costs occur regardless of the purpose of assignments or stage of globalization. Our point here is that the relative importance of these policies is not equal across all phases of globalization.

Summary

We began this chapter by saying that people are the key to global competitiveness, and that global assignments can serve three strategic functions in the utilization of people in today's global marketplace. Global assignments can play a strategic role in succession planning and management development, coordination and control of international operations, and information flow and exchange between the parent and subsidiaries and among subsidiaries. We argued that, in addition to considering global assignments as more than a "firefighting" tool, firms should include both home-country nationals and foreign-country nationals in strategic global assignments. We also pointed out that, independent of the "firefighting" or strategic role of global assignments, there are significant and sometimes devastating costs associated with poor design and management of global assignments.

Next, we presented a general framework of people management, to structure later chapters on the selection, training, cross-cultural adjustment, performance, evaluation, compensation, and repatriation of people. We also suggested that these issues become increasingly important as firms move from export patterns to coordinated MNC patterns of globalization. Consequently, executives need to examine external fit among the marketplace, pattern of globalization, and international management policies.

The remainder of this book summarizes the best thinking, practice, and scientific evidence currently available on the international management of people, and the chapters to come also discuss in more detail how general recommendations may vary according to pattern of globalization. In our attempt to make this book both interesting and realistic, by using cases and illustrations, we have tried not to sacrifice critical content and complexity for "gloss" and simplicity. We trust that executives involved in global assignment decisions, at either the strategic or the operational level, will not feel short-changed by diluted information and will be challenged by the ideas presented.

Notes

1. Bowman, "Concerns of CEOs."
2. DeYoung, "The Clash of Cultures at Tylan General," p. 149.
3. Kobrin, "Expatriate Reduction and Strategic Control in American Multinational Corporations."
4. Gupta and Govindarajan, "Knowledge Flows and the Structure of Control Within Multinational Corporations."
5. Moran, Stahl, & Boyer, *International Human Resource Management.*
6. Hall, "How Top Management and the Organization Itself Can Block Effective Executive Succession."
7. Baker and Ivancevich, "The Assignment of American Execu-

tives Abroad: Systematic, Haphazard, or Chaotic?"; Misa and Fabricatore, "Return on Investment of Overseas Personnel"; Tung, *The New Expatriates: Managing Human Resources Abroad.*

8. Harvey, "Repatriation of Corporate Executives: An Empirical Study."
9. Lublin, "Grappling with Expatriate Issues."
10. Copeland and Louis, *Going International.*
11. "GE Culture Turns Sour at French Unit."
12. Adler, "Re-entry: Managing Cross-Cultural Transitions"; Black and Gregersen, "When Yankee Comes Home: Factors Related to Expatriate and Spouse Repatriation Adjustment."
13. Baird and Meshoulam, "Managing Two Fits of Strategic Human Resource Management"; Devanna, Fombrun, and Tichy, "A Framework for Strategic Human Resource Management"; Miller, Beechler, Bhatt, and Nath, "Relationship Between Global Strategic Planning Process and the Human Resource Management Function."
14. Mendenhall and Oddou, "The Dimensions of Expatriate Acculturation: A Review"; Miller, "The International Selection Decision: A Study of Managerial Behavior in the Selection Decision Process."
15. Mendenhall and Oddou, "Dimensions of Expatriate Acculturation"; Black and Mendenhall, "Cross-Cultural Training Effectiveness: A Review and Theoretical Framework for Future Research"; Misa and Fabricatore, "Return on Investment of Overseas Personnnel"; Moran, Stahl, & Boyer, *International Human Resource Management.*
16. Adler, "Re-entry"; Adler, *International Dimensions of Organizational Behavior*; Black and Gregersen, "When Yankee Comes Home"; Clague and Krupp, "International Personnel: The Repatriation Problem"; Harvey, "The Other Side of Foreign Assignments: Dealing with the Repatriation Problem"; Harvey, "Repatriation of Corporate Executives"; Kendall, "Repatriation: An Ending and a Beginning."
17. Ghadar and Adler, "Management Culture and Accelerated Product Life Cycle."
18. Dowling and Schuler, *International Dimensions of Human*

Resource Management; Porter, "Changing Patterns of International Competition."

19. Porter, "Changing Patterns of International Competition."
20. Adler, "Re-entry"; Adler, *International Dimensions of Organizational Behavior*; Black and Gregersen, "When Yankee Comes Home"; Clague and Krupp, "International Personnel"; Harvey, "Repatriation of Corporate Executives."
21. Edstrom and Galbraith, "Transfer of Managers as a Coordination and Control Strategy in Multinational Organizations"; Jaeger, "Contrasting Control Modes in the Multinational Corporation: Theory, Practice, and Implications."
22. Black and Gregersen, "When Yankee Comes Home"; Adler, "Re-entry."
23. Bartlett and Ghoshal, "Organizing for Worldwide Effectiveness: The Transnational Solution."
24. Harris and Moran, *Managing Cultural Differences*; Stening, "Problems of Cross-Cultural Contact: A Literature Review."

Chapter 2

The Process of Making
Cross-Cultural Adjustments

If effective cross-cultural adjustment were not such an elusive target
for managers and their families, there would be little need for this
chapter or those that follow. Cross-cultural adjustment is difficult
for most people, however, and most of the first half of this book
focuses on factors that affect successful adjustment or such important outcomes as turnover and job performance. Before we tackle the
topic of cross-cultural adjustment, we need a clear idea of what
people are adjusting to.

The Essence of Culture

Many authors write about culture as if it were something in a country,
region, or firm that one can see, hear, touch, smell, or taste. People
who take this view often point to ceremonies, clothing, historical
landmarks, art, and food as examples of a country's culture. Ceremonies, clothing, historical landmarks, art, and food may indeed differ

substantially from one country to another, but the interesting question is why?

The answer lies in a much more complex view of culture.[1] The tangible aspects of a culture—thing one can see, hear, smell, taste, or touch—are *artifacts,* or manifestations, of underlying values and assumptions that a group of people share. Their structure is like that of an iceberg (see Figure 2.1). Artifacts are what we can see, but what we can see is only a small fraction of what is there. What we cannot see—the values and assumptions—are what can sink our ship.

Figure 2.1. The Iceberg of Culture.

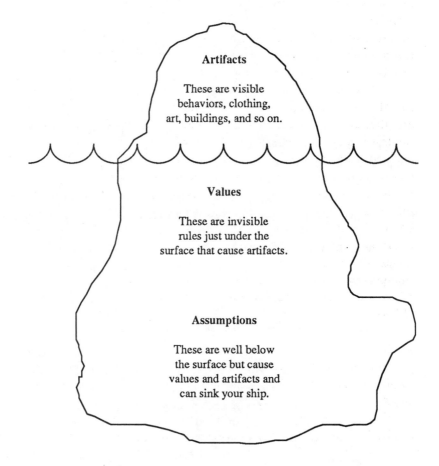

Artifacts

These are visible
behaviors, clothing,
art, buildings, and so on.

Values

These are invisible
rules just under the
surface that cause artifacts.

Assumptions

These are well below
the surface but cause
values and artifacts and
can sink your ship.

Culture, however, is not simply the total collection of a group of people's assumptions, values, or artifacts. It consists of a common set of assumptions and values that consistently influence artifacts, especially behavior, and are passed on from older to younger members of the group. How and why does this common set of assumptions and values emerge, become widely shared, and get passed on from one generation to another?

Insights come from anthropologists who have struggled with this important question for many years.[2] One of the conclusions that many scholars have come to is that there is a limited set of problems, which all people must solve. A society must figure out a way to communicate and to educate, feed, clothe, and govern its people. Societies experiment with different ways to solve these problems, and the methods and ideas that prove successful are passed on to future generations. Thus, the most important elements of a culture are intangible. They are the invisible rules that exist in people's minds.

In essence, culture amounts to a mental road map and traffic signals. The road map tells us what the important and valued goals are (they are the places marked in bold), and the ways to get there; the traffic signals tell us who has the right of way, when to stop, and so on. Imagine being put into the heart of the Tokyo freeway system with no map, no road signs, and no idea of the rules governing traffic. Suddenly, one's previous road maps and traffic rules are practically useless or perhaps even deadly, because the Japanese, like the British, drive on the left side of the road. A similar process occurs as people move from one culture to another on global assignments and they are forced to learn new maps and rules for social and interpersonal situations. That is something of what is involved when people move from one culture to another. Suddenly, one's previous social and interpersonal guides are useless or even deadly.

Violations of some traffic rules entail simple warnings or small fines; others mean time in jail. Similarly, not all the rules of a culture entail the same penalties for infractions. A helpful way of thinking about this is to conceptualize the rules on two dimensions—the extent to which they are widely shared among group members, and the extent to which they are deeply held. This conceptualization is illustrated in Figure 2.2.

Figure 2.2. The Matrix of Culture.

Narrowly Shared, Deeply Held Violations in this cell usually result in informal but sometimes significant punishments.	*Widely Shared, Deeply Held* Violations in this cell usually result in formal and significant punishments.
Narrowly Shared, Shallowly Held Violations in this cell usually do not result in uniform reactions but instead are more ideosyncratic.	*Widely Shared, Shallowly Held* Violations in this cell usually result in minor punishments or sometimes second chances.

Deep ↑ Shallow

Narrow ← → Wide

The assumptions, values, or rules of the culture that are widely shared and deeply held generally entail substantial rewards or punishments. For example, a widely shared and strongly held rule in the United States is that one does not talk to oneself constantly or loudly. When others see a person doing this, they become nervous and concerned, even if the person poses no physical threat to anyone. What happens to those who violate this rule? They get locked up in mental institutions. What about rules that are deeply held but not widely shared? In this case, rewards or punishments are often informal. For example, burping after a meal is considered by some to be a serious violation of proper behavior, but not by all. Consequently, one will not be put in jail for burping, but one may be cut out of particular social circles, at least in the United States. In other countries, one offends a host by not burping after a meal. In the case of rules that are widely shared but not deeply held, violations often entail uniform but rather mild punishments; infrequent violations may carry no punishment at all. For example, not interrupting someone who is talking to us is a generally accepted rule of conduct in the United States. If we occasionally interrupt, however, it is unlikely that this behavior will entail any significant punishment.

The Nature of Assumptions About the World

Because assumptions are the source of values, rules, artifacts, and behavior, it is important to touch briefly on the nature of assumptions and on how they differ from one culture to another. Basic underlying assumptions can be divided into five categories.[3] Table 2.1 summarizes the general nature of these assumptions and gives examples of specific forms they may take, as well as of their management implications.

Humanity's Relationship to the Environment

The first area of assumptions concerns those made about the relationship of humanity to nature. For example, in some cultures (the United States, for example), the assumption is that humans are here to dominate nature and utilize it for the wealth and benefit of mankind. In other cultures, the assumption is that humans and nature are to coexist harmoniously. The implications of these differing assumptions may be quite significant. In the United States, the dominance assumption is an important basis for the building of dams, the mining of minerals, and the logging of trees, but the implications may also reach beyond these basic activities, to strategic planning or management practices in business. Consider how most U.S. firms view the business environment and how they strategically approach it. Is the business environment viewed as something that people must accept and with which they must try to harmonize? Or is it viewed as something that must be mastered and dominated, if possible? Americans' assumption that the business environment is something to dominate is evident in the purpose of antitrust laws. Antitrust laws and regulations in the United States are there not because Americans feel that they must be submissive to or harmonize with the environment but because Americans want to counteract some of the negative outcomes of environmental domination by a single firm.

Human Nature

Different cultures also make different assumptions about the nature of people. Some cultures assume that people are fundamentally

Table 2.1. Basic Assumptions and Their Implications.

Nature of Assumption	Specific Assumptions	Management Implications
Environment (assumptions about the relationship between humans and the environment)	People are meant to dominate the environment.	Strategic plans should be developed to enable the firm to dominate its industry.
	People must be submissive to the environment.	Firms should seek positions that allow them to coexist with others.
Human nature (assumptions about human nature)	People are generally lazy.	Implement procedures for monitoring behavior and establish clear punishment for undesired behaviors.
	Work is as natural as play for people.	Provide people with opportunities and responsibilities and encourage their development.
Relationships (assumptions about how humans should relate to each other)	Individuals have certain rights and freedoms.	Individual performance should be measured and rewarded.
	People exist because of others and owe an obligation to them.	Cooperation with and contributions to the group should be rewarded.
Activity (assumptions about the proper types and targets of human activity)	People create their own destinies and must plan for the future.	People who fail to plan should plan to fail.
	People should react to and enjoy whatever the present provides.	Planning the future only gets in the way of enjoying the present.
Truth (assumptions about the nature of truth and reality)	Truth objectively exists.	Facts and statistics are presented to convince and influence people.
	Truth is what is socially accepted.	Opinion leaders are utilized to influence decisions.

good; others assume that people are inherently evil. The relevance of this area of assumptions was made clear by Douglas McGregor in his classic book *The Human Side of Enterprise*.[4] McGregor argues that every manager acts on a "theory" or set of assumptions about people. Theory X managers assume that "the average human being has an inherent dislike for work and will avoid it if he can"

(p. 33). Consequently, managers who accept this view of people believe that "people must be coerced, controlled, directed, and threatened with punishment to get them to put forth adequate effort toward the achievement of organizational objectives" (p. 34). By contrast, Theory Y managers assume that "the expenditure of physical and mental effort in work is as natural as play or rest" (p. 47). Consequently, managers who accept this view of people believe that "external control and the threat of punishment are not the only means for bringing about effort toward organizational objectives. Man will exercise self-direction and self-control in the service of objectives to which he is committed. Commitment to objectives is a function of the rewards associated with their achievement" (p. 47).

Human Relationships

This area of assumptions really deals with a variety of questions: What is the right way for people to deal with each other? How much power and authority should any one person have over another? How much of individuals' orientation should be toward themselves, versus toward others? A large-scale study by Geert Hofstede found significant differences among forty countries in the answers to these questions.[5] For example, Hofstede examined the degree to which people accepted power and authority differences among people. In his study, people from the Philippines, Venezuela, and Mexico had the highest levels of acceptance of power differences. By contrast, Austria, Israel, and Denmark had the lowest levels of acceptance. Hofstede's study also found that people from the United States, Australia, and Great Britain had the highest individual orientation, while people from Venezuela, Colombia, and Pakistan had the highest collective orientation.

Human Activity

This area of assumptions concerns what is right for people to do and whether they should be active, passive, or fatalistic. In the United States, people brag about working eighty hours a week, about having no time for vacations or watching TV, and about doing several things at once on their computers. They believe in such phrases as "People who fail to plan should plan to fail" or "Plan to do, and do the plan." In other cultures, where people believe that a preoccupation with planning only gets in the way of enjoying the present, such high-strung activity is not valued and may even be seen as a waste of time and energy.

Reality and Truth

Different cultures also form differing assumptions about the nature of reality and truth and about how they are verified or established. For example, the adversarial system in U.S. criminal law is based on the assumptions that truth exists and that the heat generated by opposing views will ultimately illuminate what really happened. In other cultures, reality is much more subjective and dependent on what people believe it to be. Consequently, opinion leaders or persuasive stories rather than "hard facts" are utilized as means of influencing people and business decisions.

Our purpose in discussing these five areas of assumptions is to illustrate two key issues. First, as mentioned earlier, assumptions are the source of values and behavior. In order to understand the visible artifacts of culture, one must understand the invisible values and assumptions. Second, fundamental assumptions, by their very nature, are not only invisible but also generally taken for granted. Their taken-for-granted nature means that they are not easy to uncover or understand, because the people who hold them are not usually conscious of them and therefore cannot easily identify and explain them to foreigners. People are as unaware of how their cultural assumptions affect their behavior as they are of the oxygen in the air around them. Breathing and following cultural norms are natural and almost automatic processes. Furthermore, the taken-for-granted nature of cultural assumptions means that they are not easily changed. Behavior may change (Japanese people may stop wearing kimonos and instead wear Western clothes), but underlying values and assumptions remain and are not easily or quickly changed.

This brings us to the heart of why cross-cultural adjustment is not easy. Although culture has visible components (artifacts and behavior) and invisible ones (values and assumptions), the invisible components are more important because they are the source of the visible aspects of a foreign culture. Unfortunately, since most so-journers have neither a mental road map nor a guide to the traffic signals, it is only natural that they encounter everything from close calls to fatal crashes. Consider the case of Fred Bailey, recently assigned to the Tokyo office of a Boston-based U.S. consulting firm.[6]

An Innocent Abroad

Fred Bailey gazed out the window of his twenty-fourth-floor office at the tranquil beauty of the Imperial Palace amidst the hustle and bustle of downtown Tokyo. It had only been six months since Fred arrived with his wife and two children for this three-year assignment as director of Kline & Associates' Tokyo office. (Kline & Associates was a large multinational consulting firm in Boston, with offices in nineteen countries.)

Fred was trying to decide whether he should simply pack up and tell the home office that he was leaving or try somehow to convince his wife (and himself) that they should stay and finish the assignment. Given how excited Fred had thought they all were to begin with, it was a mystery to him how things had reached this point.

Seven months before, the managing partner of the Boston office had asked Fred to lunch, to discuss "business." To Fred's surprise, the "business" was not the major project that he and his team had just finished. Instead, it was a very big promotion and a career move. Fred was offered the position of managing director of the relatively new Tokyo office, which had a staff of forty, including seven Americans. Most of the Americans in the Tokyo office were either associate consultants or research analysts. Fred would be in charge of the whole office and would report to a senior partner in charge of the Asian region. It was implied that if this assignment went as well as Fred's recent one had gone, it would be Fred's last step before becoming a partner in the firm.

When Fred told his wife about this unbelievable opportunity, he was shocked at her response, which was less than enthusiastic. Jenny thought that it would be rather difficult to have their two children live and go to school in a foreign country for three years, especially when Christine, the elder, would be starting middle school next year. Besides, now that the kids were in school, Jenny was thinking about going back to work—at least part-time. She had a degree in fashion merchandising from a well-known private university and had worked as an assistant buyer for a women's clothing store before the girls were born.

Fred explained that the career opportunity was just too good to pass up, and that the company's overseas package would make living in Japan terrific. The company would pay to move whatever the Baileys wanted to take with them. The company also had a very nice house in an expensive district of Tokyo that would be provided rent-free, and the company would rent their house in Boston during their absence. The firm would provide a car and a driver, money for the children to attend private schools, and a cost-of-living adjustment and overseas compensation that would nearly triple Fred's gross annual salary. After two days of consideration and discussion, Fred accepted the assignment.

The previous managing director in Tokyo had been in the office for less than a year when he was transferred to a long-established office in England. Because this transfer had occurred in great haste, Fred and his family had been given about three weeks to get prepared for their move. Given the need to reassign work at the Boston office to Fred's replacement and the logistical hassles of getting furniture and the like ready to move, neither Fred nor his family had really had time to find out much about Japan, other than what was in the encyclopedia.

Upon their arrival, the Baileys had been greeted at the airport by one of the young Japanese associate consultants and the senior American expatriate. Fred and his family were quite tired from the long trip, and the two-hour ride to Tokyo was rather quiet.

The first few weeks in Japan were hectic. It took the Baileys some time just to get settled in their new house (which was actually a luxury apartment). By Japanese standards, it was enormous; but, even though it was adequate, it was small compared to the Baileys' large house in Boston. Although Jenny missed their home, her initial reaction to the apartment was positive. The apartment was tastefully decorated and it was centrally situated in Hiro, an affluent neighborhood near downtown Tokyo. There was a grocery store nearby that carried a variety of American food products, and there was even a Baskin-Robbins next to it and a Mrs. Field's Cookies down the street. During the early days, Fred used the company car and the driver to shuttle family members around as they shopped, registered for school, and registered at city offices. It seemed as if the first month was gone before they knew it.

After that, things seemed to get worse and worse all the time. Fred would get irritated just remembering some of the problems and incidents. He remembered the time his wife called him crying on the telephone after getting lost on the subway; the time he had bought what he thought were pickles, but they tasted like spoiled vinegar; the time he asked a Japanese employee to prepare an important report and found out the day before it was due that it was not ready, and that the employee had not thought that it would be from the moment he accepted the assignment; the time he stuck his chopsticks in his bowl of rice to keep them from rolling off onto the floor at an important dinner, only to be told later that doing so was a sign of death; the many times he had asked Japanese clients simple, direct questions, only to receive vague responses; and his increasingly frequent fights with Jenny over things that they had never fought about at home.

Just as earthquakes in and around Japan can cause tidal waves, the shock of being in Japan had swept the Baileys up in frustration, anger, and anxiety. To Fred, and especially to Jenny, the only life preserver (and perhaps the only marriage preserver) seemed to be to pack up and head home.

Cross-Cultural Adjustment: The Process

The preceding case is true, and its episodes are common. Many global managers and their families experience adjustment difficulties similar to those of the Baileys. Most people recognize the term *culture shock,* but few understand its underlying process. The dynamics of cross-cultural adjustment involve the individual's *routines, ego,* and *self-image.*

Routines

Almost no one wants total uncertainty in life. Most people want a reasonably high degree of certainty and predictability. That is primarily why people establish routines. The global success of McDonald's is testimony to the general human need of a certain level of predictability in life. When we go into a McDonald's, there is a variety of items from which to choose, but we know how a Big Mac is going to taste before we order it. A Big Mac is a Big Mac. People like not only the product but also its predictability.

Routines affect all aspects of people's lives, from the mundane to the critical. For example, people establish routines for waking up in the morning—shut off alarm, get up, take a shower, get dressed, eat, run out the door. People also establish more serious routines, such as initiating or developing relationships, dealing with conflict in relationships, and forming expectations of relationships.

At this stage of human evolution, the mind cannot consciously process an infinite number of issues simultaneously. Routines and the certainty they provide create a kind of psychological economy. Because we know how a Big Mac will taste, and because we know that once we get up we will take a shower, we do not have to devote a lot of time and energy to thinking about and processing those issues. When a routine is disrupted, however, more time and energy must be devoted to processing such issues. To the extent that mental time and energy are limited, the disruption of routines means that there is now less mental time and energy for other things. Not all disruptions are equally severe, however. Severity is a function of three dimensions.

Scope. The first dimension is the scope, or total number of disrupted routines. All other things being equal, the greater the number of disrupted routines, the more difficult the process of dealing with the disruptions and the greater the frustration, anger, and anxiety that are likely to follow. It is one thing to have a showering routine disrupted, but it is quite another to have one's eating, sleeping, commuting, and working routines also disrupted by a new cultural environment. It may be inconvenient to have to give up the handshake for a bow in greeting someone, but it can be quite upsetting to have to alter most of the dimensions of how one delegates authority, makes decisions, influences people, plans and organizes the work day, and motivates subordinates.

Magnitude. The second dimension is the magnitude of the disruption. The continuum of disruption for any given routine ranges from slight alteration to total destruction. The greater the magnitude of the disruption, the greater the time and energy required to deal with it and the greater the frustration, anger, and anxiety that are likely to follow. If a shower was previously the first order of the day, having to take a bath would be a somewhat lesser disruption than not being able to do either without going to a public bathhouse. It may be somewhat irritating to have to switch from cash bonuses to days off as motivation incentives, but it can be totally frustrating to have one's ability to use incentives completely removed and placed in the hands of a labor ministry.

Criticality. The third dimension is the criticality of the disrupted routine. Some routines are critical, and others are trivial. The greater the criticality of the routine disrupted, the greater the time and energy required to deal with it and the greater the frustration, anger, and anxiety that are likely to follow. Not having one's accustomed parking spot reserved is probably less frustrating than having to change from a tell-and-sell style of leadership to one that entails consultation and joint decisions.

Culture Shock

Up to this point, the primary explanation for culture shock has been (1) that new and unfamiliar environments of foreign cultures disrupt routines, and (2) that the more routines disrupted, the more severely altered any given routine is, and the more critical the disrupted routines are, the greater the time and mental energy required and the greater the frustration, anger, and anxiety. Nevertheless, these dynamics do not completely explain culture shock and its emotional manifestations.

If it is true that for every action there is an equal and opposite reaction, would the reverse also be true? For every reaction is there an equal and opposite cause? One would expect this to be true in the case of culture shock.

Fred Bailey, six months into his assignment in Japan, found himself frequently so angry that he sometimes had to work hard not to vent his anger by striking someone. At other times, he found himself so depressed he could find very little reason to get out of bed in the morning. The extent of these emotions was not visible to anyone on the outside, and Fred worked hard to keep it that way. Certainly in Fred's case, and in severe cases like his, there has to be more than disruption of routines to explain why Fred and his family would pack up and head home, or why one in five Americans leave a foreign assignment prematurely.

The powerful cause of these severe reactions stems from a matter that is generally quite sensitive for everyone—ego, self-image, identity. The most important underlying process in cross-cultural adjustment is the maintenence and repair of one's ego and self-image. For most people, there is nothing as fragile and important as ego and self-image. It may not seem obvious, but routines are a great source of self-image. In a sense, a routine demonstrates a level of proficiency, which by the nature of its routinization is usually taken for granted. There is nothing like living in a foreign culture, however, to challenge these basic proficiencies and raise them from a taken-for-granted level to a very conscious one. In fact, the more the proficiency is taken for granted, the more severe the reaction to its loss often is.

Let us consider some specific examples from the case of the Baileys. Getting around in the city in which one lives is often a skill that is very much taken for granted. For Jenny Bailey, moving around Boston, despite heavy traffic, was something she simply took for granted. Getting lost on the Tokyo subway system, and not even being able to go from her home to a friend's house, was a severe shock to her self-image as an independent, capable person. As for Fred, someone who had been to countless important dinners with clients and had developed a rather impressive ability to deal smoothly with these situations, the mistake of sticking his chopsticks into his rice was a significant blow to his self-confidence and ego. For others like Jenny and Fred, foreign assignments involve a steady stream of incidents, from the simple to the complex, that challenge self-image. People are constantly confronted with situations that send certain messages: "You don't understand this," "You can't do that," "Even French six-year-olds know that," "You're an idiot."

People encounter such situations almost from the time they step off the plane. It takes people a while to build up the defense mechanisms that defend their egos and self-images. As these incidents build over time in number and magnitude, people get worn down and can no longer ignore them. Although the specific symptoms vary across individuals, and even within individuals from week to week, anger and frustration are common. In addition, anxiety and depression are also prevalent as the positive self-image that a person tries to maintain gets battered and confidence crumbles. Quite often, the inherent mechanisms by which people defend and maintain their egos cause them to direct their frustration toward others. This is a primary reason behind the common symptom of blaming others. In any gathering spot for Americans, one is likely to find conversations peppered with statements like these:

I can't believe how stupid these Japanese are. Their street addresses make absolutely no sense.
Europeans think they're so superior to the rest of us.
Headquarters has no idea of how things should be run in this country.
The locals are just plain lazy. It's impossible to motivate them, and they feel no loyalty to the company.
This whole thing is my spouse's fault. He has no appreciation for what I'm going through. He has his comfortable little cocoon at the office.

Unfortunately, many people never recover from culture shock. Some return home early, but not all. Many of those who never recover stay for the duration of their overseas assignments, usually fearful of the consequences of returning early, or sometimes hopeful that things will get better with time.

Most of those who stay eventually work their way through culture shock and gradually adjust to living and working overseas. The pain of making mistakes is the primary source of culture shock, but it can also be a source of adjustment. For example, it is unlikely that Fred will put his chopsticks into his rice in future meetings with Japanese clients. When a mistake is made and, more important, recognized, it is less likely to be repeated or to become a source of frustration or embarrassment to the expatriate. Gradually, through making mistakes, recognizing them, and observing what others do to behave appropriately and successfully in the foreign culture, people learn what to do and what not to do and when.

Summary

Several general statements about cross-cultural adjustment can be made. People establish routines to obtain a certain level of predictability in life and to achieve a certain level of psychological economy. Routines also provide an important means of preserving and maintaining one's ego and self-image. Living and working in new cultures generally disrupts established routines. The more routines disrupted, the more severely a given routine is altered, and the more a disrupted routine is critical, the greater the time and mental energy required to cope and the greater the frustration, anger, and anxiety associated with culture shock. Most important, however, is the fact that disruption of routines is generally accompanied by situations that challenge an individual's confidence, ego, and self-esteem. Threats to these sensitive areas cause the strongest reactions associated with culture shock—depression, anger, denial, and even hatred. In principle, then, factors that increase disruption and uncertainty tend to inhibit cross-cultural adjustment, while factors that reduce disruption and uncertainty tend to facilitate cross-cultural adjustment. Having outlined the basic process of culture shock and adjustment, we can now turn our attention to the specific processes of effectively selecting and training managers for international assignments.

Notes

1. Schein, "Coming to a New Awareness of Organizational Culture."
2. Kroeber and Kluckhohn, *Culture: A Critical Review of Concepts and Definitions.*

3. Schein, "Coming to a New Awareness."
4. McGregor, *The Human Side of Enterprise.*
5. Hofstede, *Culture's Consequences: International Differences in Work-Related Values.*
6. Black, "Fred Bailey: An Innocent Abroad."

Part Two

Before
the Assignment

Chapter 3

Selecting:
Finding the Right People

Sue Harris, director of Emanon's environmental systems division, was on the phone.

"Only five and a half weeks before I have to send *somebody* to Sweden . . . but who?"

Bill Webster responded curtly from corporate headquarters in New York.

"You know your people better than I do, Sue. Just get somebody over there fast, and make sure they put a stop to the problems!"

During the previous year, Emanon's Stockholm subsidiary, which was primarily responsible for product engineering, had missed several critical deadlines in attempting to complete necessary redesign of a market-leading pollution-control system. These delays had been costly, since the redesign was essential to Emanon's globally integrated production process. Corporate headquarters wanted an immediate management change in Stockholm, to ensure that the current redesign would be finished within three months and to set the Stockholm subsidiary on a straight course so that future engineering projects would stay ahead of production needs instead of behind them.

Sue spent the rest of the morning reflecting on who had the right technical background to manage the design process effectively for pollution-control systems. She considered calling the human resources department for input but decided against it, since this would just slow down the decision-making process. After mentally reviewing the best engineers in her division, she came up with a short list of three good candidates for the Stockholm job.

As Sue looked over the list, her mind turned again and again to Max Eisenhardt. Max was one of the best engineers she had in the United States. Perhaps more important, he also fully understood the pollution-control systems being redesigned in Stockholm. Besides, Max was a no-nonsense manager who had done a terrific job in fixing a product-engineering problem in the New Jersey plant over the previous two years. Without much more deliberation, Sue decided that Max was the right choice and called him to set up an interview.

Two days later, Max flew from New Jersey to Sue's office in Chicago. During the interview, Sue explained that the job in Sweden would not be easy. The Stockholm subsidiary had been consistently behind with product designs, and its new manager would have to turn the situation around. Max responded confidently: if he could do it in New Jersey he could do it just as well in Stockholm. Sue also said that the position was a high-visibility opportunity in the firm, since corporate headquarters knew that there were problems in Stockholm, and whoever turned the operation around could expect a hero's welcome upon returning. With that, Max decided that the international assignment would be a fantastic career move. He couldn't wait to get home and convince his wife and his family that the job in Sweden would be the opportunity of a lifetime.

Destined to Fail: The American
Approach to Global Assignments

Emanon's response to the staffing problem in Sweden reflects the way in which many U.S. multinationals approach the selection process for global assignments and how this approach is often destined to fail.[1] Basically, a crisis had arisen in a foreign operation, and there was little time to assess the situation strategically and systematically. A strong desire to put the foreign "fire" out resulted in a obsession with candidates' technical and managerial qualifications and their presumed ability to solve the short-term problem. With little time to make her choice, Sue Harris ignored the personnel department's resources and considered a narrow range of potential candidates; the people with whom she was familiar. She failed to consider the ability of the candidates and their families to adjust to and function effectively in a new cultural environment. This type of selection process can easily result in costly premature return or ineffective performance throughout an assignment—just the things that Sue wanted to avoid.

Such failures are often direct results of firms' rapid selection of technically qualified candidates who may lack the cross-cultural communication or adjustment skills to perform effectively in a foreign assignment.[2] Furthermore, the general U.S. practice of not carefully considering the spouse and the family situation often results in disaster when spouses and family members encounter severe cross-cultural difficulties. As one U.S. human resource executive told us, "For twenty-four years I have seen expatriate families come and go; many would fail or be miserable because they did not have the split level home on a dead end street, the Jell-o, the cotton bread, the prepared foods." Unfortunately, some failures could be avoided if multinational firms would stop adhering to tradition-bound selection practices.

Common U.S. Selection Practices

Sue Harris of Emanon felt pressured by corporate headquarters to quickly find and select a candidate who would definitely change the Stockholm subsidiary's performance. Sue knew that her success as division director would seriously depend on the success of her selection for this global assignment. In this situation, she undoubtedly wanted to minimize any risk that her chosen candidate would fail, since the failure would ultimately reflect on her own performance.[3] This approach is not inherently wrong; everyone wants to succeed. What was wrong was the inadequacy of the selection process. Unfortunately, Sue's attempt to minimize the risk of failure probably maximized the risk of failure.

The people with the best technical skills are not necessarily those with the best cross-cultural adjustment skills. In fact, a global assignment failure (poor performance or premature return) is generally the result of ineffective cross-cultural adjustment by expatriates and their families, rather than the outcome of inadequate technical or professional skills.[4] Our research has found that the successful completion of a global assignment is linked more closely to the expatriate's and the spouse's adjustment to the new culture than to the expatriate's adjustment to the new work role. Moreover, as we have just been saying, the exorbitant cost of global assignment failures can cycle back to hurt the parent company, the foreign operation, the expatriate, and the decision maker who selected the failed expatriate. Nevertheless, U.S. firms still rely first and foremost on technical, job-related skills when assessing candidates for global assignments, and this narrow focus on technical competence usually overshadows more critical criteria.[5]

A focus on technical skills as the only selection criterion can also result in short-circuited selection processes. Decision makers who rapidly locate technically qualified candidates are less likely to scour the organization for candidates with similar technical qualifications but better cross-cultural skills. In a very important study of global assignment selection processes, Edwin Miller of the University of Michigan examined the activities that managers engaged in before making selection decisions.[6] He found that when decision makers did not quickly identify candidates with high qualifications (technical, job-related competence), they were more likely to carefully define the range of skills required, determine more precisely how to measure performance during the assignment, search more aggressively for potential candidates throughout domestic and international divisions (by seeking references from fellow managers or reviewing personnel files), and request more assistance from human resources departments. Essentially, a paradox is inherent in the selection process of many U.S. firms. When *no* candidates with high technical and job-related qualifications are immediately accessible, line managers extend the search throughout the corporation, to locate individuals with strong professional qualifications in addition to superior cross-cultural adaptation and communication skills; but when *one or several* technically qualified candidates quickly come to decision makers' attention, the decision makers terminate their search and often miss candidates with equal technical abilities but superior cross-cultural skills.

Common Selection Practices in Japan, Europe, and Scandinavia

Selection processes used by U.S. firms are somewhat similar to those found in Japan, Europe, and Scandinavia. Rosalie Tung's study of the selection process in the United States, Japan, and Europe found that "managerial talent" was one of the top selection criteria in all three geographical areas for selection of CEOs in foreign operations.[7] In Scandinavia, professional qualifications are also the predominant criterion used by line managers in selecting personnel for global assignments.[8] Essentially, multinational firms throughout the world tend to focus their selection efforts on finding individuals for global assignments who exhibit the highest professional or managerial qualifications. This focus may well lead firms around the world to commit some of the same selection errors as firms in the United States do.

Some similarities do exist, then, between selection processes in the United States and those in Japan, Europe, and Scandinavia. There are differences, however, such as in the degree to which specific selection methods are utilized. For example, interviews are utilized almost always in the United States (99%) and Europe (100%) but less frequently in Japan (71%) and Scandinavia (75%). These differences are even more apparent when we consider how frequently the spouse is interviewed before the decision is made. The interviewing or briefing of spouses is only moderate in the United States (52%) and Europe (41%) and is quite low in Scandinavia (18%) and nonexistent in Japan.[9] We should remember, however, that these differences do not necessarily result in better or worse assessments of candidates' and spouses' abilities. The differences in interview use may well stem from unique cultural factors. In Japan, for example, the family is simply not an issue in the selection process;

if a man is advised to make an international transfer, the assignment's effect on the family is not considered relevant, because Japanese decision makers believe that a wife will not really be able to influence her husband's decision. Even if a Japanese wife rejected a decision to move overseas, her husband would still be bound to the firm and would have to take the global assignment.[10] It is important to note, however, that the cultural homogeneity and paternalistic practices of Japanese business do provide built-in, ongoing mechanisms for identifying potentially difficult situations involving the spouse and the family. Other cultural reasons may explain why so few Scandinavian firms evaluate spouses. In Scandinavia, there is strong respect for personal privacy, along with an implicit expectation that home life will not be subject to formal organizational evaluation. As in Japan, however, the smallness of the Scandinavian countries and the relative homogeneity within each one provide opportunities for Scandinavian firms to learn about potentially difficult spouse and family situations without relying on extensive formal evaluation.

There are also differences in the degree to which personality or skill tests are utilized as selection methods. Line managers and human resources professionals agree that candidates' ability to communicate with and relate to people across cultures is important to successful international assignments, but very few firms actually test these skills formally.[11] Specifically, 24 percent of Scandinavian and 21 percent of European firms rely on formal testing mechanisms to evaluate candidates' relational ability. In contrast, only 5 percent of U.S. and no Japanese firms utilize tests to assess candidates' relational skills.[12] A very recent study of 256 Fortune 500 firms by Organization Resources Counselors found that only 2 percent utilized formal testing mechanisms to assess candidates.[13] Collectively, these findings indicate that Scandinavian and European firms may be slightly more strategic and systematic in selecting international personnel, since they utilize a wider variety of evaluation methods and pay more attention to cross-cultural skills (in addition to technical qualifications). More important, if Scandinavian and European firms are indeed approaching international assignments more strategically, they are probably in a position to increase their influence in world markets through effective staffing.

Putting Strategy into Selection

To acquire or maintain a competitive position in the global marketplace, a firm must seek the highest possible return on its international assignment investments. The first step is to integrate strategy into the selection process of global employees. As the firm increases its global reach and moves through various stages of globalization, it needs to pay attention to the selection process, which becomes increasingly important. For example, a firm moving from the export stage to the coordinated multinational stage of globalization must plan strategically for the future, since the need for qualified expatriates will be much greater as the firm moves out of the export stage. Without such organizational foresight, the firm will undoubtedly reach a future global expansion point, only to discover a shortage of qualified personnel for effective staffing. Furthermore, if the firm fails to take a strategic perspective on global assignments, its selection process probably will be doomed to a short-term focus on people capable of solving current technical problems.

In Chapter One, we discussed three central strategic purposes for international assignments: coordination and control, information and technology exchange, and succession planning. In the Emanon case, discussed at the beginning of this chapter, Max Eisenhardt's assignment to Stockholm could have served the important strategic function of information and technology exchange, but his hasty selection virtually ensured that this strategic function would not be systematically accomplished. There were unique engineering designs in this case, which Max could have acquired from Swedish engineers, and which could have been forwarded to other divisions of Emanon to create market innovations and increased sales for the entire firm. To learn about and utilize this technology transfer opportunity, however, Emanon would have needed to select and send someone other than Max, someone with more effective cross-cultural communication skills. Another strategic function, succession planning at Emanon, could have been enhanced if Sue Harris had identified candidates besides Max who had both the ability to solve short-term production-design problems and the potential to develop global leadership skills and outlooks. The selection of a candidate with both abilities could have resulted in the development of a general manager with international experience, who could have assumed important executive positions in Emanon's worldwide operations. Although Max was technically quite capable, he did not possess the general management potential needed for a position as a future senior executive in the firm. Essentially, one mistake that Emanon made (one that many firms make) was to ignore strategic rationales for the global assignment and thereby sacrifice long-term objectives for short-term results. A more systematic selection process could have achieved both long- and short-term objectives.

In selecting individuals to serve strategic functions during international assignments, firms must remember that these functions are accomplished in unique cross-cultural contexts. Accordingly, we now examine specific factors that should be considered in the selection of successful international managers.

Selection Factors for Successful Global Assignments

Practicing managers and international researchers have developed relatively long lists of critical "factors" to consider in making selection decisions for global assignments. To sift through these lists, we should remember the fundamental purpose of the selection process: to choose individuals who will stay the entire duration of their global assignments and accomplish the strategic and tactical purposes of their assignments. Researchers have outlined several categories of expatriate- and spouse-related factors that decision makers should consider in order to select successful candidates for global assignments. A summary of selection criteria used in the United States, Europe, and Scandinavia is shown in Table 3.1. As the table shows, firms throughout the world use a variety of similar and different criteria for selecting expatriates. Professional-technical qualifications are the most prevalent and significant selection criterion in all three geographical regions. Rosalie Tung's study of international human resources management practices in Japan also found that managerial talent and technical skills were very important selection criteria.[14] In contrast to the consistent focus on technical skills, European firms rely more heavily on spouse- and

Table 3.1. Common Selection Criteria in the United States, Europe, and Scandinavia.

United States		Europe		Scandinavia	
Selection Criteria for Highly Qualified Expatriates	Order of Importance	Selection Criteria	Order of Importance	Selection Criteria	Order of Importance
Demonstrated performance in similar job	1	Technical expertise	1	Technical or other professional qualities	1
Direct knowledge of this particular job	2	Language	2	Previous achievements	2
		Family support	2	Motivation	3
General perceptiveness and grasp of problems	3	Managerial potential	3	Managerial talents	4
		Knowing company systems	4	Independence	5
Leadership skills, ability to command respect	4	Experience	5	Communicative talent	6
Administrative skills	5	Marital status	5	Language skills	7
		Medical status	6	Ambition and commitment	8
Willingness to accept overseas assignment	6	Independence	6	Flexibility	9
Knowledge of the company	7	Motivation	6	Adaptability of the family	10
Reputation	8	Age	6		
		Liaison skills	6		
Willingness to accept the responsibility of the job	9	Gender	7		
		Seniority	7		
Past performance in overseas assignment	10	Vulnerability to military conscription	8		
Potential for more responsible position	11				
Spouse's attitudes toward overseas assignment	12				
Ability to work with foreign employees	13				

Sources: Miller, 1973 (United States); Brewster, 1991 (Europe); Björkman and Gertsen, 1992 (Scandinavia).

family-related factors when selecting expatriates than do U.S., Scandinavian, or Japanese firms. Differences among geographical regions also seem to exist with respect to language skills and expatriates' adaptability.

Selection Factors Predictive of Expatriate Success

While decision makers may consider many potential factors when selecting individuals for global assignments, we have focused on those that are most relevant to success overseas. We chose factors that either should be related to the strategic functions of an assignment or historically have been related to the successful completion of global assignments.

"Strategic" Factors. Multinational firms must consider critical strategic aspects of each international assignment. To be accomplished successfully, each strategic function requires several types of skills, experiences, and contacts. For example, if a global assignment's primary purposes are to improve the control function between headquarters and the subsidiary and to increase the coordination function between subsidiaries, then the candidate should have broad experience in the firm, including a wide array of contacts throughout the company. Another strategic purpose of an international assignment may be the exchange of critical information between the foreign operation and headquarters. This exchange may require the movement of information not only from headquarters to a subsidiary but also from the subsidiary back to headquarters.[15] To perform this strategic function successfully, a candidate not only must have the necessary information from headquarters but also must possess excellent cross-cultural communication skills, since the information must be conveyed to the subsidiary, and important information acquired from the subsidiary must be transmitted back to headquarters. If the strategic purpose of an assignment is management or executive development, then candidates' experience within the firm and their advancement potential should be considered carefully. Of course, these strategic functions are not mutually exclusive, and the selection criteria relevant to performing one function (say, coordination) are often relevant to performing another

(say, information exchange). What is critical is that the firm pay attention first to defining the strategic purposes of the global assignment and then to carefully assessing the skills, knowledge, and experience required to accomplish those purposes.

Professional Skills. Whether the job assignment is for a CEO, a functional department head, or a technical specialist, there is no question that professional skills (either managerial or technical) are essential. These skills generally include direct knowledge of the job and a grasp of the specific problems to be solved. For example, in the Emanon case, Max Eisenhardt needed engineering and pollution-control knowledge in addition to managerial skills. Nevertheless, while technical qualifications are necessary, they are often insufficient to guarantee success and maximize the return on a firm's investment in a global assignment.

General Managerial Skills. In domestic as well as international managerial positions, approaches to conflict resolution can have a significant impact on an assignment's success. Researchers have found that a primary source of stress during global assignments is interpersonal conflict.[16] More important, the ways in which expatriates resolve conflict can have significant impacts on effectiveness. For example, studies of Japanese and Canadian managers found that dealing collaboratively with cross-cultural interpersonal conflicts was related to more effective adjustment.[17] The collaborative approach to conflict resolution is important because it helps individuals focus on understanding other parties (and cultures) instead of forcing others to see it their way.

The leadership styles of expatriate managers can also have a significant impact on their effectiveness during global assignments. Extensive research by Blake and Mouton has demonstrated that high-involvement management, which focuses not only on accomplishing tasks but also on paying attention to people, is generally superior to other managerial styles.[18] Management research has also found that trusting fellow employees and involving them in the decision-making process results in better overall decisions, greater acceptance of decisions, and increased satisfaction in domestic[19] and international management situations.[20]

Communication Skills. The ability to communicate is crucial to expatriates' success in global assignments. Most strategic functions of global assignments require individuals to communicate effectively in other cultures. Research has found several important dimensions of the cross-cultural communication process relevant to expatriate managers.

Without some level of host-country language proficiency, it is very difficult to communicate genuinely with host-country nationals in a new culture. All things being equal, language proficiency is a tremendous advantage in trying to operate in a foreign land.[21] As one American expatriate explained: "The 'key' to understanding the host country is the language. I cannot possibly understand why companies do not provide more language training to accomplish this!"

We have also found that willingness to communicate is also critical to effective adjustment during a global assignment.[22] While this characteristic may seem obvious, many expatriates are simply unwilling to try to communicate genuinely with host-country nationals; they rely on subordinates and translators to communicate the "necessary information" instead of engaging in significant two-way conversations. Furthermore, this unwillingness to communicate can ultimately frustrate the strategic purposes of the assignment, since it will be difficult to fully coordinate, control, and transfer information without effective communication. The importance of wanting to communicate is also relevant to spouses overseas, since they often have to work hard to initiate and develop social relationships and must try to communicate with others, even when others may not want to communicate with them. For example, one American spouse told us, "During both of my global assignments, I have not once received a warm welcome or strong social support from other bank wives. I knew I would have to build my own life overseas but I expected the first steps to be taken by others in England. My advice to future expatriate spouses? Be prepared and willing to develop contacts and friendships from day one."

Finally, a person's social orientation, or ability to develop significant relationships, can have a positive impact on expatriate adjustment.[23] In other words, an abiding interest in developing relationships, regardless of the situation, can help an expatriate reach out in a foreign assignment and develop significant social relationships with host-country nationals, who can provide critical work- and nonwork-related information and feedback on how the manager is doing.

Individual Characteristics. Research on international management has assessed an extensive array of individual characteristics that may be relevant to the selection process. Perhaps more important, however, our own research and that of others has found that certain of these characteristics are especially critical to cross-cultural adjustment.[24] These characteristics are especially pertinent to North American and Japanese managers but may be relevant to others as well.

How we interpret what is going on around us can have a significant impact on our adjustment in a foreign assignment. We often misinterpret and negatively evaluate the behavior of people when we cross cultural boundaries.[25] For example, a Japanese manager in a negotiation process with an older manager from Finland may think that the sound created by the Finn sucking in air through his mouth means that the Finn has a negative response to the deal, but the Finn can actually be communicating agreement by making the same sound that indicates disagreement in Japan. If an American were involved, he or she might wonder if Japanese and Finnish people have breathing problems. Using our own rules for interpreting often leads us to misinterpret behavior in other cultures. Accordingly, those expatriates who are less judgmental and less likely to evaluate behavior in the new culture have a much easier time adjusting to the new environment.[26] Moreover, those who are less rigid in their evaluations of the "rightness" and "wrongness" of others' behavior are more likely to succeed in global assignments. When individuals see their own way as the only "right" way, this characteristic is often referred to as *ethnocentricity*. The significance of this characteristic has been reinforced again and again: expatriates and spouses from around the world tell us that people on global assignments must be flexible and have open minds.

Another important characteristic to look for in potential expatriates is willingness to try new things.[27] These things might include new foods, new sports, new forms of recreation, or new ways of traveling. For example, when Americans visit Japan, are they willing to try sushi or yakisoba instead of a Big Mac and fries? When Swedes come to Miami, are they willing to substitute jai alai for hockey? Opportunities to try something new occur frequently in a foreign culture, and individuals who are adventurous enough to try new things are much more likely to adjust effectively. Families will not find the foods they are used to, but discovering new foods and things to do can actually be fun. The new culture will not be home, but if families can live with that, they will discover the new country's charm.

When individuals enter a new culture, a tremendous amount of stress may accompany a tidal wave of new experiences. An individual's ability to cope with stress can significantly buffer these stressful experiences. For example, one study[28] found that well-adjusted expatriates developed "stability zones" that functioned like harbors in a storm. These zones included such activities as hobbies, writing in diaries, and contemplation or religious worship. The activities allowed the managers to withdraw temporarily from situations and gain better perspective on the new culture or to break away from the constant struggle of trying to solve complex business problems made even more formidable by the fact that the new culture's language, business customs, political systems, laws, and people were not fully understood.

Gender-Related Factors. Up to this point, we have been discussing the importance of technical, strategic, communication, and individual factors in selecting individuals for global assignments. U.S. firms also pay significant attention to whether the candidate is a man or a woman. Fewer than 15 percent of U.S. human resources directors publicly acknowledge that they intentionally select male candidates more often than female candidates for global assignments, but the reality is that they do, more than 95 percent of the time.[29] This bias also exists in Japanese and Finnish selection practices (99 percent and 91 percent, respectively). In U.S. firms, the reasoning behind the gender-based selection criterion is twofold: foreigners are biased against female managers, and dual-career couples face insurmountable challenges.[30] Neither rationale is completely defensible. Our research in the United States, Japan, and Finland, as well as research by Adler, presents consistent evidence that women perform just as well as men do, both during and after global assignments.[31] This is even true for female expatriates in traditionally male-dominated societies like Japan and Korea. For example, a female executive sent to Japan from IBM corporate headquarters in the United States is seen by the Japanese first as a company representative, second as a foreigner, and third as a woman. The first two factors add up to the expatriate's gender becoming a nonissue for most Japanese businessmen. Even if foreigners are not used to having women in the workplace, this cultural bias does not necessarily result in performance problems for female expatriates. Furthermore, our research on U.S. expatriates and spouses has shown that expatriates in dual-career situations are just as likely as single-career couples to complete global assignments and perform effectively after returning home.[32]

U.S. firms should not discount the positive impact that female expatriates can have on profits. As firms attempt to globalize, they should cast an increasingly wider selection net throughout the company, to select the very best male and female candidates. The increased level of global competition demands that firms discard their unfounded biases and assess the potential female candidates more seriously when making international selection decisions.

Selection Factors Predictive of Expatriate Spouse and Family Success

In many ways, the basic selection factors that firms should consider when assessing expatriate candidates are equally applicable to the expatriates' spouses and family members. Although specific technical skills and those skills related to accomplishing strategic purposes for the firm are not relevant to spouses and family members, other factors, such as communication skills and individual characteristics, are as relevant to spouses and family members as they are to expatriates. For example, since spouses' effective communication with host-country nationals has been linked directly to expatriates' staying the full duration of global assignments, it seems logical that a spouse's communication skills are also critical to success overseas.[33] In addition to family members' communication skills and individual characteristics, it is important for firms to consider spouses' career situations and children's educational needs.

Spouses' Career Situations. If a spouse intends to work during a global assignment, the firm must consider whether the host country will provide work permits for both the expatriate and the spouse. If the country will not provide work permits for both partners, the firm should not immediately discount their candidacy. Our interviews and surveys of dual-career couples find that many who had dual careers before their assignments found it rewarding to become single-career couples during their global assignments.[34] Of course, there are challenges inherent in going back to work after an assignment, since the spouse will have had a break in his or her career, but the overall experience can still be rewarding. We have also found that dual-career expatriate couples are just as likely as non-dual-career couples to perform effectively during a global assignment. Essentially, the fact that a dual-career situation exists before the global assignment should not deter a firm from considering a candidate. The spouses may want to change their dual-career status, or they may both effectively continue their careers during the assignment.

Children's Educational Needs. Since more than 80 percent of expatriates around the world are married and more than 70 percent have children with them during their assignments, it is important for multinational firms to consider the educational needs of expatriate families.[35] We have worked with one Finnish firm, which was starting up a chemical production plant in a small town in Denmark. During the selection process, the firm found that many potential expatriates were not interested in the international career opportunity because English-speaking schools for their children did not exist in the Danish town. Fortunately, the firm realized that families' educational needs were influencing the availability of the best-qualified candidates. The firm collaborated with Danish community officials and arranged for the initiation of an English-speaking school program for children of the firm's expatriates, as well as for children of other expatriates in the area. Because children's adjustment to global assignments is undoubtedly linked to spousal and overall expatriate adjustment, firms must take account of children's educational needs during the selection process. Otherwise, they may get caught in the dilemma that one U.S. firm recently faced. The firm sent an American manager to Australia, never realizing that his child had significant learning disabilities. The child's schooling during the assignment was inadequate, and the whole family struggled throughout the experience.[36]

Evaluating Selection Factors for Successful Assignments

After the firm decides which selection criteria are most relevant to a global assignment, it needs to determine how to evaluate candidates effectively on those criteria. Managers have a variety of tools at their disposal for assessing candidates. Each of these tools has strengths and weaknesses, which are summarized in the answer to the following question: Is the tool reliable and valid?[37]

A selection tool is reliable if it yields similar results in the hands of different people or at different times. For example, if both the human resources department and the line manager have interviewed a candidate for a global assignment and agreed that the candidate has strong communication skills, the method is deemed reliable. If a candidate completes a cross-cultural skills test on two different days and receives very different scores each time, the test is considered unreliable.

The validity of a selection tool depends on the extent to which the tool consistently finds that a particular selection factor is predictive of success during a global assignment. For example, if language skills are deemed relevant to a particular global assignment, then candidates may be assessed with a standardized language test. Even if this test produces reliable or consistent results for a given candidate's language ability, it will be considered valid only if variations in test scores predict variations in the success of global assignments.

Methods of Selection

U.S. firms tend to rely on a very limited range of selection tools, but a variety are actually available. Some of the most effective tools are biographical data, standardized tests, work samples, and assessment centers. Selection interviews and personal references are widely used but less effective. We will discuss each of these tools here and examine how reliable and valid they are in selecting candidates for international assignments.

Biographical and Background Data. This selection tool consists of background information about candidates' personal and work histories. For example, professional-technical skills are an important selection criterion. These skills can be assessed reliably and validly by reviewing a candidate's objective job performance. In the case of Emanon, Sue Harris's selection of Max Eisenhardt was based in part on background data, which indicated that he had significant work experience in pollution-control systems, an area directly related to the problems in Emanon's Swedish subsidiary. Either a line manager or a human resources director could have determined these technical skills on the basis of a factual work history.

Standardized Tests. If standardized tests assess factors that are indeed relevant to a successful global assignment, they can be very reliable and valid selection tools. For example, engineers are often required to take standardized tests for certification in different states or countries throughout their careers. These tests are usually quite reliable and valid predictors of an engineer's knowledge base. Individual characteristics, communications competence, and managerial skills are also related to successful global assignments. Many such factors, such as conflict-resolution style or willingness to communicate, can be reliably and validly assessed with standardized psychological tests. Nevertheless, U.S., Japanese, European, and Scandinavian firms rarely use standardized tests to assess such selection criteria.[38] Specifically, 5 percent of the U.S. firms, none of the Japanese firms, 21 percent of the European firms, and 24 percent of the Scandinavian firms utilize standardized tests for assessing relational skills in potential expatriates. In our own work with multinational firms, we have developed a standardized test that assesses several important selection criteria for global assignments. The Foreign Assignment Selection Test (F.A.S.T.) survey appraises candidates along six critical criteria: cultural flexibility, willingness to communicate, ability to develop social relationships, perceptual abilities, conflict-resolution style, and leadership style. Our initial research has found that most of the F.A.S.T. criteria are indeed related to expatriate adjustment at work and outside of work in a new cultural environment.[39]

Work Samples. This selection tool takes a "slice" of the prospective job and places the candidate in the work situation. For example, one function for the director of Emanon's Stockholm subsidiary is to chair meetings and committees. For Emanon to determine whether Max was the best candidate for the subsidiary position, it might have been useful to simulate a meeting in Sweden by having Swedish managers or engineers travel to the United States or by having Max travel to Sweden and direct a Swedish meeting. Of course, this might have been a challenge for Max, since he was used to working with New Jersey employees in a very direct fashion and might have encountered difficulty working with Swedish professionals who have been known in Scandinavia for their ability to hold a meeting, discuss many issues, and make one or more decisions without a foreigner's even knowing that the decisions have been made. Max's performance in this work sample would have provided Sue with more reliable and valid information about his actual ability to manage in Stockholm.

Assessment Centers. Assessment centers are a very comprehensive and expensive method for reliably and validly evaluating a variety of technical and relational skills.[40] An assessment center typically runs from two to three days and includes in-depth interviews, standardized tests, and several work samples. Many firms, such as AT&T utilize assessment centers regularly to assess managerial talent in the organization. In addition to the typical criteria assessed in these centers, multinational firms may assess important selection criteria for future global assignments. For example, they may have candidates eat food from a variety of different cultures and evaluate their reactions. They may also try to teach them culturally new games (such as jai alai for North Americans) and assess the extent to which they catch on and enjoy it. In addition to assessing such skills as cultural flexibility, assessment centers may examine willingness to communicate in a new foreign language or stress-reduction mechanisms by placing candidates in a series of highly stressful activities. In sum, the research evidence on assessment centers suggests that they can be an effective tool for selecting more qualified candidates. Again, however, we are not aware of any U.S. multinationals that systematically take advantage of this tool in selecting candidates for global assignments.[41]

Interviews. Of all selection tools, interviews are most utilized by U.S., Japanese, European, and Scandinavian multinationals.[42] In fact, candidates for international management positions are interviewed 100 percent of the time in Europe, 99 percent of the time in the United States, 75 percent of the time in Scandinavia, and 71 percent of the time in Japan. Unfortunately, an unstructured interview is not a highly reliable or valid method for effectively evaluating selection criteria.[43] This extreme reliance on interviews as the selection method is most likely a result of the haphazard, short-term approach that managers tend to take when they are faced with staffing needs overseas.

References. Verbal or written references are frequently used by decision makers when selecting individuals for global assignments. Like interviews, unfortunately, references are quite variable in reliability and validity. Their usefulness depends highly on the degree to which the evaluator knows the specific job requirements for the international posting and understands the appropriateness of the information provided about the candidate.[44] Again, decision makers around the world rely in large part on personal references because they are inexpensive and easily obtainable forms of evaluation, even though they are not necessarily reliable or valid.

Matrix of Methods and Criteria. Clearly, there is a wide range of methods for effectively assessing candidates for global assignments. They range from very reliable and valid to relatively undependable. A summary of these methods and their relevance to various selection criteria is shown in Table 3.2. Unfortunately, the short-term approach of most multinational firms leads them to rely on a limited set of criteria (technical skills) and the least reliable and valid selec-

SELECTION METHODS

SELECTION CRITERIA	Biographical Data	Standardized Tests	Work Samples	Assessment Centers	Interviews	References
Expatriate						
Strategic factors						
Coordination and control	✓				✓	✓
Information and technology exchange	✓				✓	✓
Executive development	✓				✓	✓
Professional skills	✓			✓		✓
General managerial skills		✓	✓		✓	
Conflict-resolution approach		✓	✓	✓	✓	
Leadership style		✓	✓	✓	✓	
Communication skills						
Foreign-language skills	✓	✓		✓	✓	
Willingness to communicate		✓		✓	✓	
Relationship development		✓	✓	✓	✓	✓
Individual characteristics						
Ethnocentricity		✓		✓	✓	
Cultural adaptability		✓		✓	✓	
Stress-reduction skills		✓		✓	✓	
Spouse's career considerations					✓	
Children's educational needs					✓	
Spouse						
Communication skills						
Foreign-language skills	✓	✓		✓	✓	
Willingness to communicate		✓	✓	✓	✓	
Relationship development		✓		✓	✓	✓
Individual characteristics						
Ethnocentricity		✓			✓	
Cultural adaptability		✓		✓	✓	
Stress-reduction skills		✓			✓	
Spouse's career considerations					✓	
Children's educational needs					✓	

tion methods (interviews and references). Nevertheless, there are additional criteria and more effective means of selecting employees for international assignments.[45]

Who Should Evaluate Selection Factors?

Decision makers not only must pay attention to selection criteria and methods but also must pay more strategic attention to who performs evaluations. Most U.S. firms use a limited set of decision makers for selecting candidates to take global assignments. Most often, a decision is made by one individual, the line manager with overall responsibility for the international unit, but others can also be involved in the selection process (for example, representatives from the international unit if the assignment is to a middle- or upper-level managerial position). Moreover, the human resources department is often underutilized in the selection process and usually plays an after-the-fact role, making travel and overseas compensation arrangements. If firms want to become more strategic in their selection processes, they must learn to incorporate personnel departments' resources with those of line managers in home and host countries. In fact, human resources departments could act as decision hubs to ensure that a range of selection criteria are proposed, a variety of selection methods are utilized, and a full complement of candidates is considered.

Who Should Be Evaluated?

A relatively complex aspect of the selection process is the decision about whom to evaluate for a global assignment. Since more than three-quarters of expatriates around the world are married, most selection decisions not only involve the potential expatriate but also the expatriate's spouse and children. Even though the firm may prefer not to inquire into the family situations of its employees, an accurate understanding of the family situation and of the family's perspective on the assignment can reap tremendous benefits.[46] Basically, if the spouse and other family members have a difficult time adjusting to a new country, it is quite likely that the expatriate will either leave the assignment prematurely or perform ineffectively throughout the assignment. Either scenario creates problems for the parent company and the foreign operation. Accordingly, firms must obtain some level of accurate information about a family's willingness to take an assignment and its ability to complete it successfully. Inquiring into family matters is a delicate situation, however. A firm should be straightforward in communicating the pros and cons of a global assignment through an interview or briefing situation instead of over cocktails. This provides an opportunity for the spouse to make a more informed decision. Our research has found that when U.S. firms actively and directly seek spouses' opinions about global assignments, the spouses are much more likely to adjust to interacting with host-country nationals and to living in new cultures during assignments.[47]

Even though there are many potential benefits, relatively few multinational firms actively seek spouses' perspectives on assignments before selection decisions are made. Our research on spouses of U.S. expatriate managers in the Pacific Rim and Europe found that 32 percent had been interviewed or briefed by their firms before the selection decisions were made.[48] This percentage is lower than that found in Tung's study of the same issue, based on data collected from human resources managers.[49] In her study, human resources department heads stated that candidates' spouses were interviewed for managerial assignments 52 percent of the time in the United States, 41 percent of the time in Europe, and not at all in Japan. Scandinavian firms parallel Japanese firms: relatively few of them (18 percent) formally interview spouses during the selection process.[50]

Factors Influencing Decisions to Accept or Refuse Assignments

Until now, we have been focusing on the firm's approach to the selection process. An equally important viewpoint to consider is that of the candidate for the global assignment. What factors influence the decision to accept or refuse a global assignment offer from a multinational firm? Since many factors come into play, we have categorized them into two general groups: career implications and family implications.

Career Implications

When considering global assignment offers, potential global managers ask themselves two fundamental career questions: Will this assignment put me in a strategic business role? Will this assignment lead to my advancement? Since global managers, on the average, have over fourteen years of experience in their parent companies, they want to be certain that an overseas assignment does not leave them out of sight and out of mind. A clear indicator that a global manager will not be forgotten is the firm's having clearly thought about the strategic importance of an assignment and about how its success will produce tangible results and lead to upper-management visibility for the manager. If firms take a "put out the fire" approach to global assignments, however, then it will be hard for candidates to be convinced that such assignments present long-term career advantages.

A global assignment can be expected to lead to advancement in the organization if the assignment is clearly defined as strategic before the selection decision is made. In other words, if an assignment is strategically important to the firm's success, then the expatriate has a much higher probability of being promoted after returning home. Our research shows that relatively few global assignments have led to promotion after the return home, even though most expatriates expected them to.[51] In fact, only 11 percent of Americans, 10 percent of Japanese, and 25 percent of Finns received promotions after completing global assignments lasting at least two years. What is even more stunning, 77 percent of Americans, 43 percent of Japanese, and 54 percent of Finns actually were demoted after returning home. Other studies corroborate these results, even though some executives (such as those featured in a recent *Wall Street Journal* article[52]) attempt to convince the business world that global experience really does matter in today's multinational firms. Specifically, recent studies of Fortune 500 firms have found that executives actually pay attention to global experience as an important promotion criterion for current executive promotions only 4 percent to 7 percent of the time.[53] Collectively, these statistics paint a grim picture for potential expatriates and become very important in the selection process, since candidates for the next set of global assignments see that returning expatriates are not receiving promotions or are even being demoted. If this is indeed the case, it is quite unlikely that the selection process will result in the best candidates being posted; the best candidates will not want to jeopardize their careers with moves that result in demotion more than half the time. Firms must pay better attention to how they communicate, through words and actions, that global assignments really are strategic and really do count.

Financial incentives have played a significant role in attracting individuals to global assignments, and the individual is indeed interested in how a global assignment will affect his or her overall living situation.[54] In Finland, for example, the high cost of new cars leads many individuals to leave the country on overseas assignments in order to avoid import taxes and bring home a new automobile. For expatriates from most countries, a global assignment is often seen as an opportunity to live like a king or a queen for several years. Nevertheless, this overreliance on financial incentives is undoubtedly a function of firms' not carefully deciding and strongly communicating that global assignments are strategic and do result in positive career outcomes. This corporate emphasis on the financial rewards of global assignments has also created a strong expectation on the part of upcoming expatriates that they have a right to such royal treatment, but the increasingly competitive global business environment has forced many firms in the United States and Europe to reduce the financial incentives for taking global assignments. This compensation-reduction trend only reinforces the need for firms to consider the nonfinancial benefits of global assignments, such as completing a strategically important mission for the firm.

Finally, many candidates consider the learning aspect of a global assignment as a critical component of the decision.[55] In fact, candidates with M.B.A. degrees ranked personal growth and gaining a cross-cultural experience as the first reason for accepting future global assignments.

Family Implications

Individuals also pay close attention to how a global assignment will affect their families.[56] One of the initial questions that a spouse may

ask is, "How will this move affect my career?" A spouse must resolve the issue of whether to continue working during an
assignment. If the decision is in favor of working, will that even be
allowed in the country of assignment? Because a spouse may experience a net career loss by giving up a job to take a global assignment, firms like 3M have attempted to deal directly with the career
problems of spouses. For example, 3M provides an "employment
dislocation allowance" of up to $5,000 for working spouses leaving
on global assignments. 3M is also considering the possibility of
paying tuition in the foreign country for spouses during global
assignments in order for them to retain professional skills and obtain appropriate work when they return home. Kodak is attempting
to manage the dilemmas of spouses better by providing increased
job-finding assistance after the global assignment.[57]

In addition to dual-career issues, individuals also consider
such family needs as schooling. Will schools in the host country be
satisfactory? The question of educational quality is important not
only during but also after the assignment. For example, many Japanese families have been sent on global assignments, which typically last more than three and a half years. Expatriate Japanese
children often end up lagging behind their home-country peers and
return with gaps in knowledge and lower language skills. Given the
rigid nature of the Japanese school system, these differences can
create drastic consequences such as failing to enter a prestigious
university or being able to enter a university at all. In addition to
educational issues, the challenges for children who are forced to
leave home and develop new friendships are often great during
global assignments. In sum, candidates must often resolve these
family-related issues before accepting assignments.

Comprehensive Approach to Getting the Right People

We present here some recommendations for how multinational
firms can strategically approach the selection process for global
assignments. The first stage of this process is summarized in Figure
3.1.

Figure 3.1. Strategic Analysis of Global Assignments.

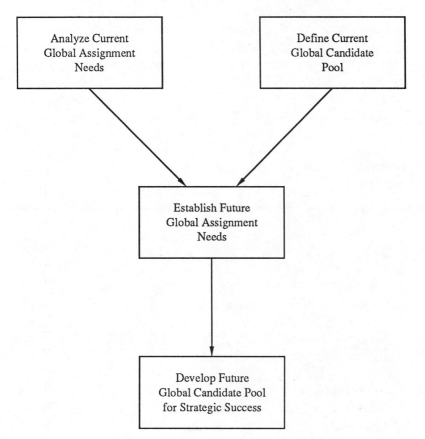

Strategic Analysis of Global Assignments

Making global assignments truly strategic requires the foresight to perform a careful analysis of the firm's overall global assignment needs, define its current global candidate pool, and, most important, assess whether its pool of global candidates will be large enough to meet future demands for effective global managers.

Analyzing Current Needs. An analysis of current needs should consider several critical factors. What stage of globalization is the firm in? Companies in the export stage have significantly fewer demands for international employees than do firms in the coordinated multinational stage. Another important consideration in assessing current global assignment needs is the strategic functions that such assignments should currently play. Does the firm need to send people from headquarters for purposes of coordination and control? Does the company need to raise the level of communication between headquarters, or between subsidiaries? Does the firm need to develop more future executives by giving them global assignments as developmental experiences? Answers to these questions can help a firm decide, from a strategic perspective, what the current needs actually are.

Defining the Candidate Pool. Multinational companies need to know the composition of the current global candidate pool. For many companies, this is a "black box" of information, since there is no centralized clearinghouse for collecting and updating information on candidates with relevant skills and linking these individuals with potential needs. Some companies, however, like Neste Oy, a major Finnish oil and gas firm, have developed comprehensive data bases that detail a manager's current assignment, technical qualifications, previous global experience, cross-cultural skills, and management potential within a firm. Such data bases clearly require an initial investment of time and resources, but they can be invaluable in searching for the best technical and cross-cultural skills to staff a specific global position.

Assessing Future Needs. Firms must plan for the future by deciding what their future global assignment needs will be. Again, these needs will be a function of a firm's future stage of globalization and of the necessary strategic functions for sustaining a global competitive advantage. If a firm is currently at the multidomestic stage, with uncoordinated operations in two or three countries, but intends to become a coordinated multinational with operations in several more countries, that company will have an increasing number of global assignment needs. In addition to its stage of globalization, a firm must consider its key future strategic functions, in order to assess future needs accurately. For example, if a firm intends to make several key strategic acquisitions throughout the world, in order to develop additional technological synergies, it will need to move technology and information from operation to operation, and from overseas to headquarters. The effective flow of information may well require additional global assignments.

Developing the Candidate Pool for Strategic Success. A firm's final strategic step in preparing for the future is the development of a candidate pool. To develop a sufficient pool of qualified candidates for global assignments, a company must implement regular assessments of employees' managerial and cross-cultural skills. In addition to examining managerial advancement potential through traditional succession-planning mechanisms, the firm should regularly assess a variety of skills and individual characteristics associated with successful global assignments. Assessments could examine communication skills, conflict-resolution skills, leadership styles, foreign-language skills, stress-reduction capacity, and cultural flexibility. An analysis of these important cross-cultural skills could be incorporated into traditional assessment center programs or management training courses. The skills could also be assessed with such surveys as F.A.S.T.[58]

In addition to regularly assessing managerial and cross-cultural skills, firms should create strategies and plans for systematically developing skills that many employees may be weak in. For example, the Lord Corporation, a medium-sized, privately held U.S. manufacturing firm, was preparing to set up production operations in France, and so the company offered free French classes on company time to any employee (secretary, line operator, or manager) and has incorporated "French Day" into corporate headquarters once a week. On French Day, the corporate cafeteria serves French foods, so that people can try previously unknown gastronomic delights. This relatively simple but strategically thought-out tradition has helped many employees develop greater cultural flexibility and better French-speaking skills. These activities may seem minor in and of themselves, but, combined with other programs, they help communicate the genuine importance of global competence to employees and provide them with opportunities to develop the necessary skills for completing international assignments.

Selection Process for Specific Assignments

After making a strategic analysis of global assignments within a firm, managers must still face the reality of effectively selecting an individual for a specific global assignment. To assist managers in the decision-making process, we have developed a flow chart of key activities that should lead to more successful and more strategic global assignments (see Figure 3.2).

Creating a Selection Team. The first step in the selection process is to create a selection team. This team should include at least three members: a home-country manager, a host-country manager, and a human resources department representative. The home- and host-country managers help ensure that headquarters and subsidiaries are both served in the selection process. Furthermore, in planning for the future (that is, for during and after the global assignment), the home-country manager can be designated as the expatriate's "sponsor" from the very beginning. The human resources representative can offer several important functions to the selection team, such as ensuring that a range of selection criteria are utilized and helping locate a broad slate of candidates for the position.

Defining Strategic Purposes for Global Assignments. The next step is for the team to carefully decide what the strategic purpose of the global assignment is. As we have said, most assignments are short-term problem-solving experiences, and firms must become more reflective in deciding what the strategic functions of an assignment are before the assignment is made.

Assessing the Context. What will the cultural context of the assignment be? If an assignment requires extensive interaction with host-country nationals, cross-cultural communication and language skills will be important. If the general culture of the host country will be unique and therefore more challenging to candidates, this factor may have a significant impact on the selection criteria and decision.

Establishing Selection Criteria. The selection team should define the criteria that match the technical needs of the job, the strategic

Figure 3.2. Global Assignment Selection Process.

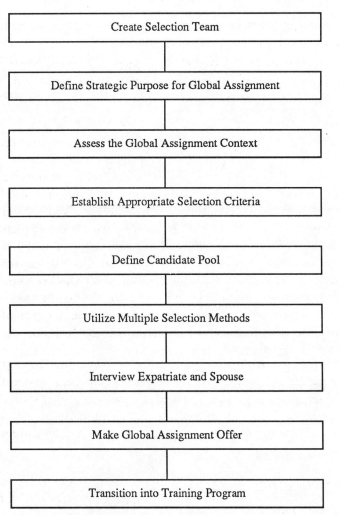

functions of the assignment, and the cross-cultural context of the position. For example, specific engineering knowledge may be needed; if the assignment is also developmental, then potential for advancement as a manager is also a crucial criterion. If extensive interaction with host-country nationals is also required, the selection team should pay attention to cross-cultural communication skills. Finally, the more difficult (or different) the general culture of the foreign country, the more attention the selection team should pay to such issues as cultural flexibility and ethnocentricity.

Defining the Candidate Pool. Once appropriate selection criteria have been developed, the firm can utilize references, internal job postings, and a global candidate pool data base (if available) to match the highest number of potential candidates with a particular assignment.

Utilizing Multiple Selection Methods. After a candidate pool has been defined, the human resources member of the selection team can facilitate the use of a variety of selection methods. Since an overseas assignment will be both costly and risky, the extra expense of utilizing multiple selection methods (such as an assessment center, standardized tests, and preselection interviews) is actually an investment in the future, rather than just an expense in the present. Since most decision makers tend to use selection methods that are unreliable and/or invalid (such as interviews alone), it is critical for the selection team to decide which selection methods are most effective for evaluating which selection criteria for a particular assignment.

Interviewing the Candidate and Briefing the Spouse. At this stage, the selection team will have narrowed the field to one or two potential candidates who, it is hoped, have both the technical and the cross-cultural qualifications for the global assignment. An in-depth interview, which outlines the strategic purpose of the assignment and its relationship to the candidate's career path within the firm, together with an honest assessment of living in the foreign country, can provide a realistic preview for the candidate. In addition, interviews or briefing sessions with the spouse, to provide him or her with realistic expectations about life in the foreign country and to determine unique dual-career and family needs, can significantly enhance the ultimate success of a global assignment. The importance of creating a realistic preview of the job and of living overseas cannot be overemphasized. Interviews must be conducted in a context where both the organization and the potential expatriate can honestly share perspectives and viewpoints on overall aspects of the job assignment and the foreign country.

Making the Offer. If the selection team approves of the candidate after utilizing several selection methods and conducting interviews with the candidate and the spouse, and if the candidate and the spouse are favorable to the assignment after having been given a realistic preview, an offer can be made. It will be based on more relevant, factual, and comprehensive information than what is usually provided before global assignments are made.

Making the Transition to Training and Preparation. The final stage of the selection process entails the transition from acceptance of the assignment to preparation for it. Generally, if the selection process has been strategic and not tactical, then the assignment will be made well enough in advance for appropriate training and preparation to be initiated.

Selection Decisions: The Key to Future Success

There are two fundamental points to make about the selection process for global assignments. First, *people must be ahead of the globalization process of the firm.* In other words, as the firm raises its level of globalization (for example, from a primarily export to a global firm), it must already have a sufficient pool of international human resources, or potentially successful international managers, to sustain its global expansion. Second, *acting strategically now is the key to keeping people ahead of the globalization process.* The strategic assessment of needs and the development of a strong candidate pool can significantly enhance the selection decisions made in multinational firms. Without this strategic component, decision makers easily lapse into ineffective selection practices, such as using technical qualifications as the only selection criterion or relying on interviews as the only selection method. With a strategic orientation to each stage of the selection process, the firm is much more likely to receive a positive return on its high-cost investment as it selects expatriates with the necessary technical and cross-cultural skills who can solve short-term problems and accomplish long-term strategic objectives.

Notes

1. Miller, "The International Selection Decision: A Study of Managerial Behavior in the Selection Decision Process"; Tung, *The New Expatriates: Managing Human Resources Abroad.*
2. Black and Stephens, "Expatriate Adjustment and Intent to Stay in Pacific Rim Overseas Assignments"; Gregersen and Black, "A Multifaceted Approach to Expatriate Retention in International Assignments."
3. Miller, "The International Selection Decision."
4. Black and Stephens, "Expatriate Adjustment"; Gregersen and Black, "A Multifaceted Approach to Expatriate Retention."
5. Miller, "The International Selection Decision"; Tung, *The New Expatriates.*
6. Miller, "The International Selection Decision."
7. Tung, *The New Expatriates.*
8. Björkman and Gertsen, "Selecting and Training Scandinavian Expatriates: Determinants of Corporate Practice"; Gertsen, "Expatriate Training and Selection"; Kainulainen, "Selection and Training of Personnel for Foreign Assignments."
9. Björkman and Gertsen, "Selecting and Training Scandinavian Expatriates"; Tung, *The New Expatriates.*
10. White, *Japanese Overseas.*
11. Zeira and Banai, "Selection of Managers for Foreign Posts."
12. Björkman and Gertsen, "Selecting and Training Scandinavian Expatriates"; Tung, *The New Expatriates.*
13. Organization Resources Counselors, *1990 Survey of International Personnel and Compensation Practices.*
14. Tung, *The New Expatriates.*
15. Gupta and Govindarajan, "Knowledge Flows and the Structure of Control Within Multinational Corporations."
16. Hammer, Gudykunst, and Wiseman, "Dimensions of Intercultural Effectiveness: An Exploratory Study"; Hammer, "Behav-

ioral Dimensions of Intercultural Effectiveness"; Mendenhall and Oddou, "The Dimensions of Expatriate Acculturation."

17. Abe and Wiseman, "A Cross-Cultural Confirmation of Intercultural Effectiveness"; Black, "Personal Dimensions and Work Role Transitions: A Study of Japanese Expatriate Managers in America"; Hawes and Kealey, "An Empirical Study of Canadian Technical Assistance."

18. Blake and Mouton, *The Managerial Grid.*

19. Cotton, Vollrath, Froggatt, Kengnick-Hall, and Jennings, "Employee Participation: Diverse Forms and Different Outcomes."

20. Negandi, Eshghi, and Yuen, "The Managerial Practices of Japanese Subsidiaries Overseas."

21. Björkman and Gertsen, "Selecting and Training Scandinavian Expatriates"; Brewster, *The Management of Expatriates*; Gertsen, "Expatriate Training and Selection"; Kainulainen, "Selection and Training of Personnel for Foreign Assignments."

22. Black, "Personal Dimensions and Work Role Transitions"; Church, "Sojourner Adjustment"; Mendenhall and Oddou, "Dimensions of Expatriate Acculturation."

23. Black, "Personal Dimensions and Work Role Transitions"; Brein and David, "Intercultural Communication and Adjustment of the Sojourner"; Church, "Sojourner Adjustment"; Hammer, Gudykunst, and Wiseman, "Dimensions of Intercultural Effectiveness"; Hawes and Kealey, "An Empirical Study of Canadian Technical Assistance"; Mendenhall and Oddou, "Dimensions of Expatriate Acculturation."

24. Mendenhall and Oddou, "Dimensions of Expatriate Acculturation."

25. Oddou and Mendenhall, "Person Perception in Cross-Cultural Settings: A Review of Cross-Cultural and Related Literature"; Triandis, Vassilou, and Nassiakou, "Three Cross-Cultural Studies of Subjective Culture."

26. Black, "Personal Dimensions and Work Role Transitions"; Ruben and Kealey, "Behavioral Assessment of Communication Competency and the Prediction of Cross-Cultural Adaptation."

27. Black, "Relationship of Personal Characteristics with Adjustment"; Mendenhall and Oddou, "Dimensions of Expatriate Acculturation."

28. Mendenhall and Oddou, "Dimensions of Expatriate Acculturation"; Hawes and Kealey, "An Empirical Study of Canadian Technical Assistance."

29. Adler, "Women in International Management: Where Are They?"; Adler, "Expecting International Success: Female Managers Overseas"; Black, "Work Role Transitions: A Study of American Expatriate Managers in Japan"; Black and Gregersen, "When Yankee Comes Home"; Gregersen and Black, "A Multifaceted Approach to Expatriate Retention."

30. Adler, "Do MBAs Want International Careers?"; Adler, "Women Do Not Want International Careers: And Other Myths About International Management."

31. Adler, "Pacific Basin Managers: A Gaijin, Not a Woman"; Adler and Izraeli, *Women in Management Worldwide*; Black and Gregersen, "When Yankee Comes Home"; Jelenik and Adler, "Women: World-Class Managers for Global Competition."

32. Stephens and Black, "The Impact of the Spouse's Career Orientation on Managers During International Transfers."

33. Hawes and Kealey, "An Empirical Study of Canadian Technical Assistance."

34. Black, Gregersen, and Wethli, "Factors Related to Expatriate Spouses' Adjustment in Overseas Assignments"; Black and Gregersen, "When Yankee Comes Home."

35. Black, Gregersen, and Wethli, "Factors Related to Expatriate Spouses' Adjustment"; Black and Gregersen, "When Yankee Comes Home."

36. Fuchsberg, "As Costs of Overseas Assignments Climb, Firms Select Expatriates More Carefully."

37. Hall and Goodale, *Human Resource Management*.

38. Björkman and Gertsen, "Selecting and Training Scandinavian Expatriates"; Tung, *The New Expatriates*.

39. Black, "Work Role Transitions."

40. Hall and Goodale, *Human Resource Management*.

41. Organization Resources Counselors, *1990 Survey*.

42. Björkman and Gertsen, "Selecting and Training Scandinavian Expatriates"; Tung, *The New Expatriates*.

43. Hall and Goodale, *Human Resource Management*.

44. Hall and Goodale, *Human Resource Management*; Miller, "The International Selection Decision."

45. Miller, "The International Selection Decision."

46. Adler, *International Dimensions of Organizational Behavior*; Black and Gregersen, "The Other Half of the Picture: Antecedents of Spouse Cross-Cultural Adjustment"; Black and Gregersen, "Antecedents to Cross-Cultural Adjustment for Expatriates in Pacific Rim Assignments"; Black and Stephens, "Expatriate Adjustment"; Stephens and Black, "The Impact of the Spouse's Career Orientation."

47. Black and Gregersen, "The Other Half of the Picture."

48. Black and Gregersen, "The Other Half of the Picture."

49. Tung, *The New Expatriates*.

50. Björkman and Gertsen, "Selecting and Training Scandinavian Expatriates."

51. Black and Gregersen, "When Yankee Comes Home."

52. Bennett, "Going Global."

53. Tung, "Career Issues in International Assignments."

54. Black and Gregersen, "The Other Half of the Picture"; Black and Gregersen, "When Yankee Comes Home."

55. Adler, "Do MBAs Want International Careers?"

56. Adler, *International Dimensions of Organizational Behavior*; Black and Gregersen, "The Other Half of the Picture"; Black and Stephens, "Expatriate Adjustment."

57. Fuchsberg, "As Costs of Overseas Assignments Climb."

58. The Foreign Assignment Success Test (F.A.S.T.), an instrument developed by the present authors that measures aptitude for cross-cultural adjustment and includes a feedback report on individuals' strengths, weaknesses, and means of improvement, has been widely used by Japanese firms and is increasingly used by firms in the United States.

Chapter 4

Training:
Helping People Learn
to Do the Right Things

Mel Stephens had not found much comfort in his commute home
from the office. Ordinarily, Mel found that ruminating over a problem during his commute, with a Mozart compact disc reverberating
through his car's interior, allowed his mind to slowly bring even the
most complicated problem into focus. Mel thought he must be out
of his league on this one. He had faced many challenges as vice-
president of human resources since arriving at Recor Engineering,
but none had troubled and nagged at him like this one.

Recor Engineering, one of the leaders in the U.S. domestic
construction industry, had just sealed a joint-venture pact with one
of Japan's largest construction firms, Dentsu Hogen. K.K. Recor, a
San Francisco–based company, had agreed to send a large team of
American experts to work in Osaka with a special group of Dentsu
Hogen's best engineers. The purpose of the effort was to team up
with Japanese counterparts and work together on bidding for the
runway project of the Osaka Airport expansion, as well as to pursue

other related ventures. This arrangement would solve two problems. For Dentsu Hogen, it would buffer pressure from the Japanese government to allow American construction firms into the bidding process for the airport expansion. For Recor, it would mean gaining experience in the Japanese construction industry, to see whether the firm wanted to attempt to enter that market in the future.

The project manager was to be designated by Recor. Larry Runolfsson was selected and had agreed to go. Larry had vast experience in all aspects of the industry and had overseen four projects in the United States, from the idea and bidding stages to completion.

All of the engineers (a total of eighteen) agreed to relocate to Japan after being assured that their families' financial position and standard of living would not suffer because of the new assignment. Most of the engineers were married. None of the engineers indicated any reluctance on the part of their spouses concerning the three-year assignment. Nevertheless, Mel's secretary—his hidden ears in the company—had told him three weeks earlier that she knew that at least eight of the wives were "less than thrilled" about disrupting their children's education and creating a new life in Japan. Five of the wives had also indicated that they were not pleased about having to quit their current jobs and follow their husbands to Japan, even though the pay was good.

Mel had put together a compensation package comparable to what most firms provided for expatriates in Japan—a task that was much easier than trying to decide what to do about predeparture training for the group. His phone calls to colleagues had yielded mixed responses. Some felt that no training was necessary, some felt a little "area briefing" was sufficient, and a few had heard of some consulting firms that offered comprehensive training packages for expatriates (but none knew whether the programs were any good or were cost-effective).

"I don't have time to figure out all the particulars of this— they leave in three months," Mel had told his training manager. "Go find out what kind of training these people need or if they need it at all." He asked the manager to give him her report in a week.

The prices she quoted from consultants on the West Coast pushed the upper limits of the quarterly training budget. She had also talked with a variety of firms that had managers in Japan.

None had done any in-depth predeparture training for their people. She concluded that Recor ought to follow the lead of others: offer a good financial package and leave it at that.

Mel ejected his Mozart disc and found a news station on his car radio. He tried to relax as he listened absently to the news, but the nagging feeling that more should be done for the team would not go away. We're sending these guys into a strange country, he thought, at least to me the Japanese seem strange—and it seems like we should do something to prepare them to go . . . other firms don't do much, if anything . . . if this joint venture melts down, I'll be in a tight spot . . . but the people being sent have all been successful here, especially Larry Runolfsson . . . they should do fine . . . besides, if they're worth what we're going to be paying them, they should be able to work through whatever problems come up. Mel put his thoughts on hold and turned his attention to the weather report.

What is the reality of training for global managers in U.S. firms? Management researchers have found the following facts to be consistent over time and across industries:

1. Only about 35 percent of U.S. firms offer any predeparture, cross-cultural, or language training for their global managers. Thus, 65 percent of U.S. firms send their "troops" into battle overseas without any "combat training."[1]

2. In the 35 percent of firms that do offer cross-cultural training, the training is not very rigorous. Such activities as watching films, reading books, and talking with people who have lived in the country of assignment are the most common approaches in use. Few firms offer their global managers in-depth, rigorous, skill-centered cross-cultural training.[2]

3. Firms do not include spouses in any training that is offered. The few firms that do are exceptions that prove the rule.[3]

4. Cross-cultural training programs have been shown in empirical evaluation studies to enhance global managers' job perfor-

mance, adjustment to the new culture, and development of cross-cultural managerial skills.[4]

No wonder so many global managers struggle in their overseas assignments. Very few of them receive any predeparture training whatsoever, even though cross-cultural training has been proven effective. The question clearly is not whether firms should spend time and resources training their global managers before they depart for their overseas assignments, but rather *how* firms can go about constructing valid cross-cultural training approaches to meet the needs of their global managers. We do not advocate the use of a "canned" program for global managers; instead, a firm's thoughtful responses to a variety of training issues should drive the nature of the training offered.

How Do People Learn and Adapt to New Cultural Situations?

The first issue in forming an effective approach to cross-cultural training is understanding how individuals learn and adjust to new cultural situations. Much research has been done on how people either adapt or fail to adjust to foreign business and social cultures. (This research is explored in detail in Chapter Two.) The process of adaptation to new cultures involves some key learning principles that affect training design.[5] These principles are presented here as a series of learning steps. Associated with each learning step is an example from the life of a global manager who was in charge of a large ranching operation in the South Pacific.

The Three-Step Learning Process

Step 1: Attention. Before managers can alter their behavior so that it conforms to the norms of the host culture, they must first see, attend to, and be aware of how the natives behave. People tend to view new behavior, think about it, and then decide whether or not they want to try it out.

For example, the Polynesian employees of the ranching operation consistently held parties on the weekends, and an integral part of the get-togethers was the *hangi*. This basically consists of cooking food on white-hot rocks in a hole in the ground. Flax leaves are put over the heated rocks, then meat is laid on the flax, then more flax leaves are put on top of the meat, then the process is repeated with different varieties of vegetables. Finally, dirt is put over the food until the hole is filled in. Later, when the food is cooked, the "oven" is dug up and the food is distributed to everyone. These get-togethers were seen as being very important culturally to the Polynesian managers, supervisors, and workers. There was a lot of singing, dancing, storytelling, and renewing of family and community ties. Being together and the warm feeling of the social unit were important; people who did not come to the parties or were unwilling to lower their inhibitions by singing, dancing, and so on, were viewed as being cold, aloof, and untrustworthy. The American manager sensed all this and saw that not merely attending but also sponsoring such get-togethers was going to be important if he was going to be effective.

Step 2: Retention. This stage deals with the degree to which managers think about what they have learned, seen, or heard regarding culturally appropriate behavior in the new country. The more one thinks about what one has seen, the more a "cognitive map" develops regarding when the behavior should be produced, under what circumstances it is acceptable and unacceptable, whether it is all right for foreigners to produce the behavior, the penalties for not producing the behavior, and so on. All one's thinking about the behavior in question becomes locked into memory and becomes a reference point for understanding and reproducing the new behavior.

During the early part of the retention process, important new behaviors and the norms that surround them are at the forefront of consciousness. Then, as the new behaviors and their norms are understood more completely, that knowledge settles into memory and spurs one's reactions in social and business situations in a natural, unconscious fashion. This process is not unlike driving around a city where one has recently moved. Without a map, one gets lost easily. One consults the map often and keeps it close while driving. Slowly, over time, one learns where the streets are, what the shortest routes to work are,. and so on, and one never consults the map anymore. One doesn't need to because the map is in one's head. It is the same with knowing what to do and say in a foreign culture; with effort, after a while, the culture becomes less vague and more predictable because of the "cognitive cultural map."

For an example, let us return to Polynesia. The American manager continued to attend the parties hosted by his workers and their relatives and carefully observed the process of the *hangi*, participating selectively when called on to do so by the Polynesians. Mainly, he blended into the group and carefully observed everything that was going on, developing an understanding of the rules, their purpose, and the behavior expected of participants. He observed that food was an important stimulant to the social norms that caused cohesiveness in the work group and among members of their extended families and friendship networks. The dances, the singing, and the conversation all revolved around the construction of the oven, the preparation of the food, the length of time the food cooked, and the eating of the food afterward. Even the cleanup of the oven provided a "quiet time" among the men who volunteered to fill in the hole. Important conversations took place at each stage of the *hangi*.

Step 3: Trying Out the New Behavior. Basically, once the behavior has been observed and a mental understanding of the rules associated with the behavior has been gained, managers must decide to try out, or not to try out, the new behavior. As managers experiment with new behavior, they check their performance against the "cognitive map" until they become expert at the new behavior. If trying out the new behavior causes embarrassment or negative reactions from host nationals, the managers may never try it again, and thus they will risk their potential to adjust to the new culture. The closer the "cognitive map" reflects true cultural reality, the more likely that the reproduction of new behavior will be successful.

Again, the American in Polynesia offers an example. The American manager determined that he was ready. He invited all the Polynesians in the community to a *hangi* at his house. When they arrived, they saw a *hangi* already under way, with the smoke arising out of the ground. The festivities began, and all were having a good time. When the *hangi* was ready to be unearthed, the Polynesians began to ask each other who had helped their American boss with the *hangi*. After a while, it became obvious that no one had. Then all eyes were on the American, who simply smiled and yelled, *"Haere Mai Kita Kai!"* ("Welcome, come and get the food!") Needless to say, his ability to influence and gain compliance from his workers increased dramatically—literally overnight—for no other American had ever attempted to prepare a *hangi* before.

Self-Confidence Influences Cross-Cultural Learning

The case just presented is a good example of a global manager going through the three-step learning process successfully. Some managers in the same circumstances would not fare as well, however. Besides cultural knowledge, there is another important factor that influences the effectiveness of the three-step learning process. It is a characteristic called *self-efficacy*.[6] Self-efficacy can be defined as the degree to which one believes that one can successfully execute a particular behavior. Another term to describe it would be *self-confidence*. In the preceding case, the American was very self-confident regarding two skill areas—getting along with people, and cooking. He liked to cook and, after observing the *hangi*, felt that he could do it. (Obviously, someone without high levels of self-efficacy in culinary techniques would probably not attempt to reproduce a *hangi*.) Self-efficacy is a vital characteristic for assignments overseas because people who are high in self-efficacy persist at imitating a new behavior until they get it right.[7] They tend to get less discouraged than people who are low in self-efficacy do. Persistence in reproducing new behavior until one gets it right is critical to success in an overseas assignment, and self-efficacy is the cause of that persistence.

Training for global managers must focus on helping managers (1) become aware of important cultural behaviors, (2) build "cognitive cultural maps," by which they can understand why the behaviors are valued by the local people and how the behaviors are appropriately reproduced, and (3) practice the important behaviors they will need to reproduce to be effective in their overseas assignments. Without training, global managers may succeed at negotiating the three-step learning process by themselves, but it is not likely. Good training can assist global managers tremendously in learning about new cultures.[8]

Key Dimensions of Cross-Cultural Training Design

Research shows that *training rigor* is critical to the success of cross-cultural training programs. The ability of a firm to determine the appropriate degree of training rigor needed for its global managers is the secret to valid cross-cultural training design.[9]

Training rigor is basically the degree of mental involvement and effort that must be expended by the trainer and the trainee in order for the trainee to learn the required concepts. Low-rigor training would include such approaches as films, lectures, area briefings, and books. More rigorous training would require the trainee actually to become involved in practicing skills that are first learned passively. Approaches that are more rigorous include role modeling, videotaped skill practice, and language training. High-rigor approaches extend the degree of participation on the part of the trainee. Examples include assessment centers, interactive language training, and sophisticated cross-cultural simulations (see Table 4.1).

Training rigor is also associated with the length of time spent on training. All other things being equal, a training program that involved twenty-five hours over five days would be less rigorous than a program that involved one hundred total hours over three weeks. It is important not to cheat global managers by offering

Table 4.1. Cross-Cultural Training Rigor.

Low Training Rigor Duration = 4–20 Hours)	Moderate Training Rigor (Duration = 20–60 Hours)	High Training Rigor (Duration = 60–180 Hours)
Lecture Films Books Area briefings	Methods in previous box, plus: Role plays Cases Assimilators Survival-level language	Methods in previous box, plus: Assessment centers Simulations Field trips In-depth language

them "quick and dirty" training programs, and not to assume that
a program is effective just because it is offered. It is also important
to remember that the investment in rigorous training is exactly
that—an investment, in both the individual and the firm. The more
rigorous the training, the more effective the training will be in
terms of trainees' being able to apply what they have learned in the
country of assignment.

Once a firm has faced up to the necessity of offering rigorous
training programs for global managers, the critical question is how
rigorous the training should be. To help firms determine the
answer, we offer a framework based on what the best research studies advocate.[10] Basically, three dimensions must be taken into account in deciding what methods should be included in a cross-
cultural training design. The degree of training rigor that a firm
should employ in its training program depends on the results of an
analysis of *cultural toughness, communication toughness*, and *job
toughness*. A careful analysis of these three dimensions is necessary
before valid training can be designed for a firm's cadre of global
managers. Otherwise, the wrong training will be given to the wrong
people.

Cultural Toughness

Simply put, the idea of cultural toughness is that some cultures are
more difficult to adjust to than others. The underlying values that
determine the way business is done are more different from American norms in some countries than in others. A manager going to
Japan is going to have a tougher time and a longer learning curve
than a manager going to Australia. Both will encounter cross-
cultural problems, but the manager in Japan will face more severe
challenges. The tougher the new culture, the more assistance
through rigorous training the global manager will need in order to
be effective.

The next logical question is how one determines which cultures are tougher than others. The research literature in this area[11]
suggests that the following regions of the world, in descending
order of toughness, are the most difficult ones for Americans to
adjust to:

1. Africa
2. Middle East
3. Far East
4. South America
5. Eastern Europe/Russia
6. Western Europe/Scandinavia
7. Australia and New Zealand

Obviously, individual countries within each region vary in cultural toughness, but this simplification of the research imparts a fairly good idea of the need, amount, and rigor of training for global managers by region of assignment.

The next step in determining cultural toughness is to examine any previous overseas experience of the specific candidate for the assignment. The more experience the person has had with a specific culture, even if that experience was in the distant past, the more the person can use that experience in coping with the challenges in his or her overseas posting. Someone who has already lived and worked in Nairobi for three years and is reassigned to Nairobi after five years back home will need less rigorous training than someone who has been assigned to Nairobi but has never lived and worked there.

Both the duration and the depth or quality of past overseas experience will strengthen what is retained. Thus, all things being equal, the Indonesian culture will be less tough for the candidate who has lived there before than for the candidate who has not. Likewise, a candidate who has had frequent, in-depth interactions with Indonesians during a three-year stay will find the cultural toughness less of an obstacle during a later visit than will one who has had infrequent, superficial contact with Indonesians during a three-year assignment. Both the quantity and the quality of a person's experience should be examined before sending him or her abroad, because it is dangerous to assume that superficial experience will lead to positive results.

Communication Toughness

How much interpersonal interaction is expected between the global manager and the local populace?[12] The more the global manager will have to interact with host nationals, the higher the level of communication toughness. For example, an oil rig expert sent to Saudi Arabia may only rarely have to speak to a Saudi, either on or off the job; a marketing manager in Peru may have to have constant contact with local clients, advertising agencies, and media people. Obviously, the first type of situation does not require substantial cross-cultural training, while the latter situation requires rigorous training. The extent of communication toughness can be examined by looking at the nature of the overseas job's requirements for communication with the local nationals:[13]

1. Are the rules and norms for communicating very different from those in the United States, or are they quite similar?
2. Will the manager have to communicate frequently or infrequently with local workers?
3. Is English the national language? If not, how difficult is the foreign language to learn?
4. Will the manager have to communicate mainly in one direction (for example, giving orders, delegating, giving presentations, and so on), or will the nature of the job require intensive two-way communication (for example, consultations, parties, business negotiations) with local nationals?
5. What will be the main form of communicating with local nationals—face-to-face communication (intimate daily discussions with subordinates) or technical communication (memos, mail, and so on)?
6. How long will the manager be in the assignment? Six months? One year? Three years?
7. What will be the main type of interaction—formal (aloofness from subordinates, figurehead authority style, authoritative order giving) or informal (personal influence with clients, relationships with government officials, and so on)?

The responses to these questions help firms understand the degree to which a global manager will have to interact with local nationals. As the intensity of interactions increases, the training program's need for rigor increases proportionately. For example, communication that will be frequent, two-way, face-to-face, and informal will require a higher level of training rigor.

Job Toughness

Most global managers are promoted when they are sent overseas. Promotion often means a job challenge because the manager is working in a new area and has more responsibilities, more autonomy, and new challenges. The tougher the tasks of the new job, the more assistance the manager will need through rigorous predeparture training. The elements of job toughness can be discerned in answers to the following questions:[14]

1. Are the performance standards the same?
2. Is the degree of personal involvement in the work unit the same?
3. Is the task the same or quite different?
4. Are the bureaucratic procedures similar?
5. Are the resource limitations the same?
6. Are the legal restrictions similar?
7. Are the technological limitations familiar?
8. Is the freedom to decide how the work gets done the same?
9. Are the choices about what work gets delegated similar?
10. Is the freedom to decide who does which tasks the same?

An examination of these job characteristics should enable a rough estimate to be made regarding job toughness in the overseas assignment. If job toughness is moderate to high, the manager will need job-specific training, as well as cultural training about how jobs get done and how people are used to being managed in the country of assignment. If the demands of the job are quite different, if the constraints are greater, and if the freedom is less, then job toughness will be higher, and so will be the required level of training rigor.

Putting It All Together

Let us return to Mel Stephens. His predicament is very common throughout the United States, across industries and firm sizes. The reader will recall that Mel was trying to put together a training program for eighteen engineers who had been assigned to Japan. Mel knew just enough about Japan to make him dangerous, but by utilizing the principles discussed in this chapter he was able to choose an effective cross-cultural training program despite time and budget constraints.

Analysis and Application

Cultural Toughness. Looking at the list of seven regions, Mel can quickly determine that the Far East is third in difficulty for Westerners to adjust to, in terms of both business and culture. After speaking with local university professors and local businesspeople who have had dealings with the Japanese, and after consulting a few recommended books, Mel finds that the Japanese accept power differences in organizations and are more attuned to hierarchy and status than Americans are. They are less risk-oriented than Americans, are more comfortable working in groups, accept traditional sex-role differences and have a stronger work ethic than Americans do. The language is difficult to learn, and few Japanese speak fluent English.

Many of Mel's people have vacationed a time or two overseas (mainly in Europe and the Caribbean), but none have lived or worked abroad or in Japan. Thus, their previous experience would not reduce cultural toughness or the need for rigorous cross-cultural training. Mel can expect his people to experience serious culture shock.

Communication Toughness. At first, Mel thought that the degree of interaction would be fairly low for his people but higher for Larry Runolfsson, the project manager. Nevertheless, the group-oriented nature of the Japanese organization and the practice of group decision making increase the likelihood that all of Recor's people will be interacting frequently with the Japanese at work. Thus, while the degree of required interaction is higher for Larry, it is also likely to be quite high for the others. Mel's team of engineers will find themselves in a business culture with different communication rules, a frequent need to interact with the Japanese, a difficult foreign language, and tasks that require two-way, face-to-face, informal communication over a period of two to three years. Communication toughness is high.

Job Toughness. On the surface, it appears that job toughness will not be high. Larry Runolfsson has managed four projects before, and all the engineers have considerable experience; they do not need to learn any new technical skills. Nevertheless, there is a good chance that performance standards, tasks concerning training or working with the Japanese, the ways in which decisions get made, and the bureaucratic procedures that have to be followed will all be somewhat different. Closer examination of the various aspects of the job suggests that job toughness will probably be moderate rather than low.

So far, Mel's analysis has focused on the engineers. What about their families? Family issues should not be overlooked; an important reason for aborted overseas assignments is the inability of the spouse and the family to adjust to the new culture. In general, cultural toughness affects family members just as much as it affects the manager, and so the family needs predeparture training, too. Children under thirteen seem to have less difficulty adjusting to new cultures than teenagers do, and so teenagers and spouses need the same level of training rigor as the manager does. Communication toughness is especially important for nonworking spouses: the inability to communicate, both verbally and nonverbally, creates depression, alienation, and loneliness, and telling people to "snap out of it" is simply not enough. All these issues are weighed in the decision about training design. There may be limits to Mel's budget, but he needs to include the spouses and other relevant family members into the training program, if he can.

What does Mel's analysis say? It can be summarized as follows:

1. Cultural toughness = high
2. Communication toughness = high
3. Job toughness = moderate

Cross-Cultural Training Cube

A framework for training program selection is shown in Figure 4.1.[15] The reasoning behind it is straightforward: the greater the cultural toughness, communication toughness, and job toughness, the greater the need for rigorous cross-cultural training. Each of these dimensions is not equally tough, however. Research shows that it is more difficult to adjust to the culture and to interacting with local nationals than to the job. This finding is represented graphically in the figure by the diagonal line labeled "training

**Figure 4.1. Integration of Cross-Cultural Training Rigor
and Main Contingency Factors.**

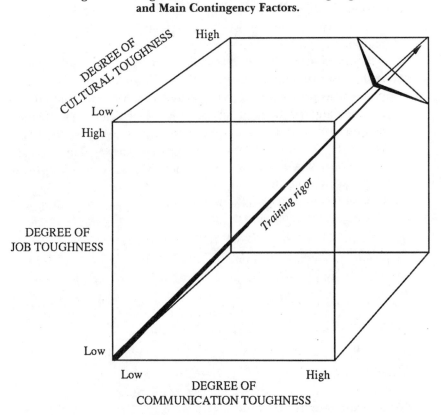

Source: Black and Mendenhall, 1989. Copyright © 1989 John Wiley & Sons, Inc. Reprinted by permission.

rigor." The seven steps that follow describe how this "training cube" works:

1. The vertical axis represents job toughness, ranging from low to high.
2. The bottom horizontal axis represents communication toughness, ranging from low to high.
3. The top horizontal axis represents cultural toughness, ranging from low to high.
4. The diagonal line, which runs from the front left corner to the back right corner, represents training rigor, ranging from low to high.
5. A point is plotted in the three-dimensional space that represents the likely cultural toughness, communication toughness, and job toughness of an impending overseas assignment.
6. The intersection of the plotted point in the three-dimensional space and the diagonal line can be determined by imagining a plane at a right angle to, and traveling on the same diagonal as, the diagonal line. (The plane is placed at a right angle because adjusting to a tough job overseas is easier than adjusting to the general culture or interacting with the local populace. Thus, in the case of a very tough job assignment where there is low toughness on the other dimensions, the highest level of training rigor is not required.)
7. When the plane intersects the plotted point it also intersects with a point on the diagonal line representing training rigor. That intersection provides a rough estimation of the training rigor required for the firm's global managers.

Now let us return to Mel's situation. He had no in-house expertise and could get the team members for only three to five days of training. After examining several cross-cultural training programs offered by various consulting firms, Mel found only one that offered a program design of high rigor. Mel encouraged the spouses to attend, and only two did not. Mel and the consulting firm agreed that the content of the training would focus on cross-cultural interaction skills. The specific methods used in the training program included role plays, short simulations, culture assimilators, and case studies. Mel arranged for the engineers and their family members to take Japanese language lessons after arriving in Japan. In addition, Mel provided them with a list of books on Japanese culture, compiled after he had his assistant consult with Japanese experts at the local university.

Mel felt that follow-up training in Japan might be useful once the engineers were settled. Later, he would decide whether to use an American or a Japanese consulting firm to provide this training. He also thought that, to reduce costs, he could send over one or two professors whom he had met at the university, to keep his people updated and to help them with any current cross-cultural problems they might have.

Mel's last idea brings up an important consideration that is overlooked by virtually all consulting firms that do cross-cultural training. Learning about cultural concepts is useful before departure, but theoretical arguments support the idea that rigorous, in-depth, cross-cultural training is most effectively delivered to global managers after they are "in country." Before they leave their home country, it is more difficult for them to imagine what the trainers are trying to convey. For example, it is one thing to imagine what it is like to have a subordinate in Hong Kong say, "Yes, I understand what you want me to do" and then do nothing because in fact he did not understand. It is another thing to have that experience first and then learn about the cultural reasons behind that behavior in a seminar. In-country training has several advantages: (1) higher levels of motivation on the part of trainees, (2) higher levels of baseline experience with the local culture as a foundation for learning deeper cultural values, norms, and ideas, (3) an environment where trainees can immediately apply what they learn, and (4) the environment itself which makes the training content real.

We believe that predeparture training should focus mostly on basic, day-to-day, survival-level concerns, and that firms should invest in in-country training for global managers while they are overseas. This idea is illustrated in Figure 4.2.

After arrival in the host country, global managers and their families will have less need over time to deal with day-to-day survival issues. With proper predeparture training, the basics will be mastered quite quickly. Mastery of culturally tough concepts is not

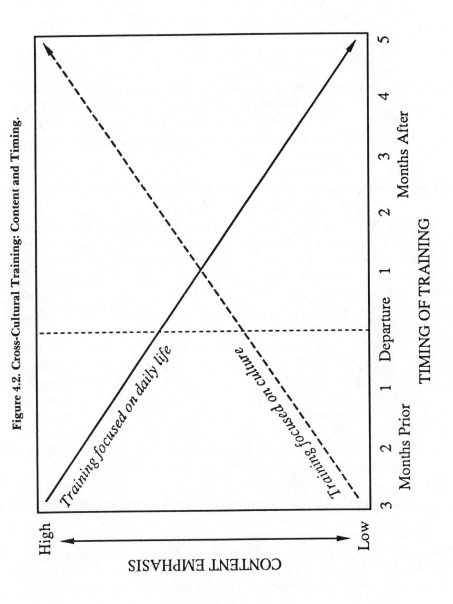

Figure 4.2. Cross-Cultural Training: Content and Timing.

automatic, however, and so postarrival training is needed. The ideal place to master cultural skills is in the host culture.

Linking Patterns of Globalization and Strategic Orientation to Training

In Chapter One, we saw that it is critical for a firm that is "going global" to maintain a fit between its stage of globalization, its competitive strategy, and its people management. Each of the five functions of people management (in this case, the training function) must support the others and not detract from them.

Internal Fit

A firm may spend a lot of time and money carefully searching for key people to send to specific countries and then lose the investment it has made in the exhaustive selection process by using an invalid, generic, ineffective training program. Ignoring global managers by offering no training at all ultimately hurts the integrity of the selection process. Thus, the training function is an important link between good selection and good management development in the process of internal fit.

A companywide, "canned" cross-cultural training program may not support the function of management development, either. Imposing a one-dimensional approach on all global managers, with no regard to their current strengths and weaknesses, to the unique situations they will find themselves in overseas, or to the kinds of skills they need to learn, will simply create frustration, unmet expectations, and poor management on the part of the global managers themselves when they are overseas.

External Fit

Cross-cultural training, like all the other functions of people management, must be designed with the firm's stage of globalization in mind. Consider two global managers, both assigned to Nigeria. One works for a firm at the export stage of globalization, while the other works for a firm at the MNC stage. Both jobs may seem similar in terms of cultural toughness, communication toughness, and job toughness, but the globalization stages of the respective firms will also influence how training should be designed, to some degree. These relationships are illustrated in Table 4.2.

The matrix is a superstructure that overarches our "training cube." The matrix assumes an identical situation for all dimensions (cultural toughness, communication toughness, and job toughness) to illustrate how stage of globalization should influence cross-cultural training design issues. In general, the more a firm is moving away from the export stage, the more rigorous the training should be. Breadth of content also increases as the firm moves away from the export stage to the global stage, and more rigorous training is needed. As firms move away from the export and multidomes-

Table 4.2. Stage of Globalization and Training Design Issues.

Export Stage	*MDC Stage*
Degree of rigor required is low to moderate.	Degree of rigor required is moderate to high.
Content emphasis is on interpersonal skills, local culture, consumer values, and behavior.	Content emphasis is on interpersonal skills, local culture, technology transfer, stress management, local business practices and laws.
Low to moderate training of host nationals to understand home-country products and policies.	Low to moderate training of host nationals; primary focus on production/service procedures.

MNC Stage	*Global Stage*
Degree of rigor required is moderate to high.	Degree of rigor required is moderate to high.
Content emphasis is on interpersonal skills, two-way technology transfer, corporate value transfer, international strategy, stress management, local culture and business practices.	Content emphasis is on global corporate operations/systems, corporate culture transfer, multiple cultural values and business systems, international strategy, socialization tactics.
Moderate to high training of host nationals in technical areas, product/service systems, and corporate culture.	High training of host nationals in global corporate production/efficiency systems, corporate culture, multiple cultural and business systems, and headquarters policy.

tic stages, global managers also need to be able to socialize host-country managers into the firm's corporate culture and other firm-specific practices, and this added managerial responsibility intensifies the need for rigorous training.

Let us take a company like Nestlé and see what kinds of training issues arise around its globalization orientation. Nestlé is a firm that responds well to local markets and whose coordination of activities across borders is relatively low. It sees itself as an international firm and is a profitable, innovative company. Thus, Nestlé fits the multidomestic stage of globalization. An organizational configuration like this requires in-depth knowledge of each culture and market where the firm operates. Production and product innovations take place in a variety of countries; thus, even though local nationals would be more expert in local cultural and market subtleties, Nestlé retains control of these operations. Therefore, the number of global managers Nestlé would send overseas would be more than in a firm at the export stage.

Given this context, when training is offered to the global managers whom Nestlé does deploy, the rigor of the training would range from moderate to high (see Figure 4.1). This is mainly because it takes a global manager with specific knowledge of the target foreign market and culture to be effective in his or her role. Thus, training content should emphasize skills related to local business practices and to cross-cultural communication, stress management, and so on. Tactics for socializing local nationals to the Nestlé philosophy, implementation of worldwide corporate systems, and other firm-homogenizing practices would not be particularly useful components of training, since such practices do not fit the globalization orientation of the firm as a whole.

Whether a firm has a pattern of globalization that requires many or few global managers to be in positions around the world, those managers need to be trained according to the contexts of their assignments. To maintain external fit, the training function must be flexible enough to deal with all potential contexts that derive from globalization patterns. A rigid, mechanistic training philosophy will not do in the global arena. The framework offered in this chapter is a training strategy by which wise choices can be made despite constraints in the organization and the environment.

Notes

1. Oddou and Mendenhall, "Succession Planning for the 21st Century: How Well Are We Grooming Our Future Business Leaders?"; Black, "Work Role Transitions: A Study of Expatriate Managers in Japan"; Tung, "Selecting and Training of Personnel for Overseas Assignments"; Baker and Ivancevich, "The Assignment of American Executives Abroad: Systematic, Haphazard, or Chaotic?"
2. Oddou and Mendenhall, "Succession Planning in the 21st Century."
3. Harvey, "The Executive Family: An Overlooked Variable in International Assignments"; Walker, "Till Business Us Do Part?"
4. Black and Mendenhall, "Cross-Cultural Training Effectiveness: A Review and Theoretical Framework for Future Research."
5. Bandura, *Social Learning Theory*; Black and Mendenhall, "Cross-Cultural Training Effectiveness"; Manz and Sims, "Vicarious Learning: The Influence of Modeling on Organizational Behavior."
6. Bandura, *Social Learning Theory*.
7. Bandura, *Social Learning Theory*; Black, Mendenhall, and Oddou, "Toward a Comprehensive Model of International Adjustment: An Integration of Multiple Theoretical Perspectives."
8. Black and Mendenhall, "Cross-Cultural Training Effectiveness."
9. Black and Mendenhall, "Selecting Cross-Cultural Training Methods: A Practical Yet Theory-Based Model"; Mendenhall and Oddou, "Acculturation Profiles of Expatriate Managers: Implications for Cross-Cultural Training Programs"; Mendenhall, Dunbar, and Oddou, "Expatriate Selection, Training, and Career-Pathing."
10. Mendenhall and Oddou, "The Dimensions of Expatriate Acculturation."
11. Torbiörn, *Living Abroad*; Hofstede, *Culture's Consequences: International Differences in Work-Related Values.*

12. Mendenhall and Oddou, "Acculturation Profiles of Expatriate Managers."

13. Black and Mendenhall, "Selecting Cross-Cultural Training Methods."

14. Black and Mendenhall, "Selecting Cross-Cultural Training Methods."

15. Black and Mendenhall, "Selecting Cross-Cultural Training Methods."

Part Three

During
the Assignment

Chapter 5

Adjusting: Developing New Mental Road Maps and Behaviors

In Chapter Two, we addressed the questions of culture and how people adjust to it when they are sent on foreign assignments. Chapters Three and Four discussed whom to select and how to train people for global posts. This chapter examines additional factors that help or hinder successful cross-cultural adjustment during global assignments.

We have argued that culture should be viewed as a set of rules, values, and assumptions commonly held among the members of the culture. These rules, values, and assumptions are passed on from one generation to another and influence behavior and other visible manifestations. We have also argued that this view of culture raises two important implications. First, the most powerful components of culture are invisible rather than visible; consequently, the most important aspects of foreign cultures are hard to recognize, understand, and adjust to. Second, being immersed in a new culture disrupts familiar and established routines and threatens the individual's self-image. This threat usually cascades into ego-defensive

115

countermeasures and feelings of anger, frustration, and anxiety. For many people, returning home is the easiest way to escape these feelings and the situations that cause them. Most people, however—perhaps because of fear, determination, or both—stay in their assignments and struggle to adjust to living and working in a foreign country.

This process of adjusting to a foreign culture consists of two interrelated components. The first component involves creating a new set of mental road maps and book of traffic rules, or what researchers call "predictive control."[1] These mental maps and rules enable people to "predict" what behaviors are expected in specific situations, how people will probably respond, what behaviors are not appropriate, and so on. These mental maps and rules allow expatriates to control the environment by being able to predict what to do in a variety of situations. The second component involves mastering new behavior, or what researchers term "behavioral control."[2] For example, it is one thing to know that the Japanese communicate in a more indirect fashion, but it is quite another thing to be able to change one's own communication behavior from a direct to a more indirect style. The challenge is equally difficult for Japanese people, who must change from their indirect style to a more direct one when they are transferred to the United States. Cross-cultural adjustment involves figuring out what the new cause-and-effect contingencies are in the foreign culture and mastering the behavior necessary to produce desired rewards and avoid punishments.

Factors Influencing Expatriates' Cross-Cultural Adjustment

Most of the scientific research that has studied the adjustment of managers working and living abroad has focused on Americans working overseas.[3] Recently, however, work has also been done on Japanese managers adjusting to international assignments and, to a much lesser extent, on European managers in foreign posts. Consequently, although the major factors we will talk about are based on the experiences of American managers overseas, we will also discuss the extent to which these factors are also true for Japanese and European global managers.

Dimensions of Cross-Cultural Adjustment

When scholars first started researching the adjustment of managers sent overseas, they focused on degree of adjustment to the more visible aspects of the culture, such as food, transportation systems, daily customs, and so on. More recently, our team of researchers has found that there are really three related but separate aspects or dimensions of cross-cultural adjustment: adjustment to the job, adjustment to interacting with host-country nationals, and adjustment to the general nonwork environment. Interestingly, research has found strong evidence that Japanese managers sent on foreign assignments experience the same three dimensions of cross-cultural adjustment.[4] These three dimensions are represented in the far right-hand box of Figure 5.1.

Adjustment to the Job. The first dimension is the adjustment to the job to which the manager is assigned. Generally, this is the easiest of the three dimensions of adjustment for American, European, and Japanese expatriate managers, primarily because job adjustment is aided by similarities in procedures, policies, and requirements of the task in the foreign operation and those in the home-country operation. Although this is the easiest of the three dimensions, it is not necessarily an easy adjustment. Often, aspects of the corporate culture of the foreign operation, as well as the national culture where the foreign operation is, are dramatically different from those back home and exert an influence on managers' tasks and responsibilities. Consequently, although a manager may be sent from New York to Hong Kong to perform basically the same task as the one performed in the United States, elements of the foreign operation and the host-country culture may make it necessary to perform the task in a slightly or even dramatically different manner to achieve similar results and success.[5] For example, a systems engineer in the United States may be able to interview workers in order to find out their needs and expected uses of a proposed computer program. In India, however, workers may simply expect to be told how they are to use the new program and may be confused by interviews asking for their input. An American expatriate may find that simply asking

Figure 5.1. Model of Cross-Cultural Adjustment.

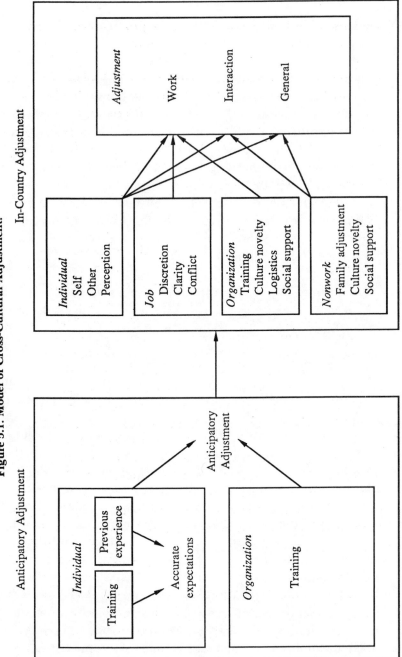

Indian workers how they would use the program will generate information that is incomplete and inaccurate.

Adjustment to Interacting with Host-Country Nationals. The second dimension is adjustment to interacting with natives of the country to which the global manager is assigned. Whether the expatriate manager is American or Japanese, this is generally the most difficult of the three adjustment dimensions, primarily because it is in interactions with host-country nationals that differences in mental maps and rules show up.

Remember Fred Bailey (see Chapter Two)?[6] Fred had an experience that illustrates how different mental maps and rules make interpersonal cross-cultural adjustment difficult. Not long after his arrival in Japan, Fred had a meeting with representatives of a top Japanese multinational firm concerning a potentially large contract. Those present included Fred; the lead American consultant for the potential contract, Ralph Webster; and one of the senior Japanese associate consultants, Kenichi Kurokawa, who spoke perfect English. The Japanese team consisted of four members—the vice-president for administration, the director of international personnel, and two staff specialists. After some awkward handshakes and bows, Fred said that he knew the Japanese gentlemen were busy and he did not want to waste their time, so he would get right to the point. Fred then had the other American lay out the firm's proposal for the project and what the project would cost. After the presentation, Fred asked the Japanese team for a reaction to the proposal. The Japanese team did not respond immediately, and so Fred launched into his summary version of the proposal, thinking that the translation might have been insufficient. Again, the Japanese team offered only the vaguest of responses to his direct questions.

After five months, a contract between the firms had yet to be signed. "I can never seem to get a direct response from the Japanese," Fred complained.

Fred decided that the reason not much progress was being made was that he and his group just did not know enough about the client to package the proposal in a way that was appealing. He called in Ralph Webster and asked him to develop a report on the client, so that the proposal could be reevaluated and changed as necessary. Jointly, Fred and Ralph decided that one of the more promising young Japanese research associates, Tashiro Watanabe, would be the best person to take the lead on this report. To impress upon Tashiro the importance of this task and the great potential they saw in him, they decided to have the young Japanese associate meet with them. In the meeting, Fred had Ralph lay out the nature and importance of the task. Fred then leaned forward in his chair and said, "You can see that this is an important assignment and that we are placing a lot of confidence in you by giving it to you. We need the report this time next week, so that we can revise and present our proposal again. Can you do it?"

After a pregnant pause, Tashiro responded hesitantly, "I'm not sure what to say."

At that point Fred smiled, got up from his chair, walked over to the young Japanese associate, extended his hand, and said, "Hey, there's nothing to say. We're just giving you the opportunity you deserve."

The day before the report was due, Fred asked Ralph how the report was coming. Ralph said that since he had heard nothing from Tashiro, he assumed everything was under control, but that he would double check. Ralph later ran into one of the American research associates, John Maynard. Ralph knew that John had been hired because of his Japanese fluency and that, unlike any of the other Americans, John often went out after work with some of the Japanese research associates, including Tashiro. Ralph asked John if he knew how Tashiro was coming along on the report.

John recounted that the night before, at the office, Tashiro had asked him if Americans sometimes fired employees for being late with reports. John, sensing that this was more than a hypothetical question, asked Tashiro why he wanted to know. Tashiro did not respond immediately. Since it was 8:30 in the evening, John suggested that they go out for a drink. At first Tashiro resisted, but then John assured him that they would grab a drink at a nearby bar and come right back. At the bar, John got Tashiro to open up.

Tashiro explained the nature of the report that he had been requested to produce. He continued to explain that, even though he had worked long into the night every night to complete the report, it was just impossible, and that he had doubted from the beginning that he could complete the report in a week. Furthermore, Kenichi Kurokawa, who was four years senior to Tashiro, had originally been involved in the project, but apparently nothing had been said to him about Tashiro's assignment.

At this point, Ralph asked John, "Why the hell didn't he say something in the first place?" Ralph did not wait to hear whether John had an answer to his question. He headed straight to Tashiro's desk.

The incident got worse. Ralph chewed Tashiro out and then went to Fred, explaining that the report would not be ready and that Tashiro had not thought it could be from the start.

"Then why didn't he say something?" Fred asked. No one had any answers, and the whole thing just left everyone more suspicious and uncomfortable.

Adjustment to the General Nonwork Environment. The third dimension of cross-cultural adjustment is adjustment to the general nonwork environment. This is the dimension that typically has been the focus of many cross-cultural adjustment researchers. This dimension includes such issues as food, transportation, entertainment, and health care. In terms of difficulty, this dimension, for both Japanese and American managers, generally falls between job and interaction adjustment.[7]

Consider an encounter that the Baileys had with a Japanese resort. Everyone in the office had advised Fred to stay at a famous hot springs north of Tokyo. Fred, Jenny, and their children arrived and were proceeding to the front desk to check in when an elderly Japanese man started making gestures with his hands and speaking rapidly in Japanese. Fred and Jenny stopped in time, but the two girls had stepped up to the main floor with their shoes on before the man could bring them their slippers. Once they all had their multicolored slippers on and their shoes securely stored in lockers, the Baileys proceeded to check in.

This accomplished, two elderly Japanese women escorted the Baileys to their room. After walking down a long hall, the women stopped in front of a wooden door, slid it back, and waited for the Baileys to enter. The hall door opened up into a small entry room, about three feet wide and five feet long. The Japanese women indicated that they should all remove their slippers, but, once again, the girls had opened the inner entry door and stepped up into the room.

After removing their slippers, Fred and Jenny gazed in amazement at their room, because that was all it was—one big room. The Japanese women showed the Baileys the closet in which the futons, or sleeping mattresses, and blankets were stored, and they rattled off several comments in Japanese. As the Japanese women prepared to leave, Fred tried to tip them. Both simply covered their mouths and waved their right hands back and forth in front of their faces.

Later, Fred decided to take a soak in one of the hot springs. He went downstairs to the locker room and took off his clothes. Strangely, there were two doors leading out of the locker room, and the signs above them were in Japanese. Fred decided to take the door on the right. He entered a large room. On the right side was a line of short wooden stools and small buckets lined up in front of a row of what looked like water faucets. At one of the faucets, a Japanese man was seated, vigorously washing his hair. In the center of the room was a large tub about the size of a swimming pool. At about the same time Fred noticed this, he also noticed the giggles coming from three young women sitting in the water on the left side of the tub.

Later that evening, Fred and his family decided to have a fresh fish dinner. After a few strange appetizers, a big fish was brought in on a large platter. As the fish was placed on the table in front of the Baileys, Fred noticed a movement. As he looked closer, Fred could see the gills of the fish slowly opening and closing in a futile attempt to breath. The body of the fish had been masterfully sliced into little fillets that lay all along its torso. Christine shrieked, "Daddy, it's still alive! They've sliced it open, and it's still alive!" Suddenly no one was hungry.

Categorization of Influential Factors

One of the important reasons for distinguishing among these three dimensions of cross-cultural adjustment is that not all important factors are related equally, or even at all, to all three adjustment dimensions. For example, a certain factor may influence work adjustment more than interaction adjustment but may not have any influence at all on general nonwork adjustment. In discussing these factors, we have first organized them into two separate categories— factors involved before departure, and factors involved after arrival. These are represented in Figure 5.1 by two separate boxes. We also further divided the factors involved after arrival into four separate categories: factors related to the individual, to the job, to the organization, and to nonwork issues. The following section discusses, in each of these categories, specific factors that research has found important and details the adjustment dimensions on which the factors tend to have the strongest influence. Figure 5.1 illustrates the various relationships.[8]

Anticipatory Adjustment

One of the most important advances in the understanding of cross-cultural adjustment is the realization that people make adjustments in advance of actually transferring overseas. The nature of these anticipatory adjustments is primarily psychological—that is, people begin to adjust their mental maps and rules before actually moving overseas. They develop what researchers term *anticipatory expectations*. For example, if individuals know in advance that the Japanese drive on the left side of the road, they can make mental adjustments before actually traveling to Japan, just as, if people know that the Swiss take gifts of flowers or chocolate when invited to dinner at someone's house, they can mentally adjust to this in advance. Generally, three aspects of anticipatory adjustment help actual in-country adjustment: (1) making a large number of mental adjustments in advance, (2) targeting those adjustments at important aspects of the new culture, and (3) refining the advance adjustments so that they are accurate.

Individual Factors. Research has found two specific factors that facilitate the formation of accurate anticipatory expectations and mental adjustments. The first factor is one that we have already discussed in some detail—cross-cultural training (in particular, issues concerning the content and rigor of training have been ex-

amined in Chapter Four). Because individuals can provide predeparture training for themselves or can have it provided by their
firms, training could actually be categorized as either an individual
or an organizational factor.

The second individual factor that can help develop accurate
anticipatory expectations is previous overseas experience. Many
writers have speculated that simply living in a foreign country
could have a positive impact on the formation of accurate expectations. The assumption is that learning how to live and work in
France is generalizable to learning how to live and work in Malaysia. Research suggests, however, that this assumption is too simplis-
tic.[9] Previous overseas experience can have a positive impact on
anticipatory adjustment, but because various aspects of living and
working in one foreign country are not always generalizable to
another, the positive impact is moderate at best.

One might expect a strong relationship between cross-
cultural adjustment and previous experience in the country of the
current assignment, but this relationship is not as strong as one
would expect unless the interval between the previous and the current residency and the degree of interaction in the culture are examined. For example, consider the case of a French manager who had
lived in Africa for a total of two years before his current assignment
there. His previous assignment to Africa was fifteen years ago, and
he lived in a neighborhood dominated by families of French diplo-
mats. He really did not have to interact with the local people and
culture at all. In his current assignment, he will be managing a
joint venture between a government ministry and his firm, and he
will be living in a native neighborhood. In these conditions, his
previous experience will tend not to have a significant impact on
the formation of accurate predeparture expectations.

Organizational Factors. Training is one of the more critical organizational factors that can affect the formation of accurate expectations in advance of being sent overseas.[10] As discussed in Chapter
Four, however, given all the logistical issues that occupy the minds
of most managers before they are sent overseas, and given that most
of them will not have had recent previous experience in the countries to which they are being sent, their level of motivation and their

general capacity to relate to deep cultural information are often not ideal just before transfer. Consequently, although research evidence suggests that predeparture cross-cultural training can have a positive impact on cross-cultural skills, adjustment, and job performance, some (if not most) of the deep cross-cultural training should be provided after the individual has been in the country for a month or so.

In-Country Adjustment

This section discusses what have been termed *postarrival* or *in-country factors* that affect cross-cultural adjustment. Many of the factors, however, especially those that organizations can influence, actually require planning and design before individuals are sent overseas. (Steps that organizations can take to facilitate successful cross-cultural adjustment are discussed in more detail at the end of this chapter.)

Individual Factors. Individual factors concerning cross-cultural adjustment were discussed in Chapter Three. Here, we simply summarize these factors in terms of three broad categories.[11]

The first category is often referred to as consisting of *self-oriented factors.* The underlying issue of these various factors or individual characteristics is the ability to believe in oneself and have confidence in one's ability to deal effectively with foreigners and new surroundings. As discussed earlier, disrupted routines hammer away at one's ego and self-image. While arrogance or an inflated self-image will not help cross-cultural adjustment, those who have a solid belief in themselves tend to persevere even in the face of mistakes, tend to ask questions about mistakes they make, tend to learn from their mistakes, and tend not to make the same mistakes repeatedly.[12] Therefore, individuals with strong, healthy self-images tend to persist in producing new behavior, even when mistakes produce negative consequences. The more they try to master new behavior, the more they have the opportunity to receive both positive and negative feedback about how they are doing.

The second group of individual factors is often referred to as *other-oriented* or *relational factors.* These are characteristics that enable individuals to meet new people, interact with them, and empathize with them. Obviously, host-country nationals are the ones who understand the mental maps and rules of their culture and are the best source for teaching foreigners how to navigate their country successfully. This is why, after a basic level of language proficiency, willingness to communicate is a more powerful factor of adjustment than absolute language abilities.

The third group of individual factors is the one usually termed *perceptual-oriented factors*. These factors focus on the individual's ability to grasp and understand the invisible cultural maps and rules. Obviously, people are not equal in this ability. For example, things that are not visible are not comprehensible to some people. Others are much better able to appreciate and understand the invisible and subtle determinants of people's behavior.

Although much research remains to be done on the relative strength of specific factors within the category of individual factors, research on both Japanese and Americans suggests that flexibility, willingness to communicate, social ability, collaborative conflict-resolution styles, and lack of ethnocentric attitudes are factors that tend to have a positive influence on cross-cultural adjustment. These factors tend to have an impact on all three dimensions of cross-cultural adjustment.[13]

Job Factors. As one might expect, job factors tend to have their strongest impact on work adjustment. In general, there tends to be little spillover effect from job factors into interaction or general nonwork adjustment.

The job factor that has the strongest impact on work adjustment is the amount of freedom individuals have in their jobs, or what researchers call *job discretion*. The major aspects of job discretion involve flexibility in determining what work to do, when and how to do it, and whom to involve. Having greater job discretion enables people to configure their work so that they can use past successful behaviors and approaches more easily. Researchers have found positive impacts of job discretion on work adjustment for both American and Japanese global managers.[14]

Another aspect of the job that helps work adjustment is the extent to which what is expected of the individual is clear and unambiguous. This is what researchers call *job clarity*. Obviously, it is hard to adjust to something that is unclear or ambiguous, and research has found this to be true for both American and Japanese managers.[15]

A third aspect of the job that influences work adjustment is the extent to which conflicting demands or expectations are placed on individuals. This is what researchers term *role conflict,* not to be confused with job ambiguity. In the case of job ambiguity, what is expected is unclear; in the case of role conflict, what is expected is clear, but different people have conflicting expectations of the worker. Research on American managers has found that role conflict generally hinders work adjustment.[16]

Organizational Factors. Research points to four specific organizational factors that are important during adjustment to an international assignment. These factors tend to have their strongest relationships with work adjustment, rather than with interaction or general nonwork adjustment.

The first organizational factor is postarrival cross-cultural training. If the content of training focuses on all three dimensions of adjustment, then training tends to have an impact on all three aspects.[17] Although training can help individuals gain the necessary mental maps and understand the rules of the culture, it can also help them practice and develop the behaviors and skills necessary to operate effectively in the foreign culture. Too often, firms simply use training as a means of conveying information. Understanding the rules of the culture is a necessary but insufficient step in becoming cross-culturally adjusted and competent. People also need to be able to do what they know they should do. (As discussed in Chapter Four, developing skills and behaviors requires rigorous training.)

The second organizational factor that can affect work adjustment is the extent to which the organizational culture in the foreign operation is different from the organizational culture of the home office. The greater the difference, the more difficult the adjustment, and the longer it ultimately takes.[18]

As anyone who has had to move from one country to another will attest, the logistics involved are tremendous, especially for a family. Logistical support from the organization can significantly reduce the uncertainty associated with finding housing, schooling, and so on. Given that much of the logistical support will concern nonwork issues, it tends to have more of a relationship with general nonwork adjustment than with work adjustment. [19]

The fourth organizational factor involves the extent to which members of the foreign operation provide social support to the newcomer. Supportive co-workers in the foreign operation can provide both information about how to get along in the organization and emotional support while the newcomers learn the ropes. We have found that American expatriates with higher levels of social support from their co-workers in foreign operations had lower levels of role ambiguity and role conflict and higher levels of work adjustment. [20]

Nonwork Factors. The research on cross-cultural adjustment of managers sent on international assignments also points to three important nonwork factors. With the marked exception of the adjustment of the family (primarily the spouse), these factors tend to be most strongly related to general nonwork adjustment.

Studies of Japanese, American, and European managers sent on overseas assignments suggest that most managers who are sent abroad are married men. [21] Studies that have examined the role of family adjustment have almost always focused on the spouse's adjustment. These studies show a consistent and strong relationship between the adjustment of the manager and that of the spouse. [22] At this point, it is impossible to determine the exact cause-and-effect relationship between the adjustment of the employee and that of the spouse. The relationship is most likely reciprocal, and the adjustment of the employee and the spouse is mutually influential.

Like differences in organizational culture, general nonwork differences increase uncertainty in questions of how to behave appropriately in the foreign culture, leading to adjustment difficulties. These general nonwork differences hinder interaction and nonwork adjustment more than they hinder job adjustment. [23] These differences have been referred to by various authors as *culture novelty, culture toughness,* and *culture distance.* Culture novelty has a negative impact on interaction and general nonwork adjustment for two reasons. The first and more obvious reason is that the greater the number and degree of differences between two cultures, the more mistakes people can make as they try to live and work in the new culture, the more depressed they can get about making these mistakes, and the more defensive and angry they can become toward host-country nationals, who are often seen as the cause of their troubles. The second and more subtle reason why culture novelty has a negative impact on adjustment is that the ways in which differences are discovered or learned, mistakes are recognized, or apologies for mistakes are made may also be different.

For example, Japanese and American cultural differences have received a lot of scholarly and popular attention. Business differences, such as merit versus seniority pay systems or individual versus group decision making, have been discussed in several popular books. Much of the academic and popular press suggests that the differences between Americans and Japanese people are so numerous and significant that conflict is inevitable when they get together. Conflicts occur among Japanese in Japan and among Americans in the United States, however, and so the fact that conflicts arise between Japanese and Americans may not be unique. A more subtle and serious problem arises when efforts to resolve conflicts cause even more conflict. In fact, this is exactly what happens in the case of Japanese and Americans, because both cultures have different rules about how conflicts should be resolved.

The final nonwork factor that has an important relationship with cross-cultural adjustment is social support outside the workplace. Support from host-country nationals outside the foreign workplace can provide both information about how to get along in the culture and emotional support while the newcomers learn the ropes. We have found that American expatriates with higher levels of social support from host-country nationals had significantly higher levels of interaction and general nonwork adjustment.[24]

Factors Influencing Spouses' Cross-Cultural Adjustment

By comparison with what is known about employees, very little is known about the specific factors that affect the cross-cultural adjustment of spouses. Nevertheless, it is clear that while the employee has the built-in structure of an organization and a job, the spouse generally is left alone to figure out how to survive and succeed in the new environment and culture. Often, this leaves the spouse feeling isolated.

We conducted a study that tried systematically to examine a number of factors and their impact on the cross-cultural adjustment of spouses.[25] We found that although expatriate candidates are often excited about the career potential of an international assignment, spouses may not be. For spouses, a move to a foreign country may simply represent a disruption of their own careers or long-term social relationships. Not surprisingly, then, our study found that the more the spouse was in favor of accepting the assignment, the more he or she tried to learn about the country and the culture of the assignment. This self-initiated predeparture training in turn was positively related to interaction adjustment. Interestingly, the spouses with the highest levels of adjustment were also those who had been interviewed by the firm before the overseas assignment.

Given the ego-bashing (or at least bruising) effect of cross-cultural adjustment, social support was expected to be an important factor in the cross-cultural adjustment of spouses. Our study found that both family support and support from host-country nationals helped spouses' interaction adjustment. Host-country nationals' support helped particularly, primarily because host-country nationals provide both emotional support and information about the culture, as well as feedback on how a spouse is doing and what changes can bring about more effective functioning in the culture.

We found two other factors that had significant relationships with spouses' general nonwork adjustment. The first was culture novelty, which hindered spouses' general nonwork adjustment. The more the home culture and the host culture differed, the more difficult it was to figure out cultural maps and rules, and the more difficult it was to operate effectively even after figuring them out. The second factor was a function of spouses' particular circumstances. Even though many spouses who had worked full-time before did find work during their assignments,[26] most spouses do not work during an international assignment. Consequently, most spouses have to deal with general living conditions all day, day in and day out. It is perhaps not surprising that living conditions in the overseas post that were equal to or better than those at home helped spouses' general adjustment to the culture of assignment.

Producing Successful Cross-Cultural Adjustment

For executives involved in or responsible for the international movement of human resources, a key question is, "What steps can we take to maximize the success and minimize the failure of international transfers?" This question is especially important, given that some factors that affect cross-cultural adjustment are not under the control of executives (for example, the level of organizational or cultural novelty is not really under anyone's control). What effective steps can be taken?

Selection and Training

Chapter Three and Four discuss at length how firms can select and train employees for global assignments more effectively. Two things are worth emphasizing here. First, most candidates for global assignments are married. The evidence suggests that the opinion of the spouse can significantly affect both self-initiated predeparture training and in-country adjustment, yet only about 30 percent of U.S. firms take the opportunity to discuss spouses' opinions about a possible global assignment.[27] Given that the motivation of an employee and a spouse to take an assignment may not be equally strong, it is probably not wise simply to rely on an employee's report of the spouse's opinion. Second, although executives cannot control the extent of organizational or cultural novelty, they can factor it into selection and training. The greater the cultural novelty, the more careful the selection decision should be, and the more predeparture and postarrival training will be necessary.

Job Design

Research clearly shows that greater job discretion and clarity and less role conflict facilitate work adjustment. Three simple steps for executives to take are to provide job discretion, make role expectations clear, and eliminate conflicting demands. The execution of these three steps is actually quite complex, however.

Let us consider the issue of role clarity. One easy but rarely utilized technique for increasing role clarity is job overlap—that is, the new expatriate and the job's previous incumbent (host-country national or expatriate) are given several days or perhaps weeks of overlap time. During this time, the incumbent teaches the new entrant. The more complex the job and the less experienced the new entrant, the longer the overlap should be. Theoretically, the incumbent should be able to help clarify all aspects of the job. In interviews, several expatriates specifically mentioned that this was a relatively low-cost means of facilitating expatriate adjustment and effectiveness. American expatriates in Japan and Korea have also mentioned that this overlap was necessary for making the proper introductions.

Let us assume that there is an incumbent capable of clarifying the new job (although this is often not the case). Our research suggests that job clarification alone will facilitate work adjustment, but this does not necessarily lead to reduction in role conflict. It is quite possible (and not uncommon) for clarification of job expectations to lead to clarification of previously hidden role conflicts. The primary source of role conflict for expatriates is conflicting expectations between the parent firm and the local operation. Consequently, clarifying the job may mean uncovering such conflicting expectations. Thus, firms must consider the need to increase job clarity and decrease role conflict simultaneously. This requires a clear understanding of what is expected of the expatriate manager from both the parent firm and the foreign operation, and both perspectives must be integrated.

Even a firm's best efforts may not eliminate role ambiguity and conflict. This is probably why job discretion tends to be the single strongest factor of work adjustment. Even if role ambiguity and role conflict exist, having a fair amount of freedom to decide what tasks to do, how to do them, when to do them, and who should do them facilitates an expatriate manager's ability to cope effectively with ambiguity and conflict. Thus, the way to solve all of these problems is simply to give expatriate managers a lot of job discretion and freedom. Unfortunately, however, this may not be as simple as it sounds. Too much discretion without clear objectives may cause expatriates to choose objectives that are not in the best interest of the parent firm, the foreign operation, or both. Therefore, the firm actually needs to consider all three elements of an expatriate manager's job simultaneously.

Even though research clearly indicates that job clarity, role conflict, and job discretion are factors important in work adjustment, we believe that these aspects of the expatriate manager's job are best thought of not as targets of manipulation but as outcomes of broader policy and strategic processes. If a firm wants to make significant, long-term effective changes in an expatriate manager's job, this goal is best achieved through a careful assessment of the following issues:

1. Why is this specific expatriate being sent to this particular post? (Because there are no host-country nationals capable of fulfilling the job? To provide a needed developmental experience for the expatriate?)
2. What are the criteria by which success in the job will be measured? What is really desired of the person in this particular position?
3. Are the objectives and goals of the parent firm and the foreign operation consistent? Are they consistent in the foreign operation and the particular department where the individual will work?
4. How much coordination and control is needed between the parent firm and the foreign operation? How much freedom and autonomy ought to be incorporated into the foreign unit? Is job discretion consistent with coordination needs?

Without an assessment of these types of strategic issues, the firm may adjust its expectations in ways that are dysfunctional for overall strategy and for the relationship between the parent firm and the foreign operation. For example, a firm may provide overlap time that only serves to clarify deep and severe expectation conflicts between the parent and the local organization, or the firm may give too much freedom to expatriate managers when much more control and coordination are required. Adjustments made independently of the broader strategy and fundamental context are likely to have short-term positive results at best and severe negative results at worst. By contrast, an analysis that begins with the broader strategy and context naturally leads to understanding of and appropriate adjustments to the expatriate manager's job, and to a higher probability of successful work adjustment.

Social Support

There is consistent evidence that social support can facilitate cross-cultural adjustment for both the employee and the spouse. The evidence is particularly strong concerning social support from host-country nationals with respect to interaction adjustment. Although the firm cannot directly control the amount of social support a particular family or employee receives, it can take steps to enhance the probability of their receiving it. Some firms have adopted the practice of asking a host-country national employee and family in the foreign operation to help the expatriate and family have a "soft landing." Generally, such assistance has focused on such logistical issues as housing, schools, and shopping. Although friendships cannot be mandated, some companies have made it clear that helping families (especially spouses) become involved in social or cultural activities is appreciated. Other firms have taken a more indirect approach. They simply provide stacks of information on local social and cultural activities and groups in which expatriate managers and families can become involved.

Summary

This chapter and Chapter Three have outlined a definition of culture, a process of adjustment, and a set of specific factors that provide a beginning framework for understanding the complexities of successfully moving human resources around the world. We have pointed to the difficulty and importance of understanding and adjusting to the invisible aspects of culture, and to the factors that either enhance or detract from that process. We have argued that such factors as organizational and cultural novelty, which are not under the direct control of firms, should at least be factored into the decisions (such as about selection and training) that are under firms' control. Chapters Six, Seven, and Eight focus on expatriates' commitment, performance, and compensation and rewards during assignments. All these aspects of the international assignment are discussed separately, but these issues are very much interrelated. Firms that enjoy the greatest success in moving people around the world have to deal effectively with them all.

Notes

1. Bell and Staw, "People as Sculptors Versus People as Sculpture: The Roles of Personality and Personal Control in Organizations"; Greenberger and Strasser, "Development and Application of a Model of Personal Control in Organizations."
2. Bell and Staw, "People as Sculptors."
3. Black, Mendenhall, and Oddou, "Toward a Comprehensive Model of International Adjustment: An Integration of Multiple Theoretical Perspectives."
4. Black, "Work Role Transitions: A Study of American Expatriate Managers in Japan"; Black, "Factors Related to the Adjustment of Japanese Expatriate Managers in America"; Black and Gregersen, "Antecedents to Cross-Cultural Adjustment for Expatriates in Pacific Rim Assignments."
5. Black and Porter, "Managerial Behaviors and Job Performance: A Successful Manager in Los Angeles May Not Succeed in Hong Kong."
6. Black, "Fred Bailey: An Innocent Abroad."
7. Black, "Factors Related to the Adjustment of Japanese Expatriate Managers"; Black and Gregersen, "Antecedents to Cross-Cultural Adjustment."
8. Black, Mendenhall, and Oddou, "Toward a Comprehensive Model of International Adjustment."
9. Black, "Work Role Transitions"; Black and Gregersen, "Antecedents to Cross-Cultural Adjustment."
10. Black and Mendenhall, "Cross-Cultural Training Effectiveness: A Review and Theoretical Framework for Future Research."

11. Mendenhall and Oddou, "The Dimensions of Expatriate Acculturation: A Review."
12. Bandura, *Social Learning Theory.*
13. Black, "Personal Dimensions and Work Role Transitions: A Study of Japanese Expatriate Managers in America."
14. Black, "Work Role Transitions"; Black and Gregersen, "Antecedents to Cross-Cultural Adjustment"; Black, "Factors Related to the Adjustment of Japanese Expatriate Managers."
15. Black, "Work Role Transitions"; Black and Gregersen, "Antecedents to Cross-Cultural Adjustment"; Black, "Factors Related to the Adjustment of Japanese Expatriate Managers."
16. Black, "Work Role Transitions"; Black and Gregersen, "Antecedents to Cross-Cultural Adjustment."
17. Black and Mendenhall, "Cross-Cultural Training Effectiveness."
18. Black, Mendenhall, and Oddou, "Toward a Comprehensive Model of International Adjustment."
19. Black, Mendenhall, and Oddou, "Toward a Comprehensive Model of International Adjustment."
20. Black, "Locus of Control, Social Support, Stress, and Adjustment to International Transfers."
21. Tung, *The New Expatriates: Managing Human Resources Abroad.*
22. Black and Gregersen, "The Other Half of the Picture: Antecedents of Spouse Cross-Cultural Adjustment"; Black and Stephens, "Expatriate Adjustment and Intent to Stay in Pacific Rim Overseas Assignments."
23. Black, "Work Role Transitions"; Black and Gregersen, "Antecedents to Cross-Cultural Adjustment"; Black and Stephens, "Expatriate Adjustment."
24. Black, "Locus of Control."
25. Black and Gregersen, "The Other Half of the Picture."
26. Stephens and Black, "The Impact of the Spouse's Career Orientation on Managers During International Transfers."
27. Black and Gregersen, "The Other Half of the Picture."

Chapter 6

Integrating:
Balancing Dual Allegiances

Each year, literally hundreds of thousands of managers all over the world find themselves torn between their allegiance to their parent firms and their allegiance to foreign operations. To understand this tension, simply consider the following situation.

A Dutch expatriate manager in a multinational consumer products firm is faced, on the one hand, with a parent firm that wants a set of products introduced to the host country (a large developing nation) as part of its global brand-image strategy; on the other hand, the host-country government wants high technology transferred into the country, not just consumer products placed on store shelves. Market research suggests that the local consumers are interested in a certain subset of the core products but not in others and are also interested in products not currently part of the parent firm's core set. The parent firm has a philosophy and a set of policies encouraging participative decision making, but host-country employees expect managers to make all the decisions and not burden subordinates with those responsibilities.

Faced with serving two masters, many expatriate managers end up directing their allegiance too far in one direction or the other and create serious costs and consequences, both for themselves and for their organizations. If individuals are too committed to a foreign operation, it is difficult for the home office to coordinate with them. A senior executive from Honda commented to us that they had incurred "nontrivial" costs trying to coordinate their global strategy for the new Honda Accord because some expatriate managers were too focused on the local situation. On the other hand, expatriates who are too committed to the parent firm often implement policies or procedures inappropriately from the home office. Today's multinational firm needs managers who are highly committed to both the parent firm and the foreign operation and who try and are able to integrate the demands and objectives of both organizations.

Unfortunately very little research has been done on the problems of dual allegiance during international assignments. One of the few studies that have addressed this issue was recently conducted by two of the present authors and involved over three hundred managers in eight different countries.[1] The good news is that there is an initial basis for identifying influential factors, underlying dynamics, and actions that firms can take to manage the dual allegiance of international managers more effectively. The bad news is that expatriate managers with high dual allegiance seem to be rare.

In this chapter, we describe the patterns, causes, and consequences of expatriates' dual allegiance. Expatriate managers can be grouped into one of four patterns of allegiance. They can be too committed to the parent firm or to the local operation; they can be highly committed to both organizations or to neither. These four basic patterns are presented in Figure 6.1. Much more important than the patterns of dual allegiance, however, are the factors that cause them and the related organizational and individual consequences. We describe the causes and consequences associated with each cell in the Figure 6.1 matrix and illustrate them with actual cases generated through numerous interviews and surveys (most of the managers asked that their names and the names of their firms be disguised). We also examine what firms are doing now and what they can do in the future to manage the dual allegiance of their expatriates more effectively.

Figure 6.1. Dual Allegiances.

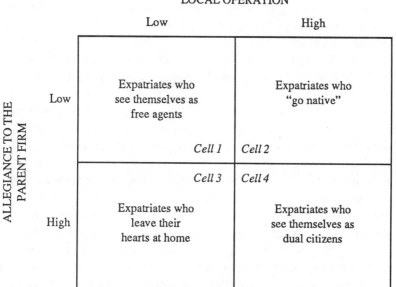

Matrix of Expatriate Allegiance

Cell 1: Expatriates Who See Themselves as Free Agents

Paul Jackson was a vice-president and general manager of the Japanese subsidiary of a large West Coast bank. This was his fourth position and firm in the ten years since he had earned his master's degree. Paul had been an Asian studies undergraduate major. He spoke and wrote advanced intermediate Chinese at the time of his graduation from college. As an undergraduate, he had also spent two years studying in Japan. In that time, his speaking and listening ability had reached a nearly professional level in Japanese. After graduate school, he was hired by a major East Coast bank. Two years later, he was sent on a three-year assignment to Hong Kong.

The compensation package that Paul and his family received made life in Hong Kong very enjoyable, but Paul felt very little loyalty to the parent firm or to the local operation in Hong Kong.

Paul was committed to his career first and foremost. Because he was such a hard charger, the bank had invested a substantial amount of time and money in his linguistic and technical training. He worked hard but always kept an ear cocked for better jobs and better pay. Two years into his Hong Kong assignment, he found a better position in another firm and took it. Four years into that assignment, he took a job with a different U.S. bank and its operation in Taiwan. After another four years, he took the job in Japan.

In the interview in which Paul related his work history, he said, "I can't really relate to your question about which organization I feel allegiance to. I do my job, and I do it well. I play for whatever team needs me and wants me. I'm like a free agent in baseball or a hired gun in the old West. If the pay and job are good enough, I'm off. You might say, 'Have international expertise, will travel.' "

Hired-Gun Free Agents

Paul was part of a network that we discovered of hired-gun free agents in the Pacific Rim. The network consisted of a group of about ten American managers, hired as expatriates (not as locals), who were either bilingual or trilingual and who had spent over half of their professional careers in the Far East (Japan, China, Hong Kong, Taiwan, Singapore, Korea, Malaysia, and Indonesia). These free agents helped one another by passing along information about various firms that were looking for experienced expatriate managers for their Far East operations.

This type of expatriate has a low level of commitment to the parent firm and to the local operation. These free agents are primarily committed to their own careers. Asked what long-term career implications this approach might have for them, these expatriates commonly indicated that it would be very difficult for them ever to "go back home" and move up the hierarchy in any firm, and most did not want to. First, they felt that the experience their children were receiving, both in private schools and in life in general, was far superior to what they would have had back home. Second, they would have been worse off financially if they had gone home and had to give up the extra benefits of their expatriate packages. Third, most were confident that they would not be given jobs back home with the status, freedom, and importance of those they held overseas. Consequently, most of these hired guns seemed rather happy with their lives and free-agent careers overseas.

Firms tend to view such expatriates with some ambivalence. On the one hand, even though these hired guns are given special benefit packages, they are often slightly less expensive to a firm than expatriates sent from home. Furthermore, these expatriates have already demonstrated that they can succeed in global settings, and they have specialized skills (such as in language) that may be lacking in the firm's internal managerial or executive ranks. This may be especially important to U.S. firms, since 15 to 20 percent of expatriate managers fail in overseas assignments, at great cost to their firms, primarily because of serious problems adjusting to foreign cultures. On the other hand, free agent expatriates often leave with little warning. Replacing them is usually costly and difficult and can have negative consequences, both for the parent firm and for the local operation. Sometimes in their commitment to their own careers, hired guns take actions that serve their own short-term career objectives but do not necessarily serve the long-term best interests of the local operation or the parent firm. Since few are willing to repatriate, integrating their general international experience or specific regional knowledge into the firm's global strategy formulation process is next to impossible.

Plateaued-Career Free Agents

Our research uncovered another type of expatriate with low commitment to the parent firm and the foreign operation. This type usually comes from the ranks of home-country employees, rather than from the ranks of hired international experts, and generally is not committed to the parent firm before leaving for the overseas assignment, in part because his or her career has "plateaued." These managers take global assignments because they do not see themselves going anywhere in "Stateside" operations and they hope that a global "stint" will change things, or they may simply be attracted by the sweet financial packages common to most overseas assignments. Unfortunately, many of the same factors that led to low commitment to the parent firm before the global assignment result in low commitment to the local operation once such managers are overseas. We think of these managers as "plateaued-career free agents."

There may be several contributing factors to this type of expatriate. If a firm simply allows candidates for overseas assignments to self-select, it opens the door for plateaued managers to nominate themselves. As one expatriate said, "I figured I was stalled in my job back in North Carolina, so why not take a shot at an overseas assignment, especially given what I'd heard about the high standard of living even midlevel managers enjoyed overseas?" A self-selection process leaves to chance the deployment of expatriates with personal characteristics that research has shown to be related to maladjustment and failure in global assignments. In combination with this practice of self-selection, a low value placed on global operations can increase the probability that plateaued managers will apply and decrease the probability that high-potential managers will volunteer for overseas assignments.[2] The high-potential managers know, since the global operations are devalued, that the place for them to get ahead is not overseas. Lack of predeparture cross-cultural training can also reinforce low commitment to the parent firm and to the local operation. U.S. firms may be particularly vulnerable to this factor, since roughly 70 percent of all American expatriates receive no predeparture cross-cultural training; the resulting attitude is, "The company doesn't care about me, so why should I care about it?" Lack of training can also inhibit the expatriate's understanding of the foreign culture and people and commitment to the local operation.

Unlike the hired-gun free agents, many of the plateaued-career free agents are not happy in their overseas assignments. Given their low commitment, they often make little effort to adjust to local operations and cultures. In the most dramatic cases, lack of effort and adjustment can lead to failed assignments and their associated costs. Generally, a failed overseas assignment does not facilitate career advancement and can strike a severe blow to individual identity and self-confidence. There are also costs to the firm. Beyond the $100,000 needed to bring the employee and the family home and send out a replacement, the firm incurs damage to relationships with clients or suppliers because of the expatriate's poor adjustment and performance while overseas. The leadership gap that often occurs during the replacement process can also damage internal and external relations, and the firm may find that failed overseas assignments generate rumors that an international post is the kiss of death for a career.

Even if this dual lack of commitment does not result in a failed assignment, it can still be rather costly to the person and the organization. An interview with a manager of a major U.S. aircraft manufacturer, stationed in Taiwan, revealed some of the more subtle but important personal and organizational costs. Bob Brown, a typical plateaued manager, had transferred overseas three years before. Bob was not excited about living in Taiwan, and neither was his family. His wife and his daughter repeatedly asked to go home. Bob pointed out that there was really no job for him to go back to. His daughter became so distraught with life in Taiwan that she began doing extremely poorly in school This and other pressures put a severe strain on Bob's relationship with his wife. Bob summed up the situation by stating that his home life was in shambles and that work was merely a paycheck, but a fat one (compensation and benefits were worth about $210,000 per year). Perhaps the parent firm and the local operation were getting their money's worth from Bob, and perhaps firms in general do get their dollar's worth, yen's worth, or pound's worth from these types of expatriate managers, but it seems unlikely.

Cell 2: Expatriates Who "Go Native"

Another pattern of allegiance is found in expatriate managers who have high allegiance to the local operation but low allegiance to the parent firm. Because the local operation is embedded in the foreign country, its culture, its language, its business practices, and its values, these expatriates usually form a strong identification with and attachment to the larger cultural context. Consequently, these expatriates are often referred to as having "gone native."

Gary Ogden had been with a large computer company for fifteen years, and Paris was his third global assignment. He was the country manager for the firm's instrument division in France and had been there for about eighteen months. Of his fifteen years with the parent firm, a little under half had been spent overseas. Since this was the family's third international post, it had not taken long for Gary, his wife, and their three young daughters to settle in. Although Gary's French was not perfect, it was decent. His girls were amazing, however. They had enrolled in regular French schools when they moved to Paris, and now they were fluent for their ages. The Ogdens frequently took trips to museums, nearby cities and villages, and other points of interest. In fact, the Ogdens loved France so much that Gary had already requested an extension, even though his contract required him to stay only another six months. When asked to describe his commitment to the parent firm and to the local operation, he responded, "My first commitment is to the unit here. In fact, half the time I feel like the parent firm is a competitor I must fight, rather than a benevolent parent I can look to for support."

Our research suggests that individuals like Gary Ogden, who have spent a number of years overseas and are skilled at adjusting to foreign cultures, are the most likely to "go native" and have high allegiance to local operations and relatively low allegiance to their parent firms. Part of the explanation of this tendency is that as managers spend more time away from home offices and the home-country operations, they begin to experience less and less of their identity as tied to their parent firms.[3] This literal and psychological distance, in combination with their ability to relate to and understand foreign cultures and people, tends to lead these expatriates to identify strongly with local operations at the expense of parent firms. The lack of formal communication with home offices, through such mechanisms as sponsors (individuals assigned to keep in touch with specific expatriates during overseas assignments) also may cause or reinforce this pattern of commitment. Firms with international divisions and cadres of career internationalists may be particularly vulnerable to this pattern.

What are the consequences of "going native," in terms of the expatriate's allegiance? Gary Ogden often felt that the parent firm was a competitor he had to fight. Because he knew that any global assignment was temporary, and that his career was to some extent a function of evaluations made of him back at corporate headquarters, he had to fight the parent firm in subtle ways. "Sometimes I would simply ignore their directives if I didn't think they were appropriate or relevant to our operations," he said. "If it's really important, eventually someone from regional or corporate will hassle me, and I have to respond. If it isn't important, or if they think I implemented what they wanted, they just leave me alone. As long as the general results are good, it doesn't seem like there are big costs to this approach." Gary also indicated that on occasion he has had to fight more overtly. While this may have cost him back home, fighting and especially winning these fights helped him gain the trust and loyalty of the French employees, and their greater loyalty made it easier for him to be effective. His effectiveness often scored points and created lenience at corporate headquarters.

Gary said that he had nearly left the firm both times he was repatriated after his previous global assignments. He complained about the lack of responsibility back in the U.S., compared to what he had enjoyed overseas, and about the general lack of appreciation and utilization of his global knowledge and experience after repatriation. Low commitment to the parent firm heightened the salience of these factors as justification for quitting. Gary said that what kept him from actually leaving the firm both times was a granted request for another overseas assignment.

From the parent firm's point of view, one common problem associated with expatriates who "go native" is the difficulty of getting corporate policies or programs implemented in foreign operations. Intense commitment to the foreign operations often leads these expatriates to implement what they think is relevant in ways they deem appropriate and then ignore or fight the rest. This approach can be very costly, especially when the parent firm is trying to coordinate activities closely in a variety of countries for the good of global objectives.

To the extent that low commitment to the parent firm contributes to repatriation turnover, the parent firm also loses the opportunity to try to incorporate the knowledge and experience of these expatriates into global strategy or to incorporate some of these individuals into succession plans. Interestingly, our research has found that most expatriates, regardless of commitment pattern, do not feel that the global knowledge and experience they gained overseas is valued by their firms (80 percent of U.S. expatriates, 65 percent of Japanese expatriates, and 60 percent of Finnish expatriates). This finding may suggest that firms in general are not utilizing valuable resources in which they have already invested substantial sums.

Despite various negative aspects of the fact that some expatriates "go native," many corporate executives recognize that these expatriates are not all bad. Their high allegiance to foreign operations generally leads these expatriates to identify with and understand host-country employees, customers, and suppliers and their feelings and values. This can mean that new products or services, or adapted products or services, are well targeted to the local market and that managerial approaches are suited to the host-country employees. The importance of a managerial style suited to host-country employees must not be overlooked, especially by U.S. firms. Most U.S. firms, assuming that good managers in New York will do fine in Tokyo or Hong Kong, select expatriates primarily on the basis of their domestic performance, but evidence suggests that the managerial characteristics related to good performance in the United States are not related to good performance in foreign countries.[4]

Expatriates with relatively high allegiance to foreign operations may be particularly beneficial in other ways, too. In the case of multidomestic firms, for example, each overseas unit usually tries to compete in its specific national or regional market independently of other units in other countries, and the primary information flow is within the local operation, rather than between it and the parent firm or between it and other foreign subsidiaries. At this stage of globalization, there is a premium on understanding local markets and the host-country people and culture. Expatriates who "go native" often have valuable insights into local operations, culture, and markets and can implement or adopt procedures, products, or managerial approaches to fit local situations. However, these expatriates rarely return home to contribute their "local" knowledge to broader regional or global strategic plans.

Cell 3: Expatriates Who Leave Their Hearts at Home

Another type of expatriate manager has high allegiance to the parent firm but little allegiance to the foreign operation. We refer to such expatriates as those who leave their hearts at home. This group identifies much more strongly with the parent firm than with the foreign operation or the foreign country and its culture, language, and business practices.

Earl Markus was the managing director in the European headquarters of the "do-it-yourself" retail division of a large building-supplies firm. This was Earl's first global assignment in his twenty-two years with the firm. He was married and had two children, both of whom were in college and had not moved with their parents to Belgium. Earl had worked his way up from store manager to Southwest regional manager and eventually to vice-president of finance over the years.

The European operations were fairly new, and Earl saw his mission as expanding the number of retail outlets, from the current nine in Belgium to fifty during the next three years, all over Western Europe. The American parent firm had assigned a sponsor, Frank Johnson, to work closely with Earl during his three-year assignment.

One year into the assignment, Earl was on schedule and had opened fifteen new outlets in three countries but was still very frustrated. He mentioned that he had seriously considered packing up and going home more than once during the past year. He claimed that Europeans were lazy and slow to respond to directives. Asked about his feelings of allegiance and commitment, he said there was no contest: he was committed first and foremost to corporate headquarters, and when the next two years were up, he would be headed back home. As an example of how things had gone, Earl described the implementation of the inventory system.

About eight months into his assignment, Frank Johnson had suggested that Earl implement the new computerized inventory system that had just been phased into all the U.S. outlets. Frank was very excited about the cost-saving and theft-reducing aspects of the new system and had high expectations of its use in Europe. For proper operation, the system required the daily recording of sales and a weekly random physical inventory of specific items. These reports needed to be transferred within forty-eight hours to the central office, where total and store-by-store reports and evaluations could be generated. The forms and procedural manuals were printed, and a two-day seminar was conducted for all the European store managers, the director of operations, and members of his staff. Two months later, when Earl asked his managers how the system was operating, he discovered that it was not. All he got from his managers, he said, were "lame excuses" about why the system would not work, especially in Belgium.

This case briefly illustrates some of the main causes and consequences of expatriates' allegiance being tilted strongly toward parent firms. Perhaps not surprisingly, our research has found that a long tenure with the parent firm in the home country is significantly related to leaving one's heart at home. All the investment of time, sweat, and heartache has been in the parent firm. High commitment to the parent firm is partly a function of expecting to receive a return on that investment. Such an investment, over time, also intertwines the identity of the manager with the parent firm. The natural consequence is high allegiance to the parent firm.[5]

Our research has also found that two other factors contribute to this pattern of allegiance. First, poor adjustment to the host country and culture, in part fostered by selection processes that primarily consider domestic performance, is an important factor. Because these expatriates cannot relate to the broader culture and people of the host country, it is difficult for them to feel strong allegiance to the local operation. Second, having a sponsor in the home office creates a formal tie back to the home office, which, in combination with the tie that many years of experience in the parent firm have created, directs attention and allegiance toward the parent firm and away from the local operation.[6]

What are the personal and organizational consequences of this pattern? Earl Markus thought about leaving several times during the first year, and it was basically his fear of negative consequences that kept him from actually doing so. Expatriates who leave their hearts at home generally fail to identify with foreign operations, host countries, host-country employees, customers, suppliers, and their values. As a result, they often try to implement and enforce inappropriate programs, or they implement them in a way that offends employees, customers, or suppliers. Earl Markus's attempt to implement the inventory system is an example. His implementation effort antagonized the employees and created an adversarial relationship that hampered the other changes and programs he later tried to initiate.

Not all the consequences of leaving one's heart at home are bad, however. Our research has found that American expatriates with high commitment to their parent firms during global assignments were more likely to want to stay with the firms after repatriation. Thus, to the extent that expatriates who leave their hearts at home are able to gain valuable experience, knowledge, and skills during their global assignments, their stronger intent to stay with their parent firms after repatriation provides the firm an important opportunity to gain future returns on substantial human capital investments. Unfortunately, however, low commitment to the foreign operations generally reduces the net return on these investments because this low allegiance inhibits knowledge and understanding of foreign countries and markets. Nevertheless, expatriates who leave their hearts at home often make it easier for home offices to coordinate activities with subsidiaries. In fact, in Earl's case, it was very easy for the corporate purchasing agent to utilize the buying power of headquarters' centralized purchasing activities for the European operations, and this coordination resulted in substantial savings over prices that the European operation could have obtained on its own.

The ability to coordinate easily with the home office may be particularly beneficial for a firm at the export stage of globalization. The primary objective of most firms at this stage is to sell, in foreign markets, products developed and manufactured in the home country, and the primary direction of information flow is from the parent firm to the foreign operation. Thus, being able to work easily with headquarters may be especially useful for a firm at the export stage because of the primacy of the home-country operations and the key coordinating role that the home office plays. An expatriate with relatively high commitment to the parent firm is less likely to resist working with and following the coordination efforts of the home office than an expatriate with low commitment to the parent firm might be.

For the individual and the parent firm there are both pros and cons to a high parent/low local level of allegiance. Expatriates who leave their hearts at home are relatively easy for the home office to work with and can be very valuable in coordinated purchasing, marketing, or other strategic activities. They are also more likely to stay with the firm upon repatriation and can be a valuable resource in global strategic planning activities or succession plans. There are negative consequences, however. Their low level of commitment to the local operation may lead them to not make the efforts usually necessary to adjust to the host culture. To the extent that these expatriates can avoid the negative career consequences of returning prematurely, they may decide to leave the foreign assignment early, which results in a host of substantial direct and indirect costs to the parent company. Finally, these expatriates may implement home-office policies in a manner that offends the local employees, clients, or suppliers, or which may be inappropriate for the local operations. The damaged relationships that result can, in turn, have substantial short-term and long-term negative consequences for both the local foreign operation and the parent firm.

Cell 4: Expatriates Who See Themselves as Dual Citizens

The final category of expatriate managers consists of those who have high allegiance to both the parent firm and the foreign operation. We describe these expatriates as dual citizens. We chose the word *citizens* because it seems to reflect the active behavior, attitudes, and emotions that this group exhibits. These managers tend to see themselves as citizens of both the foreign country and the home country, of both the foreign operation and the parent corporation. As dual citizens, they feel a responsibility to try to serve the interests of both organizations.

John Beckenridge was director of the Japanese office of a prominent U.S. consulting firm. This was John's second global assignment in his thirteen years with the firm; his first assignment had been a one-year special-project stint in Singapore, seven years before. John was one of three candidates considered for the job in Japan and had been selected not only on the basis of his past performance but also on the basis of interviews and assessments by outside consultants who assessed his personal characteristics and the demands of the job in Japan. Because the job required work in a very novel culture and a high degree of interaction with host-country nationals, John was given five months' notice before departing for Japan. During this time, he received about sixty hours of cross-cultural training. In addition, John's wife received about ten hours of survival briefing before the assignment. About four months after arriving in Japan, John also received another forty hours of cross-cultural training specifically related to Japan—its culture, business practices, and so on. He also took advantage of language training, paid for by the parent firm, after he arrived in Japan.

John had a clear set of objectives for his assignment in Japan. The foreign office of the consulting firm had been established to serve the Japanese subsidiaries of U.S. clients, but the growth of the Japanese office was limited by the slowed expansion of the U.S. client firms. John was given the job of developing Japanese clients, to serve two objectives: increase the growth potential of the Japanese office, and make it easier to secure Japanese firms' U.S. subsidiaries as clients and facilitate the growth of the large U.S. domestic operations.

John found relatively little conflict between the expectations placed on him by the parent firm and by the foreign operation. Perhaps the most significant consistency involved the time and expense that everyone realized would be needed to cultivate effective contacts and relationships in Japan. For John, there was no tension between corporate "bean counters" going crazy over entertainment expenses in Japan and local staff members constantly floating "contact opportunities."

In addition, it was quite clear how this assignment in Japan fit into John's overall career path and how his repatriation would be handled. Although he was not guaranteed a specific job or position upon repatriation, John knew what the process of repatriation would involve and what general opportunities would be his if he met his objectives while in Japan.

Perhaps most important, John was given a great degree of discretion and autonomy in achieving the objectives that were set. According to John, this job discretion often gave him the flexibility to deal with inevitable conflicts between the parent firm and the local operation or with the various ambiguities that cropped up in his job.

Asked about his commitment or allegiance to the parent firm

and the Japanese operation, John commented, "I feel a strong sense of allegiance to both. Although they sometimes have different objectives, I try to satisfy both whenever I can." When objectives or expectations were in conflict between the two organizations, John generally worked to bring them together, rather than simply choosing to follow one or the other.

The personal and organizational consequences of John's dual orientation were primarily positive. At the personal level, John indicated that it was sometimes frustrating to feel torn in two directions but that the clarity of his objectives, the latitude he had to pursue them, and the relative infrequency and small magnitude of the conflicts made it quite rewarding and personally satisfying to work for the benefit of both organizations. John did well in his five-year assignment in Japan and upon repatriation received a rather substantial promotion to a position where some of what he learned was utilized in the firm's domestic and international expansion plans. At the organizational level, John's dual orientation facilitated solid relationships with Japanese clients and governmental officials and aided the home office's efforts to establish relationships with the U.S. subsidiaries of the new Japanese client firms. John felt that he had achieved other results with his dual focus, including a greater ability to recruit high-quality Japanese employees (something the firm's competitors struggled with).

Our research has found that roughly one-fourth of our sample of American expatriate managers had high commitment to both the foreign operation and the parent firm. It would be inaccurate to say that none of these expatriates ever returned home early, left the firm after repatriation, or had adjustment or performance problems during global assignments. Nevertheless, high dual allegiance led to a higher probability that the managers would stay in their foreign assignments for the expected length of time, would stay with the firm upon repatriation, and would adjust well during the overseas stay. These expatriate managers were very interested in rigorously understanding needs, objectives, constraints, and opportunities with respect to both the foreign operation and the parent firm. They talked of trying to use their understanding to find solutions that would satisfy and benefit both organizations. This approach created two possibilities: effectively implementing home-office policies in the foreign operation, and passing information and guidance from the foreign operation to corporate headquarters, information that could shape more effective strategy and policy development in all the firm's foreign operations.

As we have seen, role conflict is an important factor in determining whether expatriate managers have low or high commitment to both the parent firm and the foreign operation: the higher the role conflict, the lower the managers' commitment to both organizations,[7] and the lower the role conflict, the higher the managers' commitment to both organizations. Interviews with dual-citizen expatriate managers indicated that the single most common source of role conflict was conflicting expectations, demands, or objectives between the parent firm and the foreign operation (in other words, it was clear what was expected of the expatriate, but the expectations of the two organizations were different). The greater these conflicts, the less managers felt responsible for outcomes, and the less they felt committed to either organization. As one expatriate put it, "It's hard to feel responsible for what happens when you're being torn in opposite directions." The greater the consistency in demands, expectations, and objectives between the two organizations, the more responsible expatriate managers felt for what happened, and the more they felt committed to both organizations.

A similar dynamic was true in role ambiguity.[8] Role conflict involves clear expectations that are in conflict; role ambiguity involves expectations from both organizations that simply are not clear. Interviews with expatriate managers indicated that poor coordination between the parent firm and the foreign operation was a common source of role ambiguity. When we asked one expatriate manager how much responsibility he felt for what happened on his job, he replied, "How can I feel responsible when I don't really even know what I'm supposed to do or what's expected of me?" The greater the role clarity, the more the expatriate managers felt responsible for what happened at work and the more they felt committed to both the parent firm and the foreign operation.

Another factor related to high allegiance to both the parent firm and the foreign operation was clarity of repatriation programs. Unfortunately, over 60 percent of U.S. firms have no systematic or formal repatriation programs.[9] When such programs do exist, however, their clear communication facilitates high commitment to both the parent firm and the foreign operation.[10] Clear repatriation programs seem to free expatriates from worrying about going home and allow them to focus on their jobs. This, in combination with clear, nonconflicting job expectations, facilitates allegiance to the foreign operation. At the same time, clear repatriation programs seem to communicate to expatriates that the parent firm cares about them and has thought about issues of reintegration. This in turn creates a greater sense of commitment and obligation in the expatriates toward the parent firm.

We found that the most powerful job factor in creating dual allegiance was role discretion,[11] which is simply the freedom that the manager has to decide what needs to be done, how it should be done, when it should be done, and who should do it. The more discretion expatriate managers have, the more they feel responsible for what happens at work, and the more they feel committed to the local operation. Because they generally view the parent firm as ultimately responsible for the amount of freedom they enjoy, however, this also translates into a greater sense of obligation and commitment to the parent firm. Part of the reason why discretion was far and away the most powerful factor lies in the fact that most expatriate managers experience some level of role conflict and role ambiguity. Greater role discretion allows the manager the flexibility and freedom to try to define more clearly what is expected and to resolve conflicting expectations.

Although dual-citizen expatriate managers are desirable for any firm at any stage of globalization, they are most critical for firms at the coordinated multinational stage. Firms at this stage need information to flow back and forth between the home office and the foreign subsidiaries and from one foreign subsidiary to another. They need managers who identify both with the people back at the parent firm and with those in the foreign operation. They need managers who try to integrate and meet the needs of both organizations. They need expatriate managers who will not leave after repatriation, so that their international experience, knowledge, and skills can serve as assets in the global strategy and policymaking activities of the corporate office. Expatriate managers who are highly committed to both the parent firm and the foreign operation are critical in filling these needs.

Guidelines for the Effective Management of Dual Allegiance

Although most multinational firms and their executives are aware of the issues concerning expatriates' dual allegiance, in our research we have found very few expatriates who said that the firm had a clear understanding of the causes and consequences of the different patterns or had systematic means of developing dual-citizen expatriates. Instead, many firms seem to have found ways to try to counterbalance expatriates' tendencies to be too committed to one organization or the other. Here, we report what some firms are doing to counterbalance "lopsided" allegiance, and we propose steps that firms can take to develop dual-citizen expatriates with balanced and high levels of allegiance.

Strategy 1: Counterbalancing the Tendency to "Go Native"

The managers who are most likely to "go native" and have high allegiance to the foreign operation and low allegiance to the parent firm are those who have had several years of previous international experience and who have been successful in adjusting to the general nonwork environment of foreign cultures. Ironically, these managers are also good candidates for overseas posts, in terms of lowering the risk and associated costs of failed assignments and premature returns.[12]

One action that Honda takes to counterbalance this tendency is to have expatriates return home to Japan for a few years before they are sent overseas again. This practice reinforces the link between the individual expatriate and the parent firm and counteracts the tendency toward overcommittment to the foreign operation. Honda's view is that it is not logical to have a cadre of career internationalists moving from one foreign assignment to the next and expect these managers to be highly committed to the parent firm.

Firms could also counterbalance this tendency by sending expatriate managers who have longer tenure in the parent firm. The longer managers have been with the parent firm, the more they have invested in it, the more they identify themselves with it, and the more they are committed to it. This recommendation becomes problematic, however, for such firms as General Electric (GE), General Motors (GM), and Ford, which increasingly utilize global assignments as developmental experiences for younger, high-potential managers.

Consequently, GE takes a broader approach to counterbalancing the tendency to "go native" through its system of sponsors. In some GE divisions, this approach even involves a prior commitment to hire the expatriate manager back to a specific position. More often, the system of assigned sponsorship involves assessing the expatriate's career objectives, choosing a senior manager (often in the function to which the expatriate is likely to return) who is willing to serve as sponsor, maintaining contact between the sponsor and the expatriate throughout the assignment (including face-to-face meetings), clarifying career objectives and abilities before repatriation, evaluating the performance of the expatriate during the assignment, and providing career advice and helping to find a subsequent position before the manager's repatriation.

We talked with executives at several firms that have sponsorship programs, and they offered additional advice. Overall, they recommended that sponsor assignment should be systematic. First, the sponsor should be senior enough to the expatriate to provide a broad view of the organization. Second, the sponsor should be given specific guidelines about keeping in touch with the expatriate (form, content, and frequency of contact). Too often, the sponsor is simply assigned, and that is all: if the sponsor takes the initiative and fulfills the responsibility, things go well; otherwise, the assigned sponsor is one in name only. Third, the responsibility of planning for the expatriate manager's return and of finding a suitable position should not be solely that of the sponsor but must be incorporated into the career systems of the firm.

Although most U.S. firms do not provide cross-cultural training for expatriates before or after their arrival in global assignments, our research indicates that such training is an effective mechanism for counterbalancing the tendency to "go native." It may seem that predeparture training could only encourage the expatriate manager to identify with the host culture; but, although the evidence consistently suggests that good predeparture training does help expatriate managers adjust to their jobs overseas and does increase their performance,[13] our data indicate that an even stronger impact of such training is the sense of obligation and commitment that it creates because it demonstrates the firm's care and concern for the expatriate. Our data reflect only the impact of predeparture training, because postarrival training was received by less than 10 percent of the expatriates, but we suspect that a similar effect could be generated by training provided after arrival, if the training is clearly seen as being paid for and sponsored by the parent firm and not by the foreign operation.

In summary, a firm can counterbalance the tendency to "go native" by having managers come home for several years before sending them overseas again, by selecting managers with longer tenure in the parent firm, by instituting a systematic sponsorship program, and by providing predeparture or postarrival cross-cultural training for managers. Once these counterbalancing moves have been taken, policies that facilitate high commitment to both the foreign operation and the parent firm can be employed.

Strategy 2: Counterbalancing the Tendency to Leave One's Heart at Home

Many executives in U.S. firms seem relatively unconcerned about counterbalancing the tendency to leave one's heart at home. Our research suggests that the negative consequences are serious, however. We draw more on our research results than on actual organizational practices in suggesting ways for firms to counterbalance this tendency.

The managers most likely to leave their hearts at home are those who have many years of tenure with the parent firm and little international experience. Thus, such firms as GE, GM, and Ford, which are increasingly sending younger managers overseas as part of career development, are perhaps unintentionally counterbalancing expatriates' tendency to leave their hearts at home.

Helping expatriate managers adjust to the general nonwork environment is another powerful counterbalancing force. Ironically, many of the perks (company car and driver, company housing, and so on) given to senior expatriate executives may isolate them and inhibit their adjustment. Another major factor related to the expatriate's adjustment to the general environment is the family's adjustment.[14] Family members (especially spouses) are often exposed more directly to the general environment because they do not enjoy the insulation that the corporate structure provides. Therefore, a firm's efforts to facilitate the family's (especially the spouse's) adjustment to the general environment can have a positive effect on the expatriate manager's adjustment and counterbalance the expatriate's tendency to leave his or her heart at home.

How can the firm facilitate the family's adjustment to the general environment? One factor that helps families also helps expatriates—interacting with host-country nationals. Because host nationals are the best source of information about their own culture, the more families interact with them in general, and the more the expatriate managers interact with them outside of work, the greater the expatriate's adjustment to the general environment of the foreign country.[15]

Ford is one of the few U.S. firms that consistently tries to provide training and preparation for families (especially spouses) of expatriates. Executives at Ford did not decide to do this in an effort to counterbalance this tendency, but our research suggests that it is a likely unintended consequence.

A preparation program can facilitate interaction between host-country nationals and newly arrived expatriate managers and their families but does not guarantee it. An additional step that a firm can take is to ask host-country employees and their families to help specific expatriates and their families during the first few months after arrival. Obviously, care should be taken to match the sponsoring host-country family's characteristics with those of the expatriate family. Several Japanese auto firms, for example, have hired Americans who speak Japanese to help Japanese expatriate managers and families adjust to life in the United States.

Strategy 3: Creating Dual Citizens

The most important steps for firms to take are those that have a strong impact on creating high dual allegiance—steps that develop dual-citizen expatriates. The results of our research suggest that the primary target for fostering an expatriate who thinks of himself or herself as a dual citizen is the expatriate's job. The specific steps to be taken may seem trivial or obvious at first, but they are probably much more involved for most firms. Greater role clarity, greater job discretion, and lower conflict are the most powerful factors related to high dual allegiance, but the enactment of these three ideas is quite complex (see Chapter Five).

Simple attention to one aspect of the job may only hurt other aspects or the overall strategic purpose of the assignment (as discussed in Chapter Five, increasing role clarity may only uncover conflicting demands). Even a firm's best efforts to increase role clarity and simultaneously reduce role ambiguity may not eliminate role ambiguity and conflict, which is probably why job discretion is the single strongest factor in high dual allegiance. Even in the presence of some role ambiguity and role conflict, having the freedom to decide what tasks to do, how to do them, when to do them, and who should do them facilitates expatriate managers' ability to cope effectively with ambiguity and conflict. Simply giving expatriate managers a lot of job discretion and freedom is not the answer, however. Too much discretion without clear objectives may cause expatriates to choose objectives that are not in the best interests of the parent firm, the foreign operation, or both. Thus, as discussed in Chapter Five, the firm actually needs to consider all three elements of an expatriate manager's job simultaneously.

The assessment and design of an expatriate's job must take account not only of the technical aspects but also of the strategic dimensions. Without an assessment of the strategic dimensions, the firm may unintentionally design dysfunctional job requirements. By contrast, an analysis that begins with the broader strategy and context naturally leads to understanding and appropriate design of the expatriate manager's job and to a higher probability of dual allegiance.

Some readers may be saying to themselves, "Our firm has moved beyond the coordinated multinational stage. We are a global firm, and we need managers who are not just capable of dual citizenship but of world citizenship. We need global managers." Clearly, many firms are moving in this direction. Our data suggest that, despite the glamour of world citizenship, most expatriate managers actually struggle to reach the level of high dual allegiance. It seems to us that the first practical step toward global firms and global managers is to develop managers who at least see themselves as dual citizens. This may be especially critical in firms that have reached or are working to reach the coordinated multinational stage of globalization. In this case, dual-citizen expatriates are best developed through careful selection processes, pre- and postarrival cross-cultural training programs, well-planned strategies that translate into career systems with clear and consistent job expectations and appropriate levels of freedom and discretion, and repatriation programs that reintegrate expatriates and effectively utilize their knowledge, skills, and experience. These steps will help firms manage dual allegiance more effectively and help expatriates serve two masters more successfully.

Notes

1. Gregersen and Black, "Antecedents to Commitment to a Parent Company and a Foreign Operation."
2. Black, "Repatriation: A Comparison of Japanese and American Practices and Results"; Clague and Krupp, "International Personnel: The Repatriation Problem"; Harvey, "Repatriation of Corporate Executives: An Empirical Study"; Kendall, "Repatriation: An Ending and a Beginning."
3. Mowday, Porter, and Steers, *Employee-Organization Linkages: Psychology of Commitment, Absenteeism, and Turnover.*
4. Black and Porter, "Managerial Behaviors and Job Performance: A Successful Manager in Los Angeles May Not Succeed in Hong Kong"; Miller, "The International Selection Decision: A Study of Managerial Behavior in the Selection Decision Process."
5. Glisson and Durrick, "Predictors of Job Satisfaction and Organizational Commitment in Human Service Organizations"; Mowday, Porter, and Steers, *Employee-Organization Linkages;* O'Reilly and Chatman, "Organizational Commitment and Psychological Attachment: The Effects of Compliance, Identification, and Internalization of Prosocial Behavior."

6. Mowday, Porter, and Steers, *Employee-Organization Linkages.*

7. Glisson and Durrick, "Predictors of Job Satisfaction and Organizational Commitment."

8. Jackson and Schuler, "A Meta-analysis and Conceptual Critique of Research on Role Ambiguity and Role Conflict in Work Settings."

9. Harvey, "Repatriation of Corporate Executives."

10. Gomez-Mejía and Balkin, "Determinants of Managerial Satisfaction with the Expatriation and Repatriation Process."

11. Glisson and Durrick, "Predictors of Job Satisfaction and Organizational Commitment."

12. Black, "Work Role Transitions: A Study of American Expatriate Managers in Japan."

13. Black and Mendenhall, "Cross-Cultural Training Effectiveness: A Review and Theoretical Framework for Future Research."

14. Black, "Work Role Transitions": Black and Stephens "Expatriate Adjustment and Intent to Stay in Pacific Rim Overseas Assignments."

15. Black, "Work Role Transitions."

◯

Chapter 7

Appraising: Determining If People Are Doing the Right Things

Compared to other aspects of international management, performance appraisal has received little attention from researchers. Nevertheless, performance appraisal has been widely studied and written about as it is practiced in the United States, and here we draw on this body of knowledge in order to chart the important issues and challenges of creating valid performance appraisal systems. Next, we look at these issues from a global perspective and see what unique challenges arise in the development of valid performance appraisal systems for international managers. Finally, we offer prescriptions for companies, to assist them in constructing sound international performance appraisal programs.

Wayne Casio, a longtime researcher in human resources management, has perhaps best summed up the problematic nature of performance appraisal systems: "Performance appraisal has many facets. It is an exercise in observation and judgment, it is a feedback process, it is an organizational intervention. It is a measurement process as well as an intensely emotional process. Above all, it is an inexact, human process."[1] Most published research in this area indicates that only the rare company has been able to design and implement a credible performance appraisal system. A plethora of studies has revealed the obstacles to good performance appraisal. We will summarize these findings shortly, but first let us briefly review the reasons for conducting performance appraisals in the first place.

The Purpose of Performance Appraisals

There are two main reasons why organizations conduct performance appraisals—evaluation and development. Unfortunately, these two purposes are often mutually exclusive and cause friction within the organization. Evaluation goals for performance appraisal systems are as follows:[2]

1. To provide feedback to managers, so that they will know where they stand
2. To develop valid data for pay and promotion decisions, and to provide a means of communicating these decisions
3. To help management in making discharge and retention decisions, and to provide a means of warning subordinates about unsatisfactory performance.

Now consider the development goals of a performance appraisal system:[3]

1. To help managers improve their performance and develop future potential
2. To develop commitment to the company through discussion with the manager of career opportunities and career planning
3. To motivate managers via recognition of their efforts
4. To diagnose individual and organizational problems

As Figure 7.1 illustrates, these two sets of goals often come into conflict. According to Michael Beer, "When performance appraisal is being conducted to meet evaluation goals, the system is a tool by which managers make difficult judgments that affect their

Figure 7.1. Conflicts in Performance Appraisal.

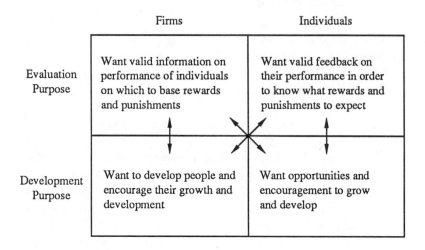

subordinates' futures. . . . The result can be an adversary relationship, faulty listening, and low trust. None of these are conducive to the coaching and development objectives of performance appraisal."[4] Figure 7.1 also illustrates the conflict within those who are being evaluated. They desire feedback about their performance, to reduce uncertainty about their standing in the organization; yet, conversely, those being evaluated want only to hear good news about their performance. This psychological tug-of-war can exacerbate poor performance due to worry, stress, and a constant focus on appearance versus substance and quantity versus quality of performance. These stresses and strains of competing purposes within the organization and of competing needs within individual employees partly cause and reinforce the knotty dilemmas and problems in designing and implementing performance appraisal systems.

Challenges to the Design of Valid Appraisal Systems

The North American research literature that has investigated performance appraisal systems is gargantuan; it would be impossible to review all the studies and their findings in this chapter. Rather than attempt to do so, we would like to distill their findings into "problem dimensions." Each dimension subsumes within it a large number of specific issues that cause performance appraisal systems to fail. The dimensions are really "umbrella" concepts, under which exist a variety of dysfunctional organizational behaviors. Management scholars generally contend that these dimensions are virtually impossible to eradicate totally in organizations. The best an organization can do is minimize how much these dimensions hurt organizational and individual growth and performance.

Invalid Performance Criteria

It is not unusual for companies to measure people on behavior that actually does not assist the organization in attaining its goals. For example, it probably does not make a lot of sense to give significant weight to punctuality in arriving at work as a performance criterion to measure the job performance of a software designer or a commercial artist. Isolating the key factors of success for any managerial position in a company is not as easy as it seems. The more complex the task, the more difficult it is to isolate what the important behaviors are that enable someone to achieve the task in an outstanding manner.

Rater Competence

The rater must have the technical background and the experience necessary to evaluate employees' behavior correctly. When raters have limited contact with those whom they evaluate, invalid ratings usually occur. The same holds true if raters do not have a clear idea of the actual complexities of the work environment. For example, it would be foolhardy to expect a manager who only understood sales results to effectively evaluate salesmen who must develop junior salesmen, jointly design systems with clients, and work with marketing research. There is often a complex system of "little things" that must be done well in order for a complex task to be accomplished. Misunderstanding of the complexity of the task tends to cause inaccurate appraisal.

Rater Bias

Rater bias occurs when the rater's values, perceptions, and preju-
dices replace organizational standards as the basis for evaluation.
This bias can take many forms. For example, a manager may "pro-
tect" a valued subordinate by giving him or her lower ratings than
deserved, so that the subordinate will not be promoted or transferred
from the rater's organizational unit; or a rater may give an employee
who is actually doing a good job a low rating because of how the
employee dresses, speaks, and generally acts around the office.
Thus, personal preference overcomes performance standards. Moreover, since raters are to some degree evaluated on the performance
of their subordinates, it is in their best interests to have subordinates
who are "above average." In this case, an entire staff may receive
undeserved positive ratings. Another rater bias is reflected in the fact
that recent events (positive or negative) tend to get more emphasis
in evaluations than past events do. The longer the interval between
evaluations, the greater the effect of this "recency bias." In short,
rater bias can take many forms, depending on the personal needs of
the rater.

Challenges to Valid Appraisal Systems
in the International Context

The problem dimensions just outlined exist in the international
arena as well as in the domestic context. The pertinent issue, however, is whether the manifestations of these problems are different
for global managers. To answer that question, we need to explore
the international aspects of each problem dimension.

Invalid Performance Criteria

The research clearly indicates that for a performance appraisal system to work, there must be a clear link between what it takes to be
successful on the job and what is measured by the appraiser. An in-
depth job analysis is vital to the creation of a valid performance
appraisal instrument. Too often, what are seen as the criteria of
success in the United States may not make sense in a foreign setting.

Common performance criteria that managers are measured on in the United States involve profit and loss, rate of return on investment (ROI), cash flows, efficiency (input-output ratios), market share, conformity to authority, and physical volumes. It would seem, on the surface, that global managers should be evaluated by the same criteria, which are easily measured and straightforward enough for clear performance standards to be derived from them. After all, companies want their managers to achieve the same sorts of things, no matter where they are in the world. Nevertheless, simply superimposing the same criteria, with similar standards for the United States and the rest of the world, can cause problems.

It is unfair to compare global managers against domestic performance standards on these criteria, because external factors often influence the financial and organizational performance of the global manager's area of responsibility. The following environmental factors can distort the appearance of financial and other performance standards in ways that the home office often cannot foresee:

- Rapid exchange-rate fluctuation
- Price controls
- Control over the revaluation of assets
- Depreciation allowances
- Costs assessed by the parent company and other associated firms against the foreign subsidiary (price of materials, general overhead charges)
- Availability of local debt financing
- Local currency evaluation of foreign-source assets invested

The problems of assessing current profit and loss from liquidation of assets and investments can sometimes cause home-office evaluators to make invalid performance evaluations of global managers.[5] Severe inflation for months or years, with no devaluation of the local currency, can help a subsidiary earn high profits, but the profits are more attributable to the inflation rate than to good management. Conversely, when currency is devalued against the dollar, the subsidiary, although well managed and profitable in terms of local currency, may show a loss in a given accounting period when its income statement is translated into dollars.

The experience of a global manager who was stationed in Chile illustrates the problem:[6]

> In Chile he had almost single-handedly stopped a strike that would have shut down their factory completely for months . . . . In a land where strikes are commonplace, such an accomplishment was quite a coup, especially for an American . . . . However, because of exchange-rate fluctuations with its primary trading partners in South America, the demand for their ore temporarily decreased by 30 percent during the expatriate manager's tenure. Rather than applauding the efforts this expatriate executive made to avert a strike and recognizing the superb negotiation skills he demonstrated, the home office saw the expatriate as being only somewhat better than a mediocre performer.

This global manager's home office placed important emphasis on sales figures, without understanding the context that influenced sales in Chile. All the other accomplishments of this manager were downgraded.

The foreign subsidiary may be measured on traditional criteria, but corporate headquarters may make it difficult to achieve the performance standards. There may be various reasons: delays in decisions from headquarters, cumbersome reporting procedures that headquarters has superimposed on the subsidiary, or complete disregard of suggestions made by the foreign subsidiary for changes that would enhance the probability of its success. Transfer pricing can force some subsidiaries to show profits that are allocated to them but have not really been earned by them. Global managers from the subsidiaries from which the profits were actually taken may be evaluated less highly than they deserve, especially if regional headquarters staff are doing the evaluating and are not informed by corporate headquarters about transfers that have taken place.

The evaluation goal of performance appraisal is to isolate the truly great performers in a company and reward them for their efforts. When this does not happen, word gets around, and global managers begin to play games with statistics, to make themselves look good to the home office instead of focusing on what really needs to be done. Sometimes the real keys to success in foreign settings are unique:

- Relationships with individuals in the local government
- Relationships with union leaders
- Public image of the firm in the local environment
- Local market share
- Employees' morale and job satisfaction
- Interpersonal negotiation skills
- Cross-cultural skills
- Community involvement

Many of these important aspects of a global manager's job are not easily quantified or measured. If they are not measured and evaluated, however, managers soon learn that it does not pay to concentrate on them.

Rater Competence

In a domestic setting, managers are evaluated by people who work fairly closely with them and with whom they have had a fair amount of interpersonal interaction. For global managers, the situation is somewhat different. The global manager may be evaluated by a regional or area executive—who may or may not be an American—with whom the global manager has had little face-to-face contact, or the global manager may be evaluated by someone at the home office with whom the global manager may have had no (or very little) face-to-face contact. Either way, there is a high likelihood that the rater may be quite unaware of the totality of the work situation of the global manager and may not have the requisite experience, insight, and knowledge to perform a valid performance appraisal. Executives at the home office may feel automatically competent to evaluate the performance of global managers. If one has not been overseas and experienced the fact that different rules operate in overseas business settings, however, and if one fails to realize that success overseas may not necessarily look like success in the United States, then it is difficult to evaluate a global manager's true performance. One study indicates that fully two-thirds of American CEOs have never lived or worked overseas.[7] Thus, there is a high likelihood that the global manager will not be evaluated by the home office from a perspective of international experience.

The example we cited of the global manager in Chile illustrates the problem. He was evaluated by someone in the home office who did not understand the business environment of Chile. A high-potential global manager sent to Japan by a large semiconductor firm had the following experience:[8]

> He barely kept his head above water because of the difficulties of cracking a nearly impossible market. On returning to the United States, he was physically and mentally exhausted from the battle. He sought a much less challenging position and got it because top management . . . believed [it] had overestimated his potential. In fact, top management never did understand what the expatriate was up against in the foreign market.

Global managers frequently indicate that their home offices deal with them from an "out of sight, out of mind" philosophy and do not understand what they are up against overseas at all. In a 1981 Korn-Ferry report[9], 69 percent of the global managers surveyed reported they felt isolated from their domestic operations and home-office superiors.

A competent rater who understands the reality of the business situation can make up for a poorly designed performance appraisal system that measures the wrong things, but the combination of a poorly designed system and a rater who does not understand the business situation of the ratee almost inevitably leads to invalid performance evaluations. When top management does not understand the realities of the overseas business environment, invalid performance evaluations, either formal or informal, are liable to occur.

Rater Bias

A large body of research has found that people from different cultures often misinterpret one another's behavior because of learned cultural differences in their perceptions and evaluations of social behaviors. For example, a research study that investigated how global managers from Britain, Japan, and the United States, and their host-country employees in Singapore perceived one another, found the following:[10]

1. American and Japanese global managers perceived themselves as being more technically competent than the British and Singaporeans perceived them to be.
2. The British global managers perceived themselves to be more technically competent than any of the other groups perceived them to be.
3. The American global managers saw themselves as being more open interpersonally than the British or the Japanese saw themselves as being, and the Americans were seen as even more open by all the other groups.
4. The British global managers were perceived as being more closed interpersonally than they saw themselves as being.
5. The Japanese global managers saw themselves as being only slightly closed interpersonally but were regarded as being very closed by all the other groups except the Singaporeans who worked for them (they thought the Japanese were only slightly closed).

This state of affairs should not surprise anyone, but when it comes to conducting valid performance evaluations, perceptual bias between people from different cultures no longer is a topic of amusement or intellectual curiosity. It can threaten performance and careers. Consider the following "close call" that an American global manager experienced in France:[11]

> In France, women are legally allowed to take six months off for having a baby. They are paid during that time but are not supposed to do any work related to their job[s]. This expatriate had two of three secretaries take maternity leave. . . . The American expatriate asked them to do some work at home, not really understanding the legalities of such a request. The

> French women could be fired from their job[s] for do-
> ing work at home. One of the women agreed to do it
> because she felt sorry for him. When the American's
> French boss found out [that] one of these two secretar-
> ies was working at home, he became very angry and
> intolerant of the American's actions. As a result, the
> American felt he was given a lower performance eval-
> uation than he deserved.

Set the scene in your mind. One secretary is in the American's doghouse because she will not do any of her work at home. The other
secretary is in the American's good graces but in the French manager's doghouse for breaking the law. The American is in the
French manager's doghouse but does not know why initially. When
he finds out why, he cannot get the French manager to understand
his reasoning. The French manager thinks that the American is
insensitive and possibly incompetent.

What happened next? The American asked his former boss,
another American, to intercede with his French superior. After a
while, the French manager came to understand why the American
had done what he did, and he modified the performance appraisal
to something more reasonable to the American. (What happened to
the secretaries is unrecorded.) The point is that the French manager
simply believed that the American manager should have been aware
of French laws governing maternity leave, and this assumption led
to problems for everyone involved. Such "war stories" are common
to all global managers; they are part of the territory. What becomes
important, however, is that if such cross-cultural misunderstandings remain unresolved, they can affect performance appraisal
negatively.

Resolving Appraisal Dilemmas in the Global Context

There are a variety of things that a company can do to lessen the
likelihood that invalid performance appraisals will be made in their
overseas operations. We would like to chart an approach for appraising global managers, an approach general enough to be ap-

plied across firms and industries yet specific enough to be of direct assistance to the people doing evaluations.

What Should Be Evaluated?

Getting to the bottom of what the key factors of success are for an overseas position is not easy. There are no shortcuts. Only careful analysis can reveal what the key factors are. It is simple to assume that profits or ROI are what the company is after, but external conditions may affect these figures, and so it is hard to know how well the global manager is doing when exchange rates fluctuate wildly, transfer pricing distorts profit pictures, and differences in accounting procedures affect financial reporting. Companies need to define what they consider success to be in Chile, Japan, the People's Republic of China, Great Britain, or Nigeria.

Obviously, business strategy largely dictates what is expected of a global manager in a specific country. It would be foolish to focus heavily on profits as a criterion of success for a global manager in the People's Republic of China, for example. If the company is in that country to make a lot of money in the short term, top management will be frustrated. More than likely, the company entered the country with a view toward building a presence there and eventually—over a period of many years—positioning itself to tap that country's gigantic consumer market. Thus, the question becomes: What does a global manager need to be doing in Peking to execute the company's strategy? Superimposing what makes sense from an American perspective will be counterproductive. The key to success in China may be close personal relationships with key government officials, it may be heavy investment in building a network of factories and training Chinese workers over a long period, so that when governmental restraints on business dissolve, the company will be ready to produce at levels the market will bear. The key may also be something else entirely. An important issue to resolve, then, is whether the firm's strategy in the country makes sense. If it does not, global managers will be between a rock and a hard place, feeling compelled to give the home office what it demands while simultaneously expending energy on what they consider to be the real issues.

Even if the strategy does make sense and the evaluation criteria are clear to everyone, the ways to meet the criteria may need to be different from those in the United States. For example, if output of production is an important criterion, it may be that in Chile the best way to ensure high output is for the global manager to spend most of his or her time on labor-management relations. In Chile, the primary key to keeping output on target may not be to focus on supply costs and inventories but simply to get the people to work on time. In locations where workforce stability cannot be taken for granted, spending time developing personal relationships with union leaders may make the difference between the workers' striking twice instead of twenty-two times during the global manager's tenure.

How can a company go about fine-tuning performance appraisal criteria to specific locations? Time simply must be spent on getting the facts. Executives must travel to the foreign locations and observe, ask a lot of questions, and ask the current global managers for their insights. Back at the home office, outside experts from universities, consulting firms, and government agencies, as well as other individuals who have lived and worked in those locations, should be brought in and thoroughly interrogated for information that could shed light on the key factors of success in the foreign locations in question.

Ideally, a manager who has returned to the home office from an overseas site should be a permanent part of the team that updates performance criteria for overseas assignments. According to Oddou and Mendenhall, "Reevaluating the criteria and their prioritization periodically will make sure the performance evaluation criteria remain current with the reality of the overseas situation."[12] It may make sense to have returned global managers travel every three to six months to their past location assignments to see how the current manager is performing and to interview him or her and gain insight into the current situation in the country's business climate, the challenges facing the firm in that country, and any changes that are needed from a strategic or an operational perspective. This way, the criteria on which the global manager is evaluated can be fluid and change according to the business climate.

Who Should Do the Evaluating?

Companies vary widely on who appraises global managers, and there are many possibilities. For example, a global manager of a U.S. firm in Brussels could conceivably be appraised by someone from the home office, someone from regional headquarters, someone from the division, branch, or subsidiary where the global manager last worked in the United States, or someone from the site to which the global manager will be assigned next. Other possibilities exist if the global manager is not the head of the overseas operation. In this case, the evaluator may be an immediate superior who is an American, an immediate superior who is a host-country national, an immediate supervisor who is a third-country national, an American superior who is two or more levels above the global manager, a superior who is two or more levels above the global manager and is not an American, a local chief operating officer who is an American, a local chief operating officer who is not an American, someone from the home office, someone from regional headquarters, or someone from the division, branch, or subsidiary where the global manager last worked in the United States.

Who should do the performance appraisal on a global manager? There is no clear answer that would apply to all firms. One study has found that U.S. global managers are most often evaluated by people from their home offices. This remains true in the case of an executive who does not head an overseas operation, but the evaluation is completed after consultation with the global manager's on-site superior. The study also revealed, however, that all the possibilities we have listed occurred with some of the global managers, and so there are distinct, company-specific differences in who evaluates global managers. [13]

We believe that a team of organization members should be involved in the performance appraisal of global managers, given the unique nature of their business activities. The team coordinator should be a senior human resources management executive, serving as the "hub" of the multiple evaluation process. This executive's task is to collect, analyze, and draft a "global manager evaluation report" that will reflect feedback from the team members. The report should then be forwarded to the individual who has direct line authority over the global manager and to other senior executives, and it should be filed at corporate headquarters, in the human resources department. The "hub manager" oversees the collection of feedback from the global manager's on-site superior (if the global manager is not the head of the overseas operation), peer managers of the global manager, subordinates of the global manager, clients of the global manager, and the global manager himself or herself.

The team members and their relationships are illustrated in Figure 7.2. Given the cross-cultural complexity of the global manager's assignment, it is necessary to access multiple raters. Ideally, those raters should reflect the differing constituencies of the global

Figure 7.2. Global Manager Evaluation Wheel.

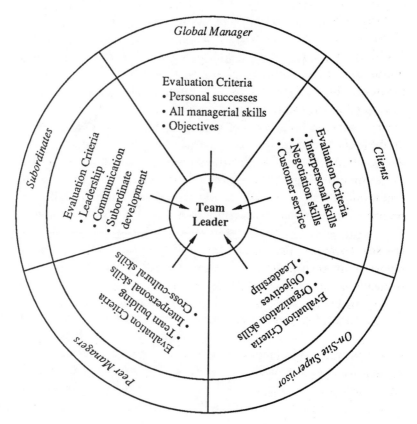

manager. Notice that no one from the home office is on the team. Research shows that the most basic prerequisite for conducting performance evaluation is the rater's having had "an adequate opportunity to observe the ratee's job performance over a reasonable period of time (e.g., six months)."[14] By definition, someone from the home office simply does not qualify. Thus, the home office needs information regarding the quality of the global manager's performance from those who have had an adequate opportunity to observe the manager in the overseas assignment.

It is dangerous to rely on just one rater's evaluation of a global manager, given possible rater bias due to cross-cultural issues. For example, if the global manager's immediate superior is an American, the superior may feel that the manager is doing wonderfully; the reality, however, may be that both the superior and the global manager may be poor performers because of their lack of familiarity with the local culture, the business climate, negotiation norms, and so on. Thus, an unwarranted "halo effect" and a commensurate inflated performance rating may occur. Conversely, as illustrated in the example of the global manager in France, an immediate superior who is a host-country national may be too tough on the global manager because of cross-cultural misunderstandings. Thus, relying solely on the rating of one person will not really give a clear picture of a global manager's performance. The performance evaluation wheel in Figure 7.2 reflects a more comprehensive approach to accessing feedback about global managerial performance.

On-Site Superiors. These individuals are in the best position to report on the relationship between the global manager's job performance and the foreign unit's organizational goals and objectives and to observe the manager's performance on important tasks, projects, and concerns of the organization.

Peer Managers. Obtaining feedback from peer managers, both Americans and host-country nationals, will reflect, to some degree, how well global managers work with others to accomplish the organization's objectives. The responses of these managers will also reflect the degree to which global managers possess managerial skills, interpersonal skills, cross-cultural skills, and team building skills.

Subordinates. Ratings from global managers' subordinates, especially if they are mostly host-country employees, will buttress "halo effect" ratings by global managers' immediate superiors. Feedback from this source will give some insight into cross-cultural managerial skills, communication skills, leadership abilities, and the degree to which global managers can work effectively among individuals who are quite different from them.

Clients. Usually part of the job description of a global manager is to represent the firm to external institutions in order to enhance the company's public image, drum up business, influence governmental decisions related to the company and its industry, foster alliances, and generally gain favor in the larger community. The only way to ascertain the success of global managers in this area is to question a sample of people who are clients of the foreign operation. Clients will not be able to provide insight into in-house managerial skills, of course, but they can provide useful feedback about global managers' expertise in negotiation, "figurehead" duties, interpersonal skills, sales skills, and alliance-building skills.

Global Managers. While the opportunity for rater bias exists in self-ratings, we feel that it is important for global managers to be able to indicate what their accomplishments, frustrations, progress, and challenges have been since the previous appraisal was conducted. Global managers' points of view are an important piece of the performance puzzle. Since global managers know that their input is only one part of the input "network," they will be motivated to try to put together reports that do not wildly exaggerate their performance in a positive vein.

When Should Appraisals be Done?

Much research has been conducted on this issue, and the results seem fairly clear. According to Casio, "Research over the past twenty years has indicated that once or twice a year is far too infre-

quent. Considerable difficulties face a rater who is asked to remember what several employees did over the previous six to twelve
months. . . . people often forget the details of what they have observed and they reconstruct the details on the basis of their existing
mental categories."[15] Managers tend to evaluate a six-month period
by their more recent memories of employees' performance. Usually
this translates into employees' performance for the last month
before the appraisal. This is the recency bias that we have already discussed, and it has a significant impact on performance
evaluation.

The dilemma that the research poses is that for the sake of
timely and consistent performance appraisals, effort is drained from
managers who could be focusing their energies on activities that
enhance profits—after all, organizations do not exist, in the main,
so that elegant performance appraisals can take place. We would
like to suggest a balance between the need for timely evaluation and
the need to use organizational time for more task-oriented activities.

The team leader should prepare a report on the global manager every six months. That does not necessarily mean, however,
that all the input should be gathered only twice a year from the
various team members. We suggest that, for global managers, performance appraisals be conducted in the following time frames,
with the following performance sources.

On-Site Superiors. Global managers should be appraised not by
chronological time periods but after the completion of significant
projects, tasks, or other organizational milestones. This allows the
superior to focus his or her evaluation within a specific task context,
rather than in a fuzzy "gestalt" context. These periodic reviews are
then forwarded to the team leader and are filed for later use, when
the team leader formally writes the "global manager evaluation
report."

Peer Managers. Peer managers should be asked to evaluate global
managers once every six months. By nature, their interactions with
the global manager will be sporadic—sometimes heavy and sometimes light—and so six-month intervals are necessary in order for

them to build up a mental data base on which they can report when asked to do so.

Subordinates. Subordinates can be asked to evaluate the global manager's activities in concert with the on-site superior's evaluations—that is, after major projects are completed. This will prompt subordinates to respond to direct task-oriented issues, rather than to their own general attitudes about the global manager.

Clients. This source should be accessed once a year. Obviously, clients are busy people and do not want to be bothered to fill out forms every three months. This raises an important question: What is the proper way to approach clients and ask them to be a part of an evaluation process? The global manager, the on-site superior, the regional superior, or executives at corporate headquarters could be asked to generate lists of clients who could be contacted. Feedback from these clients could be gathered formally, in phone interviews and surveys, or informally, over dinner—whatever makes sense in terms of the clients' personalities and cultural preferences. External observers could even be used to evaluate the global manager's dealings with the firm's clients if the act of contacting clients personally is seen as too intrusive. These observers could be in-house managers, university professors, or consultants.

Linking Patterns of Globalization and Strategy Orientation to Appraisal

Again, we would like to emphasize the point that a firm must seek a fit among its stage of globalization, competitive strategy, and its people-management practices. Another point to remember is that the five people-management functions must support and reinforce one another if each function is to be successful. For example, it does little good, in the long term, to carefully organize an elegant performance appraisal system for global managers and then, upon their return to the United States, place them in positions that do not make use of the skills they have developed overseas. The appraising function allows good management development and career planning to take place. It is an important link among functions in the people-management process.

Throughout this chapter, we have focused on ideas that will enhance a company when it goes about developing an appraisal system for its global managers. All companies have different strategies, however, and are at different stages in the globalization process. Therefore, we would like to discuss the appraisal function briefly in this light. In terms of performance appraisal, the following general principles apply.

1. *The more a company's competitive strategy moves toward differentiation, the more comprehensive and complex the performance appraisal system needs to be.* Even at the export stage of globalization, if a firm has a differentiation strategic orientation, global managers require above-average cross-cultural skills to be effective because they need to understand the foreign culture well, since products or services are fashioned to be culturally compatible with the consumers' preferences.

2. *The more a company's stage of globalization moves away from export and toward more integrative stages (MNC and global), the more comprehensive and complex the performance appraisal system needs to be.* As companies become more globally integrated, global managers find themselves not only responsible for "hard" organizational performance objectives (profits, ROI, market share, and so on) but also for "soft" organizational performance objectives (socializing foreign managers into the firm's corporate culture, coordinating and balancing the home office's and the subsidiary's concerns, representing the firm to external stakeholders, and so on). Thus, the criteria for the success of global managers increase in number and magnitude, and the team approach to performance appraisal is necessary in such conditions.

Summary

It does not matter how many global managers a firm has overseas— they have to be evaluated in a way that makes sense in the context of each one's overseas situation, the firm's strategy for that overseas unit, and the stage of globalization the firm is in. Probably the overarching principle to remember is that no matter what the context, the global manager should be evaluated on criteria that are truly important for success overseas, and not on criteria that are ancillary to success. This is probably the largest hurdle to overcome in international performance appraisal.

Notes

1. Casio, *Managing Human Resources.*
2. Beer, "Performance Appraisal: Dilemmas and Possibilities"; Casio, *Managing Human Resources.*
3. Casio, *Managing Human Resources.*
4. Beer, "Performance Appraisal," pp. 25–26.
5. Robinson, *International Business Management: A Guide to Decision Making.*
6. Oddou and Mendenhall, "Expatriate Performance Appraisal: Problems and Solutions."
7. Tung, "Career Issues in International Assignments."
8. Oddou and Mendenhall, "Expatriate Performance Appraisal."
9. Korn-Ferry International, *A Study of the Repatriation of the American International Executive.*
10. Stening, Everett, and Longton, "Mutual Perception of Managerial Performance and Style in Multinational Subsidiaries."
11. Oddou and Mendenhall, "Expatriate Performance Appraisal."
12. Oddou and Mendenhall, "Expatriate Performance Appraisal."
13. Stening, Everett, and Longton, "Mutual Perception of Managerial Performance and Style."
14. Casio, *Managing Human Resources.*
15. Casio, *Managing Human Resources,* pp. 302–303.

Chapter 8

Rewarding:
Recognizing People
When They Do Things Right

For many businessmen and businesswomen the rewards for good performance are expected to translate into $, ¥, or some other equivalent symbol. Regardless of the symbol, if it represents money, it can and will get counted by both the firm and the manager being transferred globally. Perhaps because money can get counted, and because there is a lot of it to count in the case of global assignments, compensation and benefits for internationally transferred employees traditionally receive a significant amount of corporate attention. These topics receive the lion's share of space in this chapter as well but will be placed in the context of broader objectives, where it will become clear that while compensation is important, the overall structure of compensation systems for global assignments, and other forms of rewards, are at the heart of encouraging the right things that people do. Consequently, this chapter first outlines the basics of existing reward systems and then proposes a more comprehensive and integrated reward system for employees on global assignments.

Allowances

As background for discussing general approaches to expatriate compensation, it is first necessary to review the long list of allowances that are often granted to expatriate managers. The number and variations of all the allowances offered to expatriate managers are nearly as large and varied as the firms providing them. There are a few that are quite common, however, and it is helpful to have a fundamental understanding of them before moving on to a discussion of the basic compensation approaches for global assignments and how these approaches do or do not incorporate specific allowances.

Foreign Service Premiums

A foreign service premium is simply money that is paid in recognition of the employee's and family's willingness and sacrifice in accepting a global assignment. This is compensation given in exchange for the inconvenience of living in a foreign land, with alien customs, food, weather, transportation systems, education, shopping, and health care facilities and for leaving family, friends, and familiar surroundings back home. A 1990 survey by Organization Resources Counselors (ORC) of over 250 U.S. multinational firms found that 78 percent pay a foreign service premium.[1] The policy of most firms paying this premium is to pay a percentage of base salary. This figure is generally between 10 percent and 25 percent of base pay. Some firms set a maximum for this premium—say, $50,000.

Hardship or Site Allowances

A hardship allowance is paid above and beyond a foreign service premium (if the latter is paid) in recognition of particularly difficult aspects of the specific country or site of a global assignment. Hardships may include such things as physical isolation, climatic extremes, political instability and risk, and poor living conditions due to such things as inadequate housing, education, health care, or food. The survey by ORC found that 68 percent of MNCs pay hardship allowances for U.S. expatriates, depending on the country of assignment.

Identifying and evaluating hardships and then determining a fair compensation value is a difficult task. Most firms take a two-fold approach. The first test is a simple external market test. Firms look at the competitive practices of similar firms with expatriate managers serving in the countries or locations in question. ORC found that 50 percent of U.S. firms use external experts to make this assessment. The second test is an internal market test. Firms simply assess what compensation is necessary to attract quality individuals to the country or site in question. Obviously, correspondence between external and internal market tests can range from high to low.

Several dynamics operate to influence firms when they choose the most expensive of the two market rates. Generally, firms know that, not long after arrival, their employees will compare their hardship allowances with those of employees of other firms. Consequently, even if internal market rates are lower than external market rates, firms often choose to go by the external market rates, in order to avoid feelings of inequity and complaints among their employees. Firms may also choose internal market rates over the lower external market rates in order to entice quality employees from within the firms to accept hardship assignments. Regardless of the method or methods utilized, a strong majority of U.S. firms do not phase out hardship allowances over the time of a given global assignment.

Cost-of-Living Allowances

Cost-of-living allowances (COLAs) are utilized in recognition that the costs of equivalent standards of living vary by country. ORC found that 91 percent of U.S. firms pay COLAs. Essentially, firms or their consultants must assess the cost of a comparable "basket of goods" in the country of assignment relative to some comparison country (usually the country of origin). If the country of assignment costs more than the comparison country, a cost-of-living adjustment is made. If the cost of living in the country of assignment is less than that of the comparison country, very few U.S. firms make negative adjustments.

The general method of making positive COLA calculations can be illustrated with the following example. Suppose that Janet McWilliams, a senior manager with a large accounting firm, is being transferred from Boston to Tokyo. The accounting firm contacts a consulting firm specializing in overseas COLA calculations. The consulting firm determines that it costs a single individual, without a family, 65 percent more to live in Tokyo than in Boston. Next, the consulting firm estimates that 60 percent of Janet's $100,000 salary is spendable income (goods, services, and housing) and that the remaining 40 percent is disposable income (taxes, savings, and so on). Accordingly, it determines the COLA for Janet McWilliams in Tokyo to be $39,000. It figures that, of Janet's $100,000 salary, 60 percent, or $60,000, is spendable income. Because living in Tokyo is estimated to be 65 percent more expensive than living in Boston, Janet will need slightly over $99,000 of spendable income in Tokyo, or an adjustment of $39,000. This adjustment is generally given "tax free." Most COLAs are also subject to review, in order to compare cost-of-living changes between the two referent countries due primarily to differences in inflation and exchange rates.

The timing of the inflation review and the rate of inflation can be particularly important. For example, if the annual inflation rate is 120 percent in, say, Brazil, then the frequency and timing of COLA calculations can have a significant impact. Suppose that company A evaluates inflation every three months, while company B evaluates it every month. Every three months, employees of both firms will have approximately 30 percent more cruzeiros added to their COLAs. The purchasing power of employees in company B will have been much better protected, however. If one employee from each firm receives 100 million cruzeiros in January, both employees will receive approximately 130 million cruzeiros in April. While the employee in firm A will have received 100 million cruzeiros in both February and March, however, the employee in firm B will have received 110 million in February and 120 million in March, or a total of 30 million more cruzeiros over the three months than the employee in firm A.

COLAs are also subject to changes in exchange rates. Today's foreign exchange rates can fluctuate considerably. For example, in the early 1980s, the dollar appreciated over 30 percent, in real terms, relative to the yen and then depreciated by over 35 percent in the late 1980s. To illustrate the importance of exchange-rate fluctuations, let us continue the example of Janet McWilliams. Suppose that at the time of Janet's transfer to Tokyo the Japanese yen-to-dollar exchange rate is 150¥ to $1. The total COLA for Janet in yen will be ¥5,850,000. Suppose that six months after she arrives in Japan the yen-to-dollar exchange rate changes to ¥130 to $1. Now $39,000 exchanges into only ¥5,070,000. This is a loss to Janet of ¥780,000, which at the 130-to-1 exchange rate will require an additional $6,000.

One of the important issues for firms to consider is that official exchange rates are not always accurate reflections of unofficial or real exchange rates. Especially in developing countries, in which the national currency is not freely traded on world exchange-rate markets, governments have a tendency to overvalue their currencies. Thus, while the dollar may officially only buy 415 rupiahs in Indonesia, unofficially it may buy 500 rupiahs. In particular, the combination of high rates of inflation and slow adjustments in official exchange rates can have significant and negative impacts on the true purchasing power of expatriates. Failure on the part of firms to recognize these issues can often lead to dissatisfied employees and families and to costly early returns from global assignments.

Housing Allowances

In many parts of the world, housing allowances have become the single most expensive item in expatriate compensation packages. For example, apartments in Hong Kong and Tokyo can easily cost $5,000 to $10,000 per month. There are three major methods that firms use to determine housing allowances.

The first method involves a flat allowance. In this case, the employee is given a fixed amount (which often depends on family size and organizational rank) to spend on housing. If the employee finds something suitable for less than the allowance, he or she can pocket the difference. If suitable housing costs more than the allowance, the difference comes from the employee's pocket. The firm must have accurate, up-to-date knowledge of the housing market in the country of assignment or it will either end up paying too much in housing allowances or have dissatisfied employees because it is paying too little.

The second method is to determine the housing costs of the employee in the country of origin and the cost of housing in the country of assignment. If the housing costs in the country of assignment are higher, an allowance equal to that difference is paid. The survey by ORC found that 22 percent of U.S. firms handle housing allowances in this manner.

The third method is for the firm to provide housing in the country of assignment either rent-free or at the same cost as in the employee's country of origin. Most firms that provide housing rather than housing allowances charge employees rental fees similar to those they would pay in the country of origin.

Utility Allowances

There are two general approaches to how utility allowances are handled. The first approach is simply to provide a utility allowance to the employee. As with set housing allowances, the firm must have an accurate knowledge of utility rates and reasonable usage in the country of assignment. The costs of overpaying for utilities or of not allowing enough to, say, run an air conditioner in a tropical climate can be equally high. The second approach is to assess the cost differentials between the countries of assignment and origin and provide a utility allowance equal to the difference if utility costs are higher in the country of assignment.

Furnishing Allowances

There are three major ways in which firms handle furnishing allowances. The first involves shipping the employee's furnishings to the new location. There is usually a maximum weight limit, such as 15,000 pounds, set on what can be shipped. The benefit of this approach is that employees and their families have their own home furnishings. This approach can become quite expensive, however, and both damage and delays can lead to dissatisfied and sometimes angry employees.

As a second approach, many firms either purchase or, more often, lease household furnishings and then provide them free to international managers. This approach is often accompanied by a shipment of less than 1,000 pounds of personal belongings. Firms often pay for storage of furniture during an assignment. This may seem to be a simple task, but if it is poorly done, employees can become as dissatisfied as one American expatriate did: "Almost all of our personal effects were ruined while in storage. It was difficult and extremely stressful to straighten the mess out. The company didn't really offer much help—we were on our own."

The third approach is simply to provide the employee with a fixed sum of money ($8,000–$10,000) with which furnishings can be purchased. (If the desired furnishings cost less than this amount, the employee is free to keep the difference. If they cost more, the employee must cough up the extra yen, pounds, rupiah, or lire.)

Education Allowances

Children's education is a critical issue in the minds of most parents who are asked to transfer to a foreign country. Most firms' internal markets are such that the firms would find very few quality people willing to accept global assignments if the children were simply forced to attend local schools in the countries of assignment. Consequently, most firms provide an education allowance that covers the normal costs (tuition, books, supplies) of attending local "international" schools. If adequate educational facilities are not available in the country of assignment, many firms provide assistance that covers part of the cost of boarding schools back in the country of origin. In the more comprehensive education allowances, this will also include one or two round-trip tickets for the children to visit the parents. In the more limited allowances, only air fare is provided, without boarding school support or assistance.

Home-Leave Allowances

Most companies provide executive employees and their families business-class air fare between the countries of assignment and origin once a year. Employees strongly favor being given the equivalent sum in cash, to use as they please. This allows them to purchase less expensive economy-class tickets and pocket the difference, to take their home leave away from home by visiting some other place or country, or to select an inexpensive plan that allows them to do both. Most U.S. firms do not require employees to take home leave in their home country.

Relocation Allowances

The relocation allowance is provided in recognition of the fact that a variety of expenses cannot be predicted accurately, and they vary by individual. These miscellaneous expenses associated with moving are typically covered by a fixed allowance equal to one month's salary or $5,000, whichever is less. ORC found that 43 percent of U.S. firms pay a flat sum, most often at the beginning and at the end of an assignment.

Rest-and-Relaxation (R&R) Allowances

Rest-and-relaxation allowances are most often associated with hardship assignments. Generally, they are provided in order for the employee and the family to get away and recover from the hardships of the country of assignment. These trips are often necessary in order for the employee and family to purchase goods or receive medical care not available in the country. Many firms have a "use it or lose it" policy with R&R allowances because they do not want employees or their families to make the trade-off of risking physical or emotional health for the allowance money.

Medical Allowances

The health of employees and their families is not something that firms can afford to put at risk. Consequently, most firms pay for all medical expenses (but often excluding optical and dental). Some firms prefer to pay for any medical expenses in excess of those covered by insurance. In developing countries, this can often mean that firms pay for employees or members of their families to receive adequate medical care in countries other than the country of assignment.

Car-and-Driver Allowances

Except for senior executives, most firms provide a car allowance, based on the differential between owning and operating a car in the country of assignment and in the country of origin. External market pressures seem to be the biggest determinants of whether a car or a car and driver are provided to senior executives. ORC found that 22 percent of U.S. firms provide a company car for all expatriates from headquarters, while 67 percent provide company cars when they are essential. In Pacific Rim countries, American executives are often provided cars and drivers to which they would not be entitled even in similar-level positions back in the United States.

Club Membership Allowances

In many countries, club memberships are the only (or often the least expensive) means of employees' and families' gaining access to normal recreational facilities, such as tennis courts, swimming pools, exercise rooms, and so on. In other locations, club memberships are essential for gaining access to the informal but important contexts of business decisions and political and business contacts. ORC's survey found that 6 percent of U.S. firms pay for club memberships for expatriates, and that 42 percent pay on a case-by-case basis.

Taxes

The first thing to say is that taxes are a complex issue in the case of managers working in global assignments; the details and specifics are best handled by experienced professionals. With this said, there are a couple of important issues to understand that will enable firms or individual managers to be better consumers of expatriate tax-consulting or tax-preparation services.

There are two major approaches to tax policies and global assignments. The first approach is commonly referred to as tax protection. Under this policy, firms reimburse employees for taxes paid in excess of what they would have paid if they had remained in the country of origin. There are several things to keep in mind. Many of the benefits and allowances previously described add to the employees' taxable income, making it greater than it would be if they had remained at home. The extra money reimbursed to compensate for these additional taxes is itself taxable income, generating additional taxes and creating the need to provide even more reimbursement. Carried to the extreme, this can become a never-ending cycle of compensation and tax-reimbursement escalation. Consequently, the firm must make decisions about whether to limit this cycle to one or two rounds. Another major issue is that it is possible for employees transferring from higher-tax home countries to lower-tax assignment countries to actually owe less in taxes than they would have if they had stayed home. In this case, the firm must decide if it will allow employees to keep the benefit or require employees to reimburse the firm for the difference. Most firms in this situation find it difficult to require employees to reimburse the difference.

The second major approach is commonly termed *tax equalization*. The objective of a tax-equalization policy is to see that employees pay no more and no less than they would have paid in the home country. Under a tax-equalization policy, the tax that the employee would have paid is subtracted from the salary. The firm then pays all actual taxes in the home and the host country that employees owe. There are several advantages to the tax-equalization approach. First, subtracting the hypothetical home-country tax from the total salary reduces actual taxable income. ORC found differences in how this hypothetical tax was computed. Roughly 25 percent of U.S. firms estimate it on base salary alone, 54 percent estimate it on base salary plus bonus, and 8 percent estimate it on base salary, bonus, and all premiums. The benefit to the firm of tax equalization can be quite substantial, especially with respect to employees originating from high-tax countries. This is probably why nearly nine in ten U.S. firms take this approach. Second, it reduces problems upon repatriation. For example, if an employee from the United States were sent to Saudi Arabia (which has virtually no personal income tax) and were allowed to keep the tax windfall, the employee would experience a significant shock upon repatriating.

The person could easily experience a drop in disposable income of 30–50 percent. Third, making adjustments for different tax policies in different countries through tax equalization makes it easier to motivate employees from low-tax countries, such as Saudi Arabia, to go to high-tax countries, such as Sweden. Fourth, if the majority of the firm's employees sent on global assignments originate from relatively high-tax countries, the firm often receives a net benefit (or cost reduction) due to differential tax rates.

The Problem of Rewarding *A* While Hoping for *B*

One of the common problems that these various allowances create is what is commonly referred to as "rewarding *A* while hoping for *B*."[2] Essentially, this phrase captures the problem of rewarding one behavior while hoping that the person will actually exhibit another. For example, professors hope that students learn the material and expand their understanding, but they often only reward students' ability to regurgitate memorized facts and figures. In business, employees are often quick to point out that although their bosses hope they will show initiative and solve problems, they often reward employees for simply following orders and sticking closely to "standard operating procedures." Because this problem is so commonplace, examples abound. Two reasons for this pervasive problem are that (1) objectives often are not clear or are not clearly understood and that (2) even when objectives are clearly understood at the outset, the means of achieving them eventually supplants the original objectives and becomes an objective itself. International assignment reward systems are just as vulnerable to this phenomenon as to any other.

To avoid the trap of rewarding *A* while hoping for *B*, it is important to consider two critical objectives of global assignment reward systems and the special issues involved when people are moved around the world.

Attracting and Retaining Quality People

One of the first objectives that reward systems are used for is to attract and retain quality people for global assignments. Although there are positive and appealing aspects of living in a different country and culture, there are also numerous uncertainties and negative consequences. Leaving family, friends, familiar and comfortable living conditions, education and health care facilities, entertainment and recreational opportunities, favored foods and shopping areas, and so on, is not something most people want to do. Consequently, money is often used as a means of "buying off" the loss of the things left behind or as a means of simply "buying" them, or paying for them to be brought along. As one manager in Jakarta pointed out, "the normal grocery store here doesn't carry Wheaties, but with enough money, I can get my Wheaties."

Consequently, while firms may hope that quality people are attracted to international assignments and may hope that these individuals will adjust effectively to the foreign cultures, many of the rewards of accepting a foreign assignment (for example, the different allowances) often encourage the expatriate and the family to transport or purchase a life-style quite similar to the one they had back home, and not to make much effort to adjust to the foreign culture and country. This is rewarding *A* while hoping for *B*.

Enhancing Feelings of Equity

International reward systems are designed to enhance feelings of *equity*, which should not be confused with feelings of *equality*. Most organizations are not built on the principle of equality—that is why firms are generally structured like pyramids, with various levels of hierarchy, and why financial compensation almost always moves up as the person moves up the pyramid. The notion of equity assumes that people make comparisons of the *ratio* between what they "put in" or contribute and what they "get out" or receive. This means that employees at the same organizational level, performing at virtually the same level of performance, would expect quite similar rewards. In the international context, this means that there is a need to avoid significant differences in pay between expatriates originating from different countries but assigned to the same location and performing equally well at similar jobs, or to avoid significant differences in pay for expatriates performing equally well at the same job in different locations.

Unfortunately, the financial incentives that are used to attract quality people to international assignments often create quite a strong sense of *inequity*. Host-country nationals just one level below expatriates frequently see large gaps between what they contribute and receive and what expatriates contribute and receive. Many of the rewards that expatriates are given are lost if not used, which only encourages expatriates to use them or lose them, and this adds to feelings of inequity between local nationals and expatriate managers. Poorly designed reward systems can also create inequity between expatriates originating from different countries but assigned to the same location. For example, a country manager in Japan heading up the local office for a large U.S. multinational commented, "I have a German expatriate working two levels below me, with a compensation package equal to mine and twice as large as a British expatriate's one level above him." Firms may hope for equity, but many of their reward systems encourage the maximization of inequity. Consider the following comment from the spouse of an American expatriate:

> I feel this firm does not really care about its people and their families as well as it should. Everything is done "on the cheap," which makes adjusting to the new country so much harder, which in turn makes their employees even more stressed out. Comparing this assignment to those of other major New York banks' employees, our benefits were extremely below standard and embarrassing! For example, the housing allowances of many people we met were 25 percent higher than ours. Home-leave airfares were only economy in our company, while other firms were business class. Significantly higher bonuses were given by other firms. Our bank has lost and will continue to lose a great many excellent people should they continue to deal in this way. By the way, my husband left the bank for these reasons since our repatriation.

Basic Compensation Approaches

As long as there are expatriate employees, they will make both internal and external comparisons of compensation packages. These packages are more than the individual allowances that have been discussed, however. They are a composite of both monetary and nonmonetary reward systems. As a final preliminary step before we discuss both aspects of effective reward systems, we will examine the basic approaches for fitting these individual allowances into a general monetary reward system.

Balance Sheet

The balance sheet arguably represents the dominant approach in the United States. The basic objective of this approach is to ensure that employees can maintain a standard of living in the country of assignment similar to what they enjoy in their home country. This keeps the shock from changes in standard of living relatively small throughout the entire international assignment cycle. Figure 8.1 provides a rough illustration of how this approach is designed.

This approach works relatively well when the conditions are right. Because the objective is to keep the standard of living constant before, during, and after the international assignment, it assumes that individuals return to the home country after completion of the assignment. This condition is true in many firms, but others have systems in which a cadre of career international managers move from one international assignment to another. In this case, it becomes difficult to determine both the home country of employees and the rationale for making their living standard abroad equal to that of an arbitrary home country.

This approach works better when most of the firm's expatriates originate from the same country. If expatriates originate from different countries with different standards of living and yet work together in the same country of assignment, the balance sheet actually serves to highlight the imbalance or unequal standards of living that these individuals enjoy (or suffer). Consequently, expatriates of equal responsibility may find it quite difficult to accept unequal compensation packages due primarily to accidents of birth.

Figure 8.1. Balance Sheet.

Approximately Equal Overall Standard of Living

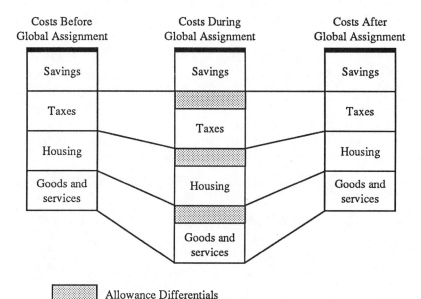

Allowance Differentials

This method is most effective if reliable, detailed figures for calculating and comparing standards of living are available. Take the case of a biotechnical firm with headquarters in Salt Lake City and regional headquarters in Geneva, Switzerland. The firm recently transferred one of its leading managers, married with two small children, to Switzerland from Los Angeles. The company's director of corporate personnel made some inquiries about how much the annual rental costs would be in Geneva for a three-bedroom house or apartment. The estimate came back that annual rental costs in Geneva would be approximately $25,000 per year. The director knew that annual homeowner costs in Salt Lake City for a three-bedroom house were about $13,500. This translated to an $11,500 housing adjustment that needed to be made in favor of the employee. Instead of using these figures, however, the director could easily have relied on national averages for Switzerland and the United States in making an assessment of the necessary housing allowance needed to bring about a balance. The point is that standards of living (and the expenses associated with them) vary, not just by country but also by region, city, and even neighborhood. This particular expatriate's annual housing costs were $16,500 per year for his three-bedroom house in Los Angeles. The average annual rental cost for a three-bedroom apartment in Switzerland in general was $21,000, or $4,000 less than in Geneva. Thus, the figures that are available, how they are calculated, and which ones are used can make a significant difference in the amount that is needed to "balance" living standards.

Unfortunately, firms utilizing the balance sheet tend to create situations in which employees experience significant changes in compensation upon returning home. Consider the following comments from American expatriates:

> When I returned, my base salary was reduced 16.7 percent versus the stated policy of a maximum of 10 percent. In the last twelve years, I have received consistent outstanding performance reviews. These ratings have been by eight different managers, three of whom were senior vice-presidents. In the last three years, I have received the maximum bonus available under the performance incentive plan.

> I was generally very happy to return to the U.S. after living in Toronto, where the cost of living was less than in New York. As a result, even though I did get a raise and the additional benefit of a second lease car, I now have much less disposable income (higher taxes, higher housing costs) and in fact can't even afford *one* lease car, because I can't afford parking for it! I am being hurt financially because I moved back to a much more expensive city, and my company has no policy to handle that. It hurt particularly in contrast to the fact that I felt my overseas assignment benefited me financially.

The balance sheet currently represents the most utilized approach. Most employees considering global assignments see it as reasonable and fair, and therefore it can be an effective means of attracting quality people to these assignments. It works best, however, when employees return to their home countries upon completing their assignments, when most expatriates originate from the same country, and when accurate and specific data exist on the standards of living for both locations.

Parent-Country Equivalency

This approach is in many ways quite simple and straightforward. With this approach, the compensation of all expatriate employees (or all expatriate employees above a certain level) is based on market rates in the home country. For example, a U.S. chemical MNC provides all expatriates, regardless of country of origin, the same salary and benefits as for employees in the U.S. This approach reduces the inequality that expatriates from different countries of origin who are working in the same location often feel with other approaches.

The effectiveness of this approach is also subject to several important conditions. It works well when the home country of the parent firm has relatively high wages and a fairly high standard of living, because it is easier to convince individuals to accept pay scales and standards of living that are greater (but not less than) what they would otherwise have.

This approach also works well when the expatriate managers in global assignments are career internationalists and move from one foreign assignment to another. This reduces the negative impact that the loss of cost-of-living adjustments creates when individuals return home to countries with lower pay scales and lower living standards.

This approach works best when there is a relatively small number of managers (fifty or fewer) on international assignment, or a cadre of career international expatriates. Paying parent-country wages and ensuring parent-country living standards, especially when they are high relative to world standards, for a large group of expatriate managers can become very costly. Moreover, large groups of managers trotting around the globe and enjoying relatively high wages and standards of living can intensify the inequity that host-country managers and employees feel and can hurt an expatriate manager's ability to work effectively with local staff people.

Regional or Composite Markets

Some companies have found an approach based on *regional* or *composite markets* attractive. This approach involves the calculation of an average salary and standard-of-living index for a set of countries. The term *regional market* is generally used to refer to a set of countries determined by their geographical proximity (for example, those in Central America, in the Middle East, in Scandinavia, and so on). The term *composite market* is used to refer to a set of countries grouped not by geographical location but by some other criterion, such as market importance to the firm. This approach is often less costly than the parent-country approach because it allows the firm the opportunity to arbitrage the difference in wages and cost of living between the parent country and other countries.

This approach works well when expatriate managers come from and stay within regional or market boundaries. The more employees move between regions or markets, the greater the chance that feelings of inequity will emerge. This approach works best when regional or market boundaries are drawn around countries that have wage and living-standard levels that are more similar than different. For example, drawing a boundary around Canada, the United States, and Mexico as the North American region would create feelings of inequity because of the significant wage and living-standard differences between Mexico and the other two countries.

Local Markets

The fourth major approach to expatriate compensation starts from the premise that there is nothing special about being sent on an international assignment, and so no special compensation or benefits should be expected or paid. Accordingly, all employees, whether they are working in their home country or not, are paid according to local market rates. A slightly less absolute version of this approach involves providing some allowances for the first year or two and then dropping them and treating the transferred employee as a host-country national. A slight variation involves a "one-time premium" that is paid at the beginning of the assignment (or sometimes at the beginning and at the end). The obvious implication of this basic approach is that quality employees will accept global assignments to countries in which wage structures and standards of living are higher than those of the country of origin. It is quite difficult to entice employees to make the opposite move, however.

This approach can work under some fairly restrictive conditions. First, if the firm in general takes a multidomestic strategic approach to business and desires little transfer of information into or out of countries, then its need for expatriate managers will be relatively low. Second, if the firm is expanding into countries that are more rather than less developed, by comparison with the country of the parent firm or the country of origin of the most desirable expatriate employees, then this approach can work.

An Integrated Solution

What sense can be made of these basic approaches, allowances, and fists full of money? Many multinational firms have simply decided that it is all too costly and too complicated and are taking drastic measures to reduce the costs and complexity of global assignments, but these firms may be throwing the baby out with the bathwater. After reviewing the strengths and follies of some cost-reduction and simplification approaches, we will outline an approach that can be both less costly and more effective for a wide variety of multinational firms.

Anorexic Versus "Lean and Mean"

As is clear from all the common allowances that most firms provide to internationally transferred employees, these employees can be quite expensive. One multinational U.S. firm with 500 employees in global assignments estimated that the incremental cost for these employees was $80 million. Consequently, most firms direct their cost-cutting activities at slashing the number of expatriates, in order to reduce total expatriate costs. The fastest way for a firm to cut $40 million from its $80 million total in incremental costs is to cut the number of expatriates from 500 to 250, as one West Coast bank did recently. This may be an appropriate step, but there are a few things to consider, so that the firm will not be penny-wise and dollar-foolish.

If future key leaders of the organization need international experience in order to be prepared to lead the firm in a global environment, then cutting the number of global assignments just for the sake of reducing costs may be a short-term sacrifice of the firm's long-term future in a global marketplace (see Chapter One and the discussion of strategic roles of expatriates).

One can also think about the flow of knowledge[3] throughout the global network of the firm and the strategic role that expatriates can play in these knowledge flows. To put the matter simply, knowledge can flow into and/or out of a foreign subsidiary, as illustrated in Figure 8.2. If the flow of knowledge both into and out of the subsidiary is low, then the unit is basically isolated and autonomous. If this is true of most foreign subsidiaries for the multinational, then the knowledge-transfer role of expatriates (knowledge they carry with them in their heads when they are transferred in, or when they leave) is reduced, and therefore reducing the total number of expatriates may be an appropriate cost-cutting step.

If the flow of knowledge into the subsidiary is high but the flow out of it is low, then the unit is primarily an implementer and utilizer of knowledge from the parent firm or other "big brother" units. If this pattern is the dominant one for the multinational, then there is an important knowledge-transfer role for expatriates, especially from the parent or "big brother" organization. In this case, fewer expatriates may mean that less knowledge is being transferred into the "implementer" unit. Consequently, if reductions in the number of expatriates are made, careful attention should be given to which people and what knowledge are *not* sent.

If the flow of knowledge into the unit is low but the knowledge flow out is high, then this unit can be thought of as a source of innovation and ideas. If this organizational unit is not the parent firm, then the dominant pattern of international transfer is likely

Figure 8.2. Knowledge Flows.

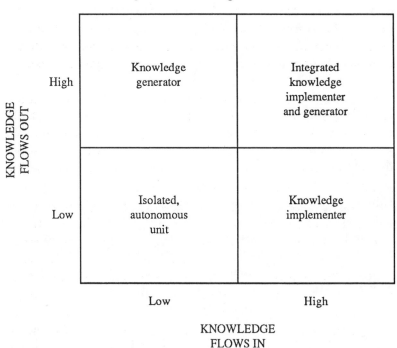

Low   High

KNOWLEDGE
FLOWS IN

Source: Adapted from Gupta and Govindarajan, 1991.

to be one of third-country nationals or managers from one foreign country being transferred to other foreign countries (but not the country of the parent firm). Although the pattern of international transfers would look different from the typical parent-country expatriate pattern, the transfer of people and of the knowledge they have in their heads may be quite important. Once again, careful thought should be given before wholesale slashing of the total number of international managers is undertaken.

Finally, if the knowledge flow into and out of subidiaries is high for the multinational as a whole, then the knowledge-transfer role of expatriate managers is quite critical. In this case, the firm is likely to have parent-country nationals being transferred to various foreign countries, to have foreign nationals being transferred to the parent country, and to have third-country nationals being transferred all over the world. To some extent, this "cross-pollination" can be achieved only through international transfers. Consequently, substantial slashing of the number of expatriates may significantly reduce total short-term expatriate costs at the expense of the firm's global competitive position.

In addition to the strategic roles of succession planning and knowledge transfer, the coordination and control function should also be carefully considered before the total number of managers on global assignment is cut. Many authors have recently talked about the role that corporate culture can have in reducing coordination and control costs.[4] Often the shared values of a strong corporate culture are referred to as *second-order control mechanisms*. This notion simply suggests that the costs of directly monitoring, reporting, and evaluating (first-order controls) the behavior of employees worldwide is more costly than having employees internalize a set of values that then guide their decisions and behavior (second-order controls). Although the content of cultures and values differs the world over, one common element is that people are socialized by other people to accept certain values. Therefore, if the organization wants to establish or maintain a strong corporate culture, it will need people who accept the desired values and can socialize other people to them. Effective socialization generally requires significant and direct periods of contact. This means, quite simply, that the firm that wants a strong worldwide organizational culture will need to move managers throughout its worldwide operations. Any given firm may have too many expatriates to accomplish this effectively, but careful consideration of the necessary number should be given before numbers-cutting programs are initiated.

Expatriates are expensive; international assignments are costly. No one will debate these two statements, but executives and policymakers should carefully consider succession planning, knowledge transfer, and coordination and control before launching programs to significantly cut the number of expatriates. Reducing programs should leave the organization "lean and mean" but not anorexic.

Leaping Ahead to the Past

Just as no one will argue that expatriates are expensive, no one will argue that expatriate compensation systems can be complex. This, in combination with the expense, may explain why more firms would like to simplify things by merely setting a percentage premium and leaving it at that. Increasingly, policymakers are saying, "Give these managers an extra 20 percent, and send them." These changes in expatriate compensation actually represent a return to the past. In the early days of expatriate compensation—say, in the 1950s—most managers were given a little extra, and off they went. However emotionally appealing this simplification may be to frustrated personnel directors and other executives, it is likely to be quite disappointing for the problems it does not solve. For example, it will not solve the problem of attracting quality people to take international assignments. It will not solve the problem of the significant effect that exchange-rate fluctuations can have on real purchasing power in another country. It will not solve the problem of lowered standards of living due to high inflation rates in the country of assignment. It will not eliminate the sense of inequity that employees feel when they compare themselves to other expatriates at similar organizational levels in other firms.

Expatriate compensation systems are expensive and complex, but the focus should be on the entire reward system first and then on the effectiveness of the compensation system. From a strategic perspective, simply cutting the number of employees in global assignments may do nothing positive and may actually have negative consequences for organizational and individual effectiveness. Likewise, merely simplifying the compensation system may increase efficiency at the expense of effectiveness. Many people and systems are expensive and complex; that is not the issue. The real issue is how to make sure that costly and complex assets are worth the trouble and expense.

A Broader Perspective

One way to take a broader view of the issue is to answer a seemingly narrow question: Why do we have to pay so much extra to get people to accept overseas assignments? The simple answer is that, human motivation being what it is, the anticipated benefits must be greater than the anticipated costs before someone can be induced to do something. To the extent that the firm is perceived by employees as taking an out-of-sight, out-of-mind approach to international assignments, the career costs can be substantial. We surveyed 174 American managers recently returned from overseas assignments to over twenty-six different countries and found that 80 percent felt that their international experience was not valued by their firms, and that only 11 percent had been promoted upon returning.[5] Facts such as these, and horror stories about so-and-so's being caught in a holding pattern for six months after returning from overseas, only serve to raise the career costs, in people's minds, of accepting a global assignment. Some people are willing to accept these career costs for extra compensation. The greater the career potential of the individual, the greater the costs, and the greater the compensation that firms must provide to induce the individual to accept the assignment.

There are, however, many positive aspects or benefits of accepting an international assignment, independent of the monetary compensation. Most employees expect—and actually experience— greater job autonomy and responsibility while abroad. They develop market knowledge, language skills, contacts, and global perspectives. Certainly, these are positive factors in the cost-benefit analysis; for most employees, they would be. It seems unlikely, however, that these expected short-term benefits could simply cancel out the long-term anticipated career costs, especially if these acquired skills and experiences were unlikely to be utilized by the firm in the future. Money may be the second-best means of balancing the equation.

The point is not to try to examine all the potential costs or benefits that might go into employees' decisions to accept or reject global assignments; rather, the point is that employees do make these judgments, and both monetary and nonmonetary factors are included in the decisions. This is why simply focusing on monetary compensation for global assignments is a formula for rewarding A (maximization of short-term monetary benefits over costs to the individual) while hoping for B (inclusion of both long-term monetary and nonmonetary factors in the decision and performance). One simple means of reducing (but not necessarily eliminating) the escalating costs per individual manager sent abroad is to increase rewards for successful completion of a global assignment. In Chapters Nine and Ten, on repatriation, we specifically discuss how to redesign repatriation policies so as to maximize their positive influence on employees' perceptions of potential rewards. We argue that at least some of the extra monetary rewards could be replaced by such nonmonetary rewards as better expatriation policies, career systems, and repatriation procedures. If employees thought that expatriation policies would enhance their ability to perform well during overseas assignments, and if they believed that their performance abroad would be rewarded upon repatriation, then they would be motivated to accept global assignments with lower levels of immediate monetary inducements. Notice that we say they would accept *lower* levels, but not that they would be willing to forgo all monetary inducements. These ideas can be illustrated with the framework of a well-known theory of motivation: expectancy theory (see Figure 8.3).

A firm's reward system will be most successful when the efficiency and effectiveness of both monetary and nonmonetary elements are consistent with the goals and objectives of the firm, as well as with its circumstances. Most of the previous chapters of this book have outlined specific steps that can be taken to enhance the efficiency and effectiveness of expatriation policies. These can also serve the double purpose of enhancing employees' belief that their efforts will result in good performance during a global assignment. Later chapters provide more detail on how to enhance the repatriation and career development systems and thereby enhance the reward system and further motivate international managers. Even with these important additions to the reward system, there are still several ways of increasing the cost-effectiveness of monetary compensation structures and policies.

Three-Step Approach

While effective compensation policies must attract quality people and enhance feelings of equity, these policies must also cut unnecessary costs. What we outline here provides both a general strategic approach and specific tactical tips for designing international compensation systems. Our proposal in itself is not totally new, nor is it a panacea. Still, it suggests some interesting issues to consider

Figure 8.3. Expectancy Theory and Global Assignments.

Overall Motivation	Effort	Performance	Outcomes

M —— E —→ P

What is the probability that if I put forth effort I can achieve a desired level of performance?

What is the probability that a specific outcome will occur if I achieve a certain level of performance?

How much do I positively or negatively value each outcome?

Good selection systems enhance probability

Good training programs enhance probability

Good adjustment support systems enhance probability

O_1 Money

O_1 Value

O_2 Promotion

O_2 Value

O_3 Responsibility

O_3 Value

Good compensation systems enhance probability of O_1 (money).

Good career path systems and repatriation policies enhance probability of O_2 (promotion).

Good assignment design systems enhance probability of O_3 (responsibility).

in the design or redesign of compensation systems for global assignments.

Step 1. This general approach assumes that most people will not be willing to move to a foreign country if they must experience a significant decrease in their standard of living. Consequently, as in the "balance sheet" approach, the first step requires estimating what it takes to maintain a reasonably similar standard of living in the country of assignment, compared to the country of origin. Firms must be careful to make accurate calculations for individuals. For example, comparisons can be made between living in the United States and living in Japan, or between living in Boston and living in Tokyo. In many cases, the difference between general and specific comparisons is substantial. We have already seen that the differential between average U.S. housing costs and average Japanese and Swiss housing costs was much larger (and therefore more costly to the firm) than specific housing differentials between Boston and Tokyo and between Los Angeles and Geneva. Although such detailed comparisons are not always available, they are clearly the most accurate. Therefore, if outside consultants are utilized, how they compute living costs (especially housing) and the level of detail they can provide are two important issues. This first step also requires that each individual be assigned a country of origin. For most employees, this will simply be the home country. For career internationalists, however, there may not really be an easily defined "home country." In this case, they need to be assigned "career" home countries.

Step 2. Once the cost of living for the individual in the country of origin and in the country of assignment has been computed, the country-of-origin cost of living should be subtracted from the individual's normal base salary. This usually involves the cost of housing, utilities, food, clothing, transportation, medical care, entertainment, education, and taxes. The remainder is the individual's disposable income. This disposable income is paid to the employee through the normal system and in the currency of the country of origin.

Step 3. The estimated cost of living in the country of assignment is paid to the employee in the currency of the country of assignment. This significantly reduces the exchange-rate adjustments and risks that currently frustrate many international compensation managers. Employees are paid, in the foreign currency, only what they are estimated to need for living costs in the assignment country, but they are free to transfer money from a home-country bank account to the assignment country and individually bear the risk (or enjoy the rewards) of transferring the money.

This three-step approach, especially in the context of well-designed nonmonetary rewards, ensures in principle that people will not experience significant drops in standard of living. The risks and rewards of increasing their standard of living by transferring money into the country of assignment is their decision. This basic approach also reduces the inequity between expatriates and host-country nationals, or among expatriates of different countries of origin, because international managers will receive, in local currency, amounts pegged to the costs of living in the country of assignment. The differentials that certainly will exist in disposable income among expatriates from different countries of origin (or even from different regions in a single country) will generally be "out of sight" in home-country bank accounts during the international assignment. At the same time, the firm is likely to reduce its overall expenses.

In our discussion of other basic approaches to compensation, we examined the conditions under which the specific approaches would be more or less effective. These general conditions involve (1) having many or few expatriates, (2) having expatriates who return to the home country or move from one international post to another, (3) having expatriates come from the same or from similar countries of origin, and (4) having detailed figures for cost-of-living differentials. Accordingly, it is fair to examine the extent to which this three-step approach is dependent on or independent of these conditions.

The first condition that this approach depends on is the availability of accurate and detailed cost-of-living information. The three-step approach can certainly be used even in the absence of detailed information, but its effectiveness will be a function of how well the general cost-of-living information matches the specific situations of the employees involved. This approach is relatively independent of the other three major conditions, however. Although the total savings of this approach will generally be larger the more expatriates a firm has, it can be used independently of the total number of expatriate managers. This approach can also be used independently of whether expatriates return home or are career internationalists; the only thing required in the case of career internationalists is that they need to be assigned "career" home countries. One large U.S. firm selects the "career" home country on the basis of the country in which the individual believes he or she is most likely to retire. Finally, because what expatriates receive is only estimated "spendable income" during their global assignments, whether expatriates in a given country come from different home countries with different wage structures or standards of living is not a critical factor. (As just mentioned earlier, disposable income differentials remain "out of sight" in the individual's home-country bank account.) Thus, even though the other basic approaches discussed can be effective under certain conditions, this approach is much more context-independent and generalizable.

One implication of utilizing this three-step approach is that a tax-equalization policy is required. Under a tax-equalization policy, the individual's hypothetical home-country tax is subtracted from base salary, reducing the total taxable income, and then the firm pays all taxes due. Under the three-step approach, in addition to the individual's hypothetical tax, the individual's hypothetical home-country cost of living is subtracted from the base salary, which significantly reduces taxable income. This substantial savings accrues to the firm, at no cost to the individual.

Another important implication of this approach is that expenses for similar quality of education for children are paid by the firm. In many cases, this will mean that the education costs deducted from the country-of-origin base salary will be less than the expenses paid in the country of assignment. Our experience and belief is that it will be hard to entice quality people to accept international assignments if they must pay the increased cost differential of similar-quality education for their children, or if children will experience a drop in educational quality.

The final implication of this approach is that inflation in the country of assignment must be monitored and factored into COLAs. Although splitting the spendable and disposable income of internationally assigned employees nearly eliminates the risk and the complex adjustments entailed in exchange-rate fluctuations, it does nothing to eliminate the need to monitor the impact of inflation on purchasing power. Each firm should carefully consider the frequency with which COLA changes are made, but some general rules apply. If the rate of inflation in the country of assignment is greater than 15 percent per year, employees are likely to feel significant losses of purchasing power and some disappointment with the firm if semiannual adjustments are not made. Inflation rates of 30 percent or more should be accompanied by at least quarterly adjustments. Cost-of-living adjustments should be made monthly if the inflation rate is 80 percent or more. Inflation rates of 350 percent are likely to require weekly adjustments. If the inflation rate is greater than 1,000 percent, expatriate employees will need almost daily adjustments.

Allowances

Even if this three-step approach is adopted, there are still several decisions about allowances that must be made, and there are tips that can reduce the cost of allowances without hurting the effectiveness of compensation systems.

Hardship Allowances. The first allowance to consider is the hardship allowance. Unless the firm has a strong internal market, it is unlikely that hardship allowances can be totally eliminated. Nevertheless, there are many cities for which external markets pay hardship allowances that could be eliminated without severe costs to the effectiveness of international assignment compensation systems. For example, many firms in the Pacific Rim still provide hardship allowances of $1,000 to $5,000 for such cities as Hong Kong, Seoul, Singapore, Taipei, and Tokyo. While arguments concerning issues of safety, health, and pollution can be made for such allowances in

Bangkok, Manila, or Mexico City, these arguments are much harder to make for clean, safe cities like Tokyo.

Housing and Utility Allowances. Under the three-step approach, an allowance for similar housing and utilities in the assignment country must be provided. In such cities as Tokyo and Hong Kong, this expense can sometimes be greater than the individual's base salary. Where patterns and numbers of expatriates are somewhat predictable and consistent, firms may save considerable sums of money by purchasing houses and apartments rather than simply laying out rental cash. In many cases, providing housing can also reduce the tax burden for the firm. Finally, firms should generally discourage employees from purchasing houses in the country of assignment or selling their houses in the home country, especially during high-inflation periods. Many American managers sent overseas in the 1970s sold their houses, only to find when they returned that inflation had totally priced them out of the U.S. housing market. The survey by ORC found that only 27 percent of U.S. firms discourage their employees from selling their houses when they leave for an overseas assignment. Most firms cannot afford to buy and sell employees' homes, but they may be able to facilitate their rental during assignments.

Furnishing Allowances. In moves of any significant distance, it is generally cheaper to provide a lump sum for furnishings and an allowance for shipping less than 1,000 pounds of personal items than to ship the individual's belongings and furniture. Although care should be taken in determining this lump sum, it is generally between $7,000 and $10,000, with which people are free to buy or rent what they choose and pocket or pay the difference. If expatriates are expected to stay three to five years, as opposed to one to two years, paying a lump sum at the beginning is usually much cheaper than providing a rental allowance for furnishings over the entire duration of the assignment.

Home-Leave Allowance. Expatriates generally prefer to be given a lump sum equal to round-trip business-class flights and hotel expenses when they travel between the assignment country and the home country. Expatriates and their families should be required to spend some time in their home country if they are planning to return after the current international assignment. We would not recommend taking the parental attitude of providing actual plane tickets, but reporting requirements should be such that expatriates return home at least once a year.

Relocation Allowances. We have interviewed many American expatriates, who consistently pointed out unexpected expenses associated with the move over to and back from a global assignment. Very few consistently pointed out unanticipated "moving" expenses during the assignment, however. Therefore, if firms provide an annual relocation allowance, they are probably overpaying. The ability of firms to attract quality people may be reduced if no relocation allowance is provided at all, but providing a lump sum at the beginning and at the end is probably all that is needed for cost-effectiveness.

Summary

Sending people on global assignments is costly, and the reward systems are complex. The critical issue, however, is the cost-effectiveness of global assignments and their associated reward systems. The overemphasis on monetary rewards has been partly responsible for problems of "rewarding *A* while hoping for *B*"—of rewarding maximization of monetary incentives while hoping for recognition of nonmonetary incentives. We have argued that good selection, training, adjustment, and repatriation policies not only can serve to enhance the probability of effective performance during and after the global assignment but also can be effective in promoting a focus on the nonmonetary rewards of a global assignment and increasing an individual's motivation to accept and do well in an assignment. A good reward system must contain both monetary and nonmonetary rewards, however. Although many firms want to reduce total expatriate costs, we have argued that they should be concerned first with the cost-effectiveness of individual expatriates. We have proposed a three-step approach to expatriate compensation that is much more situation-independent than other basic approaches and has the potential for substantial savings per expatriate. The number of globe-trotting expatriates may indeed be too high and should be reduced. Nevertheless, reductions, as well as the selection of expatriates in the future, must be considered in light of the strategic roles that these employees can play in the global competitiveness of their firms.

Notes

1. Organization Resources Counselors, *1990 Survey of International Personnel and Compensation Practices.*
2. Kerr, "On the Folly of Rewarding *A* While Hoping for *B.*"
3. Gupta and Govindarajan, "Knowledge Flows and the Structure of Control Within Multinational Corporations."
4. Edstrom and Galbraith, "Transfer of Managers as a Coordination and Control Strategy in Multinational Organizations"; Ouchi, "A Conceptual Framework for the Design of Organizational Control Mechanisms"; Ouchi, "Markets, Bureaucracies, and Clans"; Ouchi, "The Relationship Between Organizational Structure and Organizational Control."
5. Black and Gregersen, "When Yankee Comes Home: Factors Related to Expatriate and Spouse Repatriation Adjustment."

Part Four

After
the Assignment

Chapter 9

Repatriating: Helping People Readjust and Perform

Many expatriates and their families expect a hero's welcome after returning home from a successful global assignment,[1] but research has found that many expatriates are lucky to receive any welcome at all when they come home.[2] As one spouse of an American expatriate put it, "If you look at repatriation as a 'homecoming,' you're setting yourself up for failure. My husband's company left him dangling in the wind, so to speak. I think that is wrong. He took a real demotion when we came home. No one in the company volunteered anything. He had to initiate everything. He fell through the cracks in the system . . . if indeed there was a repatriation system in this company. Why can't companies deal more efficiently and compassionately with employees returning from overseas assignments?" We interviewed one American expatriate who actually lost his "identity" during repatriation: apparently he did not exist on company records for up to three months after his return; he found out about the problem through a credit firm when he was denied two critical loans (house and car) because he was unemployed. While this may seem like an atypical case, our research and consulting have taught us quite the opposite. In fact, most expatriates returning home to America, Japan, and Finland are functionally unemployed once the plane lands. They might be on their employers' records, but they do not have permanent positions in their firms.[3] Indeed, we have found that expatriates and families from many countries face significant challenges when returning home. A small sample of these challenges is captured in the following comments:

> Be mentally prepared for enormous change when coming home. Expect repatriation culture shock to surpass the culture shock you might have experienced when you went overseas.
> —American expatriate returning from
> seven-year assignment in Indonesia

> Coming back home was more difficult than going abroad because you expect changes when going overseas. It was real culture shock during repatriation. I was an alien in my home country. My own attitudes had changed, so that it was difficult to understand my own old customs. Old friends had moved, had children, or just vanished. Others were interested in our experiences, but only sort of. They simply couldn't understand our experiences overseas, or they just envied our way of life.
> —Finnish expatriate spouse returning from
> three-year assignment in Vietnam

> Treat coming home as a "foreign assignment" and spend time getting the "lay of the land." Don't expect any special treatment—you're basically a "new hire." Look out for yourself, because no one else will. After being home for nine months, and after giving thirty-three years of my life to this company, I still have no office to work in—just a "bullpen" with a temporary assignment.
> —American expatriate returning from
> one-year assignment in England

> Now that I'm home, it seems like my overseas assign-
> ment is a punishment, a real "ball and chain," in
> terms of my career.
>   —American expatriate with fourteen
>   years of international experience

To some top executives and line managers (especially those without international experience), these comments may seem a bit overstated, but our research on repatriation found that 60 percent of American, 80 percent of Japanese, and 71 percent of Finnish expatriates experienced some degree of culture shock during repatriation. Our results are similar to those found in Nancy Adler's decade-old study of American expatriates, in which the culture shock of coming home was usually more difficult than the culture shock of going overseas.[4]

Unfortunately, most executives have little sympathy for repatriation problems. In fact, the home-office response often goes like this: "Culture shock coming home? What's the big deal? After all, they are coming home." The problem with this perspective is that it contains elements of both fact and fiction. It is true that people moving from one city to another in the same country have to establish new routines, friendships, schools, and so on, but these transfers do not entail the degree and types of changes that expatriates face when transferred home from international assignments. These changes may include contending with new political systems, transportation systems, social groups, eating habits, languages, and so on. It is also true that when expatriates return from an international assignment they are returning to their home country, but it is not true that they and their home country are the same after a typical international assignment of three to five years.

The Repatriation Process

Without a doubt, expatriates and home countries change throughout the duration of an international assignment. Some major components of these changes are outlined in Figure 9.1. Before an international assignment, expatriates have consciously and unconsciously acquired the mental maps and behavioral routines that work effectively for them in the home country. Furthermore, when

Figure 9.1. Components of Change.

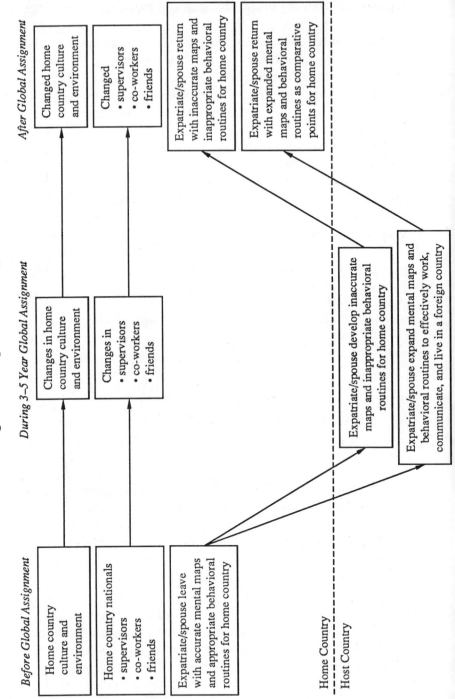

expatriates embark on a global assignment, relatively few have previous work experience in the country of assignment, and even fewer receive any sort of cross-cultural preparation or training.[5] Thus, they enter the new country with little prior knowledge of what to say and how to act in a foreign country. After living in a foreign country for several years, most expatriates acquire new mental maps and behavioral routines for how to act and what to say in the new familiar "foreign" culture.

As expatriates adjust and change overseas, many objective aspects of the home country simultaneously change. For example, consider the economic cycles that occur in any country, or the sweeping political changes of the late 1980s and early 1990s. Besides the potentially dramatic changes at home, there are, perhaps more important endless little changes in the home country during a global assignment. These changes can occur in a host of contexts—for example, previous home-country neighborhoods (people move in and out), friendships (old friends get new friends), and schools (funding levels may shift, or teachers change). Accordingly, one American told us that repatriates should "treat repatriation as another 'foreign' assignment. Returned managers rapidly feel like aliens in their native land. They also should not expect their home country to stay the same as they remembered it." Finally, dramatic and simple changes can also occur at the employing firm in the home country (restructurings, strategic shifts, managerial advancements, and so on). Some of these corporate changes and their potential impacts on adjustment are reflected in this American expatriate's experience after working in the parent company for more than eighteen years: "The division I worked for was reorganized, and the subsidiary I worked for was placed under stringent cost-cutting guidelines. My reentry was very cold, with little support in finding a job, since previous management had been fired. Instead of placement, I had strong feelings of displacement when coming home."

At the same time that objective changes are occurring in the home country and the parent company, expatriates' subjective perceptions of what used to be in the home country and company and what may still be in the home country and company can also change throughout a global assignment. There are several reasons for these changes in mental maps.

Individuals have difficulty remembering exactly what used to be in their home country, and if they do remember, these memories often tend to focus on the ideal aspects of home. This process could be called the Dorothy Syndrome, after the Dorothy who lived in the land of Oz and felt that there was "no place like home" as she fondly recalled her life back in Kansas. Reflecting this perceptual distortion of the past, one spouse commented, "All of the years that I lived overseas (largely in underdeveloped countries), I always thought that the U.S. was really better, more efficient, and so on, than anywhere else in the world. For twenty-six years and four global assignments, I carried this idea around. Now that I am finally back home, I am finding out that things in general are just as inefficient in the U.S. as in other countries. This has been a very difficult reality to accept."

We must also remember that most expatriates work and live in foreign countries and cultures with different languages, attitudes, and behaviors for three to five years. If they have successfully integrated themselves into the foreign environment, they have undoubtedly changed in both attitude and behavior. For example, many American families find it uncomfortable to leave their shoes on whenever they go into someone else's home after assignments in the Pacific Rim. Other changes during global assignments are much more challenging. For example, Japanese men often gain a new sense of family, with stronger bonds to their wives and children, during global assignments, but these relationships are often lost when they return to Japan. Many Japanese expatriates become quite bitter and resentful toward their firms for "stealing" away their newfound roles of husband and father. Yet another Japanese example of change is reflected in the experience of one Japanese spouse we interviewed. She cried every day for six months after returning to Japan, and she begged her husband to get transferred back overseas. During her husband's assignment in Britain, her social role as the wife of a vice-president had given her the opportunity to interact, entertain, express opinions, and discuss world events. These activities were not possible or accepted when she returned home to Japan.

In addition to changes at home, changes occur in the workplace. For example, most expatriates find it difficult to unlearn the autonomy they had in their global assignments and relearn the nuances of corporate bureaucracies.[6] One Japanese expatriate said, "When I first went overseas, I was scared to make decisions without a big group around me. Now that I'm back home, I've not only forgotten how to effectively manage consensus decision making, I'm not sure I even like it."

Another example of the influence of changed perspectives is captured quite well in one American expatriate's experience: "It is still difficult to deal with the attitude of American people at work: managers, clerks, sales people, and so on. I never realized the apathy that exists in our society until I lived and worked in Japan for three years." Indeed, we have found that the new reference points gained through global assignments often cause more negative than positive evaluations of the home country. For example, a Finnish manager returning home from Germany stated, "I became quite critical of my home country after having the opportunity to compare our way of living to the continental European way. People seem very materialistic, even though things are so terribly expensive in Finland."

When expatriates and families actually return home after three to five years abroad, supervisors, co-workers, and friends have also changed but often incorrectly assume that the expatriates and their family members have not. One spouse returning to Finland after a six-year assignment described this dynamic well when she said, "Family and friends didn't want to admit that I had 'grown up' during the years in a foreign country." An American expatriate expressed similar sentiments: "Previous friends expected me to return unchanged and resume life *as if I had not left.*"

In sum, the changes in home countries and in individuals (expatriates overseas and friends and co-workers at home) over the course of a global assignment produce many of the same dynamics of cross-cultural adjustment that were discussed in Chapters Two and Five—even though people are coming home. Specifically, people often return home from global assignments with incorrect mental maps of what to do, learned inabilities regarding how to do it, and uncertainties about what the results of their actions will be in the now "foreign" home country.

Repatriation Adjustment and the Bottom Line: Performance

In our work with multinational firms around the world, executives frequently ask, "Why should multinational firms pay attention to the adjustment of expatriates and their families during repatriation?" Our response, based on research and experience, is that failure to pay attention to repatriation adjustment can have a negative impact on the bottom line—in other words, reduced executive and managerial performance. Specifically, we found that when American, Japanese, and Finnish expatriates adjust effectively during repatriation, they are better performers.[7] Furthermore, when the family of an expatriate adjusts during repatriation, there is a positive "spillover" effect in which the productive home situation spills over to work and increases an expatriate's effectiveness.[8] Spouses' repatriation adjustment to interaction and the general culture were significantly related to repatriates' work performance in the United States ($R=.42$, $p<.01$; $R=.19$, $p<.05$), Japan ($R=.22$, $p<.01$; $R=.01$, $p<.10$), and Finland ($R=.24$, $p<.01$; $R=.15$, $p<.10$).[9] The realities of adjustment spillover and performance failure were emphasized in this American expatriate's experience: "My spouse has had a very difficult time coming home from Europe and living in the suburbs of America. She hates it. Her adjustment difficulty has made my life less than wonderful and my work performance less than excellent."

Dimensions of Repatriation Adjustment

To parallel cross-cultural adjustment during international assignments, we have identified three basic areas that expatriates and their families adjust to when returning home.[10] First, expatriates need to adjust to new jobs and work environments. Even though most expatriates have almost fifteen years of experience in a parent company, they still make comments such as, "Be prepared for corporate culture shock when you come home!" One American expatriate with twelve years of experience in the parent company commented; "Our organizational culture was turned upside down. We now have a different strategic focus, different 'tools' to get the job done, and different buzz words to make it happen. I had to learn a whole new corporate 'language.' " Interestingly, work-related adjustment challenges during repatriation were one of the most frequently mentioned problems by repatriates in America, Japan, and Finland.[11]

Second, expatriates and their families need to adjust to communicating with home-country co-workers and friends. After a global assignment, home-country people often seem more like foreigners. For example, Americans are well known for making small talk at the beginning of a conversation, while people from other cultures may find this mode of conversation insincere. After a Finn spends several years in America and learns small talk, he or she returns home to fellow Finns who react quite negatively to such "trivial" talk. Another common challenge of communicating with home-country people during repatriation is their general lack of interest in repatriates' international experiences. Finally, children of Finnish and Japanese expatriates often encounter significant language difficulties during repatriation. This was especially true for younger children born during global assignments, who failed to learn the complexities of their home-country language, and for teenagers, who are very aware and self-conscious of their differences in terms of non-native accents, outdated knowledge of slang and wording, and some loss of correct syntax and intonation. In sum, communicating effectively with home-country people during repatriation is a challenge for expatriates, spouses, and children. Some of these difficulties are reflected in the following comments:

> After coming home, my daughter felt neither British nor American from a cultural standpoint. She went from being president of the school overseas to being a new face at home. Nine months after our return, she still feels quite "different" from the other students.
> —American expatriate returning from fourth global assignment in nine years

> Treat the return like the arrival at any other foreign assignment. It will be the same hard work to integrate all over again. Friends and co-workers have changed, you have changed, and you have to start building all those relationships afresh.
> —Finnish spouse returning from France

I had very little in common with "home-country nationals" after being away for fourteen years. Customs,
attitudes, and behaviors were so different. Maybe I had
just idealized them and never knew it.
—American expatriate returning from Singapore

Third, expatriates and their families face the problem of
readjusting to the general living environment (food, weather, housing, transportation, schools, and so on), even though they have
usually lived in their home country for most of their lives. These
adjustments to the general culture are often the most challenging,
as reflected in our research, which found that 64 percent of the
American, 55 percent of the Japanese, and 57 percent of the Finnish
expatriates experienced significant general culture shock during repatriation.[12] The following comments describe some of the specific
dilemmas of coming home:

It was challenging to return home and find housing,
locate stores, and make friends. Even though I'd lived
in the same metropolitan area and country before, this
was like moving into a new world, and I had to start
from scratch. I never realized that in returning home
I would not be *instantly* home.
—American spouse after six years in Europe

I was totally unprepared for the long, harsh, cold win-
ters . . . even though I had grown up in Finland.
—Finnish expatriate after three years in Australia

I never realized how difficult and exhausting simply
commuting to and from work is in Japan until now.
I hate it.
—Japanese expatriate after five years in America

The cost of living is so high in Japan. It's been very
difficult to adjust to spending so much of my income
on necessities like food and housing.
—Japanese expatriate after seven years in Wales

Factors Influencing Repatriation Adjustment

Repatriation adjustment is a significant challenge for most expatriates and their families. Adjustments fall along three general lines: work, communicating with home-country co-workers and friends, and the general culture of the home country. Our research on these facets or aspects of adjustment has found that certain factors either facilitate or inhibit one or more aspects of repatriation adjustment. Accordingly, we have summarized in Figure 8.2 those factors that affect repatriation adjustment before individuals return home and those factors that influence adjustment after they return home. Furthermore, these factors are categorized into several groups. There are important sources of information about changes in the home country and the parent company, and there are individual, job, organizational, and nonwork factors that affect cross-cultural adjustment after returning home. We will discuss each of these factors and how they influence the adjustment of expatriates and their families during repatriation.

Prereturn Repatriation Adjustment

Just as people make anticipatory adjustments before embarking on a global assignment (see Chapter Five), individuals also make adjustments before transferring home from a global assignment. These anticipatory adjustments just prior to repatriation are primarily mental or psychological in nature. In other words, people begin to make changes in their mental maps of what work and living will be like in their home country *before* they actually return home. Such changes in mental maps are generally helpful, since the home country and the individual have usually changed during the global assignment. Accordingly, there are several potential sources of accurate information about the home country, which can help modify and mold expatriates' and their families' mental maps of the home country before they actually return.

Managerial and executive jobs often require extensive interaction between company headquarters (in the home country) and a foreign operation, which often causes significant information to be passed on to expatriates. Job- or task-required interaction and in-

Figure 9.2. Basic Framework of Repatriation Adjustment.

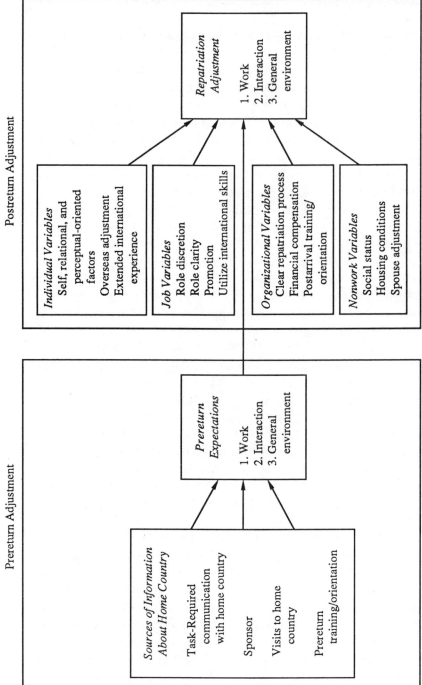

formation exchange is especially relevant to multinational and global firms, where coordination needs between the home country and the foreign operation are typically higher than in export and multidomestic firms. For expatriates in managerial and executive positions, the coordination requirements of a job may cause a reasonable level of accurate information to be passed on. It is important to remember, however, that most of this information is undoubtedly focused on changes in the parent company, and relatively little of this information is related to changes in previous neighborhoods, children's schools, and friendships outside of work. Accordingly, information acquired through job-required interaction is most likely to facilitate expatriates' adjustment to work but will have less impact on interaction or general environmental adjustment.[13]

Another source of primarily work-related information is an organizational sponsor, mentor, or "god-parent."[14] Fundamentally, a formally or informally assigned mentor can provide an expatriate with important information about structural changes, strategic shifts, political coups at work, promotion opportunities, and general job- and company-related knowledge. This information is not likely to help people adjust to the general culture; it is more likely to help them effectively adjust to work and to communicating with home-country people during repatriation.[15] Without an effective sponsor during and after a global assignment, an expatriate can be caught in a dilemma like this one: "After spending nine years in Venezuela, fitting in is difficult if you have no ongoing contacts. There is tremendous insecurity, since no one knows you or cares, and you can easily get caught in the next job-reduction plan. Some reward for all the sacrifice of going abroad!" In this repatriate's case, an effective sponsor might have reduced some of the apparent problems encountered during repatriation. Even though sponsors can provide important adjustment-related information during global assignments and helpful support during repatriation, relatively few expatriates actually have such sponsors throughout an assignment. In fact, our research found that only 22 percent of American, 22 percent of Japanese, and 51 percent of Finnish expatriates had sponsors while in foreign assignments.[16] More important, our research found that expatriates from Japan and Finland who did have sponsors were better adjusted at work after repatriation than those expatriates who were without sponsors during international assignments (R=.15, .17; p<.05, respectively). This relationship did not hold, however, for American expatriates returning home.[17] Given the tight social and political networks in the relatively homogeneous societies of Japan and Finland, it appears that sponsors play an even more critical role in the repatriation process there than in the United States.

Still another important source of information about the home country and company is periodic visits to the home country during a global assignment.[18] Visits provide expatriates and families the opportunity to acquire information about changes at work, among friends, and in the home country throughout the course of a global assignment. Conversely, visits also allow co-workers and friends to observe changes in the expatriate. While 65 percent of the U.S. expatriates we studied received paid home leave for themselves and their families throughout the international assignment,[19] a study of approximately 250 American and Canadian multinational firms found that only 35 percent of expatriates and families are required to take their "home" leave at home.[20] As a result, the informational and relational benefits of home leaves are often not realized as expatriates use home-leave money for trips to more exotic places.

Prereturn training and orientation provided by the firm is another source of information.[21] In earlier chapters on training and overseas adjustment, we discussed the potential effectiveness of training and the range of approaches that firms can take to cross-cultural training (see Chapter Four specifically). Clearly, the same principles can apply to the repatriation process, when people recross cultural boundaries and reenter their home country, which often feels quite foreign. Repatriates from the United States, Finland, and Japan have told us about the importance of such training. In fact, except for help in locating an appropriate job after a global assignment, training during repatriation was what expatriates most frequently wanted from multinational firms.[22] Such training can facilitate adjustment not only at work but also in communicating with home-country people and in living in the new environment.

Given the relative importance of prereturn training and the research support for the utility of such training, it is somewhat

surprising that relatively few multinational firms provide training
or orientation during repatriation. In fact, our studies found that
64 percent of American, 92 percent of Japanese, and 77 percent of
Finnish expatriates received absolutely no training before returning
to their home countries. Furthermore, approximately 90 percent of
all spouses received no repatriation training.[23] After returning
home, one spouse suggested that "a repatriation meeting should be
provided to families, like the orientation meeting before going overseas, since many changes occur at home in three to five years."
Without such training, many expatriates and spouses inefficiently
search for (and often do not find) accurate information about their
home country during repatriation.

Postreturn Repatriation Adjustment

After expatriates return home, there are several factors that can facilitate or inhibit their adjustment to work, to communicating, and
to the culture in general. These factors are grouped into individual,
job, organizational, and nonwork categories.

Individual Factors. Many of the important individual factors relevant to effective cross-cultural adjustment were outlined in Chapters Three and Five. We believe that many of these factors apply
equally well to the repatriation adjustment process. Specifically, the
self-oriented factors (strong self-image), relational-oriented factors
(language proficiency and willingness to communicate with home
nationals), and perceptual-oriented factors (ability to understand
and grasp invisible cultural maps and rules) are likely to have a
positive impact on all facets of repatriation adjustment, just as they
are expected to facilitate all aspects of expatriation adjustment.

   While the self-, relational-, and perceptual-oriented factors
can facilitate cross-cultural adjustment during an overseas assignment, successful overseas adjustment can ultimately result in more
significant adjustment challenges during repatriation.[24] This is especially true for expatriates and families who have completed assignments in cultures very different from the home country and who
have stayed overseas for extended periods, either through sequential
global assignments or unusually long stays in individual assign-

ments. Essentially, the more people acquire the maps and rules of an overseas culture, the more difficult it is to revert back to the maps and rules relevant to the home country. One American expatriate with extensive international work experience found that "twenty-one years overseas was terribly hard to 'shake' after coming home." In many ways, the challenges of multiple global assignments or long global assignments result in feelings of being an "alien" in one's native country. Extensive international experience also makes it more difficult for American[25] and Japanese[26] expatriates and spouses to adjust to all aspects of the home country during repatriation.

Job Factors. For expatriates, one of the most pivotal components of successful repatriation is the selection of a return job assignment. We found this to be true for expatriates returning to America, Japan, and Finland,[27] but only 4.3 percent of North American multinational firms were found by one study to give more than six months' notice to expatriates that they would be returning home; 30 percent received approximately three months' notice, and most (64%) received random notification, reflecting little planning for repatriation.[28] This relatively short-term return horizon is also reflected in the significantly negative job experiences of repatriates whom we studied:

> After being home three months, I am still waiting for a permanent office. All this after thirty years of experience in the company and three international assignments!
>
> —American expatriate

> My job description did not even exist when I came home. I felt as though I had no status in the company. In fact, everybody was asking, "Hey, what are you doing here?" It seemed like I was just a temporary "extra" for at least nine months.
>
> —Finnish expatriate with nine years of experience in the parent company

No one accepted responsibility for placing me back in the organization. I ended up without a job, when I was expecting a promotion! My wife also gave up her job with the same company to go overseas (she had twelve years of experience). We were promised a job for her upon our return. Again, no one has helped us find one.

—American expatriate with fifteen years
of experience in the parent company

The major problem of repatriation was in the area of locating my next position after returning home. It was totally up to me and networking connections. The official process stinks.

—American expatriate with sixteen years
of experience in the parent company

From these accounts, it is clear that the first step in effective adjustment at work is having a job. Nevertheless, between 60 and 70 percent of American, Japanese, and Finnish expatriates in our research did not even know what their assignments would be before they returned.[29] Because return assignments were so infrequently planned, expatriates often referred to "holding pattern" return assignments, which resembled airplane holding patterns over congested airports when no runways are available. It should come as no surprise that when expatriates did get jobs after returning home, these positions were rarely optimal. In fact, they were frequently ill-defined, low-impact "make work" positions intended to keep the expatriates occupied and out of the way.

When permanent positions are located, they are often positions with reduced autonomy and authority in comparison to the positions the expatriates held during their most recent overseas assignments.[30] This was true for American, Japanese, and, to some extent, Finnish expatriates in our repatriation study. Specifically, 46 percent of American, 50 percent of Japanese, and 33 percent of Finnish managers had less autonomy and authority back home,[31] as illustrated by these comments:

When I was overseas, I felt I had an impact on the business. In the U.S., I felt as though the impact . . . if any . . . is minimal.

When I came home, I was assigned to a newly created, undefined staff job, where I had no friends, no contacts, and no access to management. Firms need to realize that expatriates have developed independent decision-making skills, have become accustomed to having final authority, and are conditioned to having their business judgment given a lot of credibility by top management. In my new job, my business judgment is much less valued than when I was overseas. Until firms change, expatriates should expect the worst when coming home, to avoid disappointment.

The overall importance of providing repatriates with high-discretion jobs was reinforced by our study of American, Japanese, and Finnish expatriates.[32] The results of that research found that in all three countries those with high job discretion were more adjusted at work during repatriation. Furthermore, Americans with high job discretion were also more adjusted to interacting with home-country people and to the general home-country environment.[33]

Our research has also found that providing repatriates with clear job descriptions, or high role clarity, was also relevant to effective repatriation adjustment at work. This was the case for expatriates from all three countries in our repatriation study.[34] Undoubtedly, the first step in clarifying jobs for repatriates is finding them something better than "holding pattern" positions. Otherwise, it is a given that the temporary positions are going to be highly ambiguous, since they will be essentially "make work" assignments.

Many expatriates took their global assignments with the hope of promotion after successfully working overseas. Unfortunately, this romanticized myth of global assignments does not usually match the reality of repatriation. As one Finnish expatriate with twenty years of international experience in eight assignments said, "When you go overseas, your firm absolutely forgets you in terms of promotions. In fact, my overseas assignment seems more like a punishment, in terms of my career." In the American context, the picture is not much brighter; "I went on my foreign assignment to the U.K. as a favor for the department. In return, I received nothing special for the ten months I spent away from my family and the hardship I put them through. I really expected a promotion after coming back home and did not receive it." In reality, fewer than 25 percent of the Finnish expatriates returning home received promotions and only 11 percent of the Americans and ten percent of the Japanese did.[35] To some extent, these low levels of promotion may reflect the significant restructuring and downsizing of many multinational organizations in the late 1980s and early 1990s. It is unlikely, however, that the high level of demotion for repatriates was matched in the managerial cohort at home. Specifically, upon repatriation, 77 percent of American, 43 percent of Japanese, and 54 percent of Finnish managers were demoted to lower-level positions than they had held overseas.[36]

Expatriates often gain unique country knowledge, language proficiency, and international management skills during global assignments. In fact, one of the strategic purposes of such assignments is to develop such skills and knowledge in the executive and managerial ranks of a firm. After expatriates return, however, such skills are utilized inconsistently.[37] Specifically, 39 percent of American, 54 percent of Japanese, and 53 percent of Finnish managers had the opportunity to utilize international experience after repatriation. After making million-dollar investments to send, support, and bring home each expatriate, it is surprising that firms are willing to obtain such minimal returns on so many of those investments. Expatriates feel similarly, as these comments suggest:

> Firms must value international expertise . . . not only appreciate it but actually put it to good use. Don't let a corporate headquarter's environment destroy the lessons, "business savvy," negotiation skills, and foreign-language proficiencies that expatriates learned from the real world . . . a global marketplace.
>
> —American expatriate

This company places little value on my international
skills. In fact, I am now fluent in Japanese, but the
company has shown no interest in placing me in a
position to use my recently acquired language skills.
What a waste!

—American expatriate

I hope I will be able to use my knowledge about Europe in my company in the future, but now I don't feel
as if this knowledge is appreciated.

—Japanese expatriate

My husband is given no credit for knowledge and
skills that were obtained overseas. Ten years of overseas experience now count for zero at home! He sac-
rificed a lot to go overseas for the company, and it's
just not right that those years count against him now
that he's back.

—Finnish spouse

Organizational Factors. The parent company's overall approach to
the repatriation process and its provision of adequate financial
compensation can have a significant impact on adjustment after
expatriates return home.[38] In our research, we found that a minority
of firms pay systematic attention to clarifying the entire repatriation
process. Most American and Finnish expatriates felt that their companies had communicated a very unclear picture of the repatriation
process.[39] Specifically, 60 percent of American, 27 percent of Japanese, and 59 percent of Finnish managers indicated that their firms'
repatriation processes were unclear. In general, many expatriates in
each country were uncertain and concerned about return positions,
career progression, compensation equity, taxation assistance, and so
on. This overall sense of uncertainty is reflected in this American
expatriate's comment: "What was it like coming home? No clear
direction in my job, no clear direction in my career, and no assistance during the return. You are on your own around here!" Undoubtedly, the overall ambiguity of the repatriation process within

firms is largely a reflection of a nonstrategic approach to global assignments.

In addition to clarifying the repatriation process, firms need to pay special attention to financial compensation packages when expatriates return home. Because nonmonetary rewards received during repatriation are generally quite low (temporary job, demotion, and so on), repatriates pay particular attention to monetary rewards and to potential shifts in living standards after global assignments. Some of these financial dynamics are captured in the following remarks:

> The cost of everything—from housing to the basic necessities—was so much higher in New York that it was literally shocking, even though we expected it. Everything is so expensive in New York City. In Mexico and, before that, Brazil, my family and I lived quite well. After returning to the states, it was back to reality—purchases had to be budgeted, something we hadn't done for years.
> —American expatriate

> When you are overseas, you receive many benefits, such as maybe a free car, or free gas, or a nicer home than you had back in your home country. You become accustomed to these benefits. Then, when you return to your home country, things return to normal, and lots of these benefits you were accustomed to disappear. It's like being Cinderella, and midnight has struck.
> —American spouse

For these two families, the balance sheet on expatriate compensation (see Chapter Eight) is clearly *out* of balance. Apparently, they received many of the allowances available to expatriates during an international assignment, but these allowances are generally unavailable after the assignment. Much like drug addicts, expatriates and their families often experience financial "withdrawal" during repatriation. Specifically, most American, Japanese, and Finnish expatriates had to cope with significant decreases in standard of living after returning home.[40] In fact, 75 percent of American, 64 percent of Japanese, and 78 percent of Finnish expatriates experienced reduced standards of living upon repatriation.

Since many international firms do not pay systematic attention to repatriation compensation and fail to clarify the repatriation process, it is no surprise that very little training and orientation is provided to expatriates after they return home. The overall lack of company-provided training and orientation is well reflected in this American spouse's comment: "Give more information about the home country, and about all the things the company is willing to help with—no matter how small. Only one or two of the wives I know received any formal information from the company. Most of what we found out had to be dug up and passed on by word of mouth, from one to another. As a consequence, much of the information we received was too late to do most of us any good." Training and orientation after a global assignment can enhance repatriation adjustment.

Nonwork Factors. Our studies have identified two primary factors associated with repatriation adjustment in America, Japan, and Finland: shifts in social status, and changes in housing conditions.[41] After coming home, expatriates and their families lose the formal status of being foreigners. In our repatriation study, 54 percent of the American, 47 percent of the Japanese, and 27 percent of the Finnish expatriates and spouses experienced a significant drop in social status, while fewer than 4 percent of the expatriates in all three countries experienced an increase in social status relative to their status during the overseas assignment.[42] These statistics indicate that repatriated expatriates and spouses are less likely to be treated as guests of honor at social and recreational functions (dinners, receptions, and so on) or as "guests" in their neighborhoods, with other families and children interested in their language, culture, and country. As one spouse said, "The biggest surprise of coming home was that I simply didn't realize how specially we were being treated in all aspects of life during our international assignment."

During an overseas assignment, expatriates typically feel like big fish in a little pond. After coming home, they are little fish in a big pond. The demotion, loss of financial perquisites, and absorption into corporate headquarters that typically accompany repatriation can easily increase the sense of lowered social status. According to one American expatriate returning from a nine-year executive position in the United Kingdom, "If you have been the orchestra conductor overseas, it is very difficult to accept a position as second fiddle when coming home." In general, our research found that net losses in social status had a negative impact on adjustment at work and on adjustment to the general environment for American repatriates and a negative impact on all facets of adjustment for Japanese and Finnish repatriates[43] and spouses ($R=$ $-.16, -.19$ [$p<.05$] for Japanese spouses' interaction and general adjustment; $R=-.22, -.20$ [$p<.05$] for Finnish spouses' adjustment).

In addition to shifts in social status, changes in housing conditions can significantly influence repatriation adjustment for expatriates and their families. Specifically, appropriate housing was positively related to all three facets of expatriates' adjustment and to the general adjustment of spouses during repatriation to America.[44] Three major issues influenced perceptions of repatriation housing. First, if expatriates had rented their home-country house during the global assignment, they usually returned home to live in a hotel for two to fifteen weeks, in order to repair destruction caused by renters. For some, these costs were over $15,000 for repairs (after only two-year assignments), and relatively few firms were willing to fully compensate repatriates for these losses. Second, if repatriates had sold their homes before the global assignment, company policies and/or the challenges of living in hotels often led them to find suitable housing as soon as possible after repatriation. In some cases, firms were forcing expatriates out of the "expense" column of the balance sheet by cutting off hotel allowances before housing loans had even been approved. In other cases, the sheer hassle of hotel accommodations for an entire family led expatriates to make less than optimal housing purchases. Third, if repatriates had sold their home before the global assignment, housing prices had generally risen in their home country, but no house-purchase allowance was provided during repatriation by 60 percent of North American multinational firms.[45] Our research found that Japanese

expatriates were much more likely to experience a significant de-
cline in housing conditions than were their American or Finnish
counterparts.[46] In fact, almost 70 percent of the Japanese expatriates
stated that their housing conditions were less than satisfactory during repatriation. (The Japanese face a somewhat unusual challenge
in that their home-country housing is generally much smaller than
overseas housing.)

Unique Aspects of Spouses' Repatriation Adjustment

Many of the predeparture and postarrival factors that we have discussed were relevant to expatriates and spouses alike during repatriation. Nevertheless, some important and unique aspects of a
spouse's repatriation are a function of the spouse's career before,
during, and after the global assignment. In our repatriation study,
we found that 55 percent of American spouses worked before, 12
percent worked during, and 30 percent worked after global assignment. In the case of Finnish spouses, 72 percent worked before, 20
percent worked during, and 75 percent worked after a global assignment.[47] Collectively, these data suggest that many American and
Finnish spouses make significant career sacrifices in order to go on
global assignments, but many still seek employment afterward. In
addition, some Finnish spouses feel "forced" to find employment
after returning home because it is very unusual to stay at home with
children in Finland. Regardless of the reason for seeking employment after a global assignment, many spouses find if difficult to
return to work during repatriation, as these comments attest:

> The biggest challenge of coming home was going
> back to work again. Years without training and
> schooling resulted in a big career loss . . . not to men-
> tion the pension losses.
> —Finnish spouse returning from
> three-year assignment in Saudi Arabia

> My contacts and visits with work colleagues in the
> home country were very occasional during the inter-
> national assignment, and the reestablishment of those

contacts and my return to professional life have de-
manded even more effort than was required during
expatriation.

—American spouse returning from
four-year assignment in France

In many situations, spouses have difficulty finding work immediately after global assignments. Sometimes these challenges are
related to the loss of professional skills or political contacts. Other
spouses are challenged in the job-finding process when potential
employers wonder whether they will go on other global assignments in the near future. Still others struggle with establishing the
home and helping children adjust, which leaves little time for the
job search. Given the potential difficulty of finding appropriate
work after repatriation, it is unfortunate that very few multinational firms offer any job-finding assistance to spouses after the
spouses have made significant career sacrifices to complete global
assignments. More specifically, while 15 percent of the repatriated
spouses received job-finding assistance in Finland, only 2 percent
received assistance from U.S. firms.[48]

In contrast to the significant career-related challenges many
American and European spouses face during repatriation, Japanese
spouses (almost all women) face equally difficult but somewhat
different circumstances when they return home. Before, during, and
after international assignments, Japanese wives generally have three
major roles: household manager, mother/educator, and neighborhood member.[49] The role of household manager is important to
most Japanese wives. Husbands usually turn their paychecks over
to their wives, who handle all financial matters (including investments) and provide their husbands with monthly allowances. During repatriation, 54 percent of the problems described to us by
Japanese wives focused on the role of household manager.[50] These
problems ranged from moving and family finances to housing and
living conditions. Generally, Japanese spouses' repatriation adjustment problems stemmed from the difficulty of running a house
back in Japan, because many things were better overseas. For example, Japanese wives living in America during a global assignment

usually became accustomed to larger living quarters. After returning home, they had to adjust to much less space.

The mother/educator role is probably the most important
role for Japanese wives. In Japanese society, the direction of much
of one's adult life is a function of one's education. Because the
government and major corporations offer lifetime employment
primarily to the graduates of Japan's elite universities, much of
grammar school, middle school, and high school is geared to doing
well on college entrance exams. In fact, nearly all successful applicants to the country's top university have also spent several years
attending after-school "cram" courses, called *juku*. The primary
contact with schools and teachers, as well as the main motivator and
coach at home, is the mother. The popular phrase in Japanese is
kyoiku mamma, or "education mother." Because the educational
system in Japan is so rigid, the problems that schoolchildren had
upon returning to Japan had a significant impact on the Japanese
spouses' adjustment. These challenges usually resulted in the wives'
making tremendous efforts to speed up their children's assimilation
and learning, so that the children would not be permanently stig-
matized as foreigners and permanently evaluated as educationally
impaired.[51]

The role of neighborhood member comprises a Japanese
wife's membership in various social groups, not just the immediate
neighborhood. Fundamentally, Japanese wives gain much of their
self-identity through the groups to which they belong and through
their ability to belong. In Japan, such groups may include mothers
who take their preschool children to the neighborhood park each
day, local flower-arranging clubs, and so on. Overseas, the Japanese
wives usually experienced an entirely new set of roles and situations, such as accompanying their husbands to company dinners
and events, hosting dinner parties in their homes, or attending
dinner parties in the homes of their husbands' business associates.
In Japan, wives are not at all involved in these types of business and
social activities, even if they have been involved in them overseas.
The sudden withdrawal from these roles is often frustrating and
difficult, since many many Japanese wives have learned to enjoy
these activities and gained a new sense of identity and self-esteem
during overseas assignments.

The lack of systematic support for repatriates is reflected in the lack of support for spouses during repatriation. Some executives may feel that firms should not intrude into the family lives of employees, but the reality is that the families were asked to accompany the expatriates, and the families face significant challenges after international assignments. Perhaps most important, our research has found that the more easily spouses from Japan and Finland adjusted to interacting with home-country people, and the more easily spouses from Japan, Finland, and the United States adjusted to the general environment and culture during repatriation, the more easily the repatriates adjusted at work. Moreover, the better adjusted the repatriates are at work, the better their overall performance is for the firm.[52]

Steps Toward Successful Repatriation Adjustment

Up to this point, our discussion of repatriation adjustment has focused primarily on the multitude of challenges and dilemmas that firms face in bringing expatriates and their families back from international assignments. These challenges often leave repatriates and their families with the sense that firms do not care about their success as they "dangle in the wind" at work and at home. To get beyond these problems, we now shift our focus from what firms do not do about repatriation problems to what firms can do to create a strategic approach to the process of coming home.

Starting in the Home Country

Defining the Strategic Functions of Repatriation. The first step toward effective repatriation is an analysis of the strategic functions that expatriates can accomplish after they return home. Before the assignment, the firm should have defined one or more of the three primary purposes for sending a particular expatriate abroad: executive development, coordination and control, and transfer of information and technology. If the strategic purpose of the international assignment was executive development, the return assignment should be a critical next step in the development of additional executive skills and knowledge. If the strategic purpose of the international assignment was coordination or control, the return assignment could utilize the expatriate's overseas contacts, in order to continue effective coordination or control between headquarters and foreign operations now that more effective relationships have been established. If the strategic purpose of the international assignment was the transfer of information and technology, the firm should seriously consider what home-country units of the company would benefit most by receiving the information and technology from the repatriate. Unfortunately, corporate headquarters often underestimates what home-country units can learn from overseas operations, which limits the probability that effective information and technology transfer will occur.

The reason why executives must define the strategic purposes of a return assignment is that, without a planned purpose in repatriation, the investment of more than one million dollars to send the expatriate overseas is likely to be completely squandered. Put in economic terms, it seems unlikely that any firm would be willing to accept a zero or negative rate of return on a million-dollar long-term investment; yet, without a strategic purpose for the repatriation process, many firms get that kind of return from their repatriates. Furthermore, without a strategic purpose for the return, there are few compelling reasons for the firm to pay significant and systematic attention to the multitude of problems the repatriate and the family face. What happens then is that a cost-reduction logic tends to overpower the entire repatriation process because there is no strategic purpose that could push the firm to pay attention to the repatriate's effectiveness. If there are no significant, well-defined strategic reasons for bringing an expatriate home (except that the contract has expired), why should a firm want to deal with the repatriate's problems?

Establishing a Repatriation Team. After a clear strategic purpose for the return has been defined, a team should be formed, consisting of a human resources department representative and the expatriate's supervisor (if in the home country) and/or sponsor. These individuals should initiate preparations for the return at least six months before actual repatriation. If possible, it is helpful for the human resources department representative to have had firsthand experience with expatriation and repatriation. This opinion was expressed by managers from all three countries in our study:[53]

> It would have helped, at least, to have personnel with *some* understanding of the experience of repatriation. Most of these people have no appreciation of what needs to be done in coming home. Since we had lived internationally and moved back one time before, we knew what to expect and basically had to manage it ourselves.
>
> —American expatriate

> Have a human resources department that understands the trauma of repatriation. In the best-case scenario, the human resources department would be made up of former expatriates.
>
> —Finnish expatriate

> Most people in the personnel department have not had any international experience. Consequently, they cannot understand the process. This is a big mistake.
>
> —Japanese expatriate

The supervisor or the sponsor will play an important role on the repatriation team by becoming primarily responsible for locating the appropriate return position for the repatriate. For example, the medical systems division of GE requires sponsors to play this active role in the repatriation process, and the sponsors are formally evaluated on the extent to which they effectively perform this function.

Targeting Resources on High-Risk Repatriates. Once the strategic purposes for a return assignment have been defined and the repatriation team is in place, it is critical to target resources on high-risk repatriation candidates, who are likely to have the most problems coming home. Two characteristics of expatriates (and spouses) place them in the high-risk group.[54] First, expatriates and spouses with extended international experience (either multiple assignments or long individual assignments) are likely to have the most difficult repatriation process. Second, expatriates and spouses who return from an international assignment in a country very different from their home country (for example, a German returning from Japan) are at higher risk coming home than are those returning from a similar country (for example, an American returning from Canada). These expatriates are most likely to have inaccurate perceptions of the home country and the home company because of their extended time overseas or their experiences in very different environments.

Managing Expectations with Accurate Information. Since the expatriate, the parent company, and the home country have all probably changed during the global assignment, there is a strong likelihood that numerous aspects of the expatriate's perceptions of home are inaccurate. Accordingly, it is critical for firms to manage and mold expectations before individuals arrive home, so that the expatriates will be more likely to have their expectations fulfilled and more likely to adjust effectively to work and nonwork issues after coming home.[55] The relative importance of managing expectations during repatriation is portrayed well in this expatriate's experience:

> I am Austrian by birth and lived in Germany until I was eighteen years old. Then I moved to the U.S., and my ties to Austria and Germany have remained strong all these years. When I had the opportunity to work in England and Germany for the last two years, I happily accepted the German part of the assignment. It seemed like going home. When I went back there, I took with me all my expectations about a country that I remember mostly through holiday visits and through the eyes of my parents and relatives. In contrast, I had no opinion about England before going there. I just went. I went to England first and, much to my surprise, I loved it. I had no real problem adjusting, even though the differences from my life in the U.S. were great. Then came a Germany that I didn't recognize. I found the people very rigid and

inflexible. I felt like a foreigner in a country where I had expected to feel very much at home. If I had trouble adjusting, it had nothing to do with the differences between the U.S. and Germany; I expected those. The differences that caused me the most difficulties were the ones between the Germany that I had lived in years ago and the Germany I was returning to.

Establishing Home-Country Information Sources. There are several mechanisms that firms can utilize to mold the expectations of repatriates before they come home. These are sponsors, prereturn training and orientation, home-country visits, and general home-country information.

Throughout the global assignment, and especially just before return, sponsors can provide important information to expatriates. If an expatriate has not had a sponsor during the assignment, it is still important to assign one, in order to make the coming-home process more effective. The information a sponsor provides will generally focus on company-related changes but may also include news concerning changes in the home country. Several spouses in our study suggested that firms consider "family sponsors," who would be in active contact with families of expatriates during and after international assignments. If this were arranged, family sponsors could provide a significant amount of information about general changes in the home country.

Training and orientation can provide essential information about the entire repatriation process to expatriates and their families. As one expatriate said, "Don't just give expatriates a brochure and walk away." Expatriates need information about changes in their jobs, about how to interact with home-country people, and about changes in the general living environment. Job-related information could focus on structural and political changes in the firm, technological innovations, procedural changes, and so on. Communication-related training could focus on the differences in interaction styles between the country the expatriate is currently in and the home country. This training could also include warnings about the general lack of interest that people at home will have in the expatriate's international experiences. This lack of interest will be felt at work and after work. These may seem like simple things, but they are significant to expatriates who return home expecting others to sit fascinated for hours as they recount their overseas adventures. Finally, training and orientation can be provided about housing, financial compensation changes, tax laws, school systems, price levels, and so on. While the rigor of repatriation training will generally be lower than in training before the international assignment, it is still an important tool for molding more accurate expectations.

     · It is also important to remember to provide spouses and other family members with information relevant to their return process. One spouse from Finland reinforced the importance of formally provided information. After spending eight years overseas in four different assignments, she stated, "In big companies, it seems so easy to forget that getting information through training and orientation is important for the well-being of people when they are overseas *and* when they come home!"

     One question that executives often ask us about repatriation training is, "Who will provide the training when expatriates do not return home in groups?" Clearly, it would be expensive and time-consuming to send trainers to all parts of the world in order to provide custom repatriation-training programs. If there are groups of expatriates coming home from concentrated areas, this strategy might work. For many firms, however, individuals return from global assignments individually. To cope with this problem, one of our client firms in high technology is developing a video-based training system that can be sent to expatriates and their families before they return home. This video will provide company-specific information, as well as general information relevant to repatriation.

     Along with sponsors and training, visits to the home country throughout the global assignment, and especially just before return, provide expatriates and spouses with opportunities to develop more accurate expectations. As we mentioned earlier, two-thirds of the expatriates we studied received paid home leave from their companies, but only one-third of companies required expatriates to take home leave in the home country. This is an important issue, since requiring home leave to be taken at home can benefit firms by providing expatriates and their families the opportunity to acquire information about home during the global assignment. Restrictions on home leave can be problematic in global firms, however. For example, many of the European firms we have worked with employ expatriates with spouses who are not from the expatriates' home countries. If this is the case, where is home leave to be taken? Regardless of the potential policy problems associated with home leave, visits to the home country before repatriation by either the expatriate or the spouse can play an important role in the acquisition of accurate information relevant to all three facets of repatriation adjustment.

Another important source of information about the home country is home-country newspapers and magazines. As one spouse from Finland suggested, "When you know you are going back, you should make time to read newspapers and magazines from home. Then you have a much better idea of what is happening." Newspapers and magazines can be expensive, but there are creative ways to use them. Some firms send only Sunday editions of a major home-country paper. Others send only weekly magazines, while others provide single copies to groups of expatriates in the same office (one problem with the latter approach is that the newspapers and magazines are unlikely to make it home for spouses and children to get updates on home-country changes). Regardless of the method, the purpose is to provide information about the home country in order for expatriates and spouses to develop accurate expectations.

Preparing the Home-Country Job Environment

To avoid many of the problems associated with repatriation, the repatriation team, in consultation with the expatriate, needs to explore the expatriate's career path and options after repatriation. Ideally, the return job will provide the repatriate an opportunity to accomplish one of the three strategic objectives for global assignments; otherwise, firms can expect a low return on the investment in people sent abroad and brought home. The return job should also contain some element of challenge, with a reasonable level of autonomy. Most executives or managers want these attributes in their work, but repatriates are especially attuned to them after working overseas in very responsible positions with high levels of autonomy. In addition to creating challenging jobs, with discretion to make things happen, it is important to assess the match between what the employee learned in the global assignment and how those skills can be utilized after the return home. As one returning expatriate suggested, "Expatriate employees who were successful in various worldwide assignments have considerable and varied insight into conducting business. Firms should treat such insight and perspective as an asset, rather than discarding, wasting, and hindering such contributions." We concur with this position, as does our research. When this skill match occurs, the employee is much more likely to adjust well to the return job. As an excellent example of this process, consider the following executive's experience after returning to Ford: "After coming home, I took a position that gave me the opportunity to use what I learned while working at Mazda in Japan for the last three years. The new job is terrific. Overall, coming home has been easy, since I returned to an area that deals specifically with international activities. In my new group, it is critical to know how Mazda works, and I have that knowledge." In this situation, the job appears to be challenging and utilizes specific skills that the expatriate acquired overseas. More important to the firm, however, the return assignment seems to have accomplished a critical strategic objective: information transfer. Knowledge gained by this Ford expatriate was effectively utilized by the parent company after the global assignment.

In some firms and some industries, it may not be possible to provide expatriates with ideal jobs when they come home, because of downsizing, restructuring, and so on. In this case, it is better to communicate the situation to employees clearly and early instead of leaving them in the dark overseas. One expatriate from a large U.S. energy firm described this "mushroom-growing" approach to return assignments: "Why can't firms provide at least some information about the progress, or lack of it, in finding a new assignment while expatriates are waiting to come home? Correspondence I sent home from Jakarta during the last three months of our stay was never answered. Being in the dark for months is very hard when you know you are going to repatriate!" Basically, if there are not good jobs waiting for expatriates when they return, they should be told before they return. Otherwise, they come home with inflated, inaccurate expectations that cause adjustment problems.[56]

After an appropriate job is selected, the firm should consider the backgrounds and experience of the repatriate's future supervisor and co-workers. Often these people have little or no international experience, and so they have difficulty understanding and working around the challenges of repatriation. In our repatriation study, for example, we found that very few American repatriates had supervisors with any international experience. In fact, only 29 percent of the Americans had supervisors with international experience, while Japanese and Finnish repatriates had somewhat better situations (64 percent and 56 percent, respectively).[57] Generally, supervisors with no previous international experience can be expected to have little understanding of or empathy with the challenges of repatriation. In some cases, supervisors and co-workers have actually inhibited the adjustment process. An American expatriate confided, "When I came home, co-workers were very jealous of my assignment, even though my responsibilities were vastly decreased in comparison to my recent overseas position." In Finland or Sweden, co-workers and supervisors may be less jealous of the assignment but more jealous of the repatriate's new tax-free automobile and the repatriate's previous tax-free earnings, since cars and earnings are heavily taxed in Scandinavia. Taking a different perspective, one American expatriate returning to a firm in the U.S. transportation industry said, "I was shocked at the animosity of co-workers because I had learned to work successfully with the Japanese during my international assignment." After experiences like this, repatriates learn to keep their mouths shut about their international expertise. Home-country co-workers or supervisors can frustrate the strategic purposes of a global assignment and return position, as happened in this American expatriate's case: "There was a lack of knowledge of and interest in what is happening in the world outside this company. No one really cared what I had done or learned overseas. It seemed like everything had to be 'homegrown' in the U.S.A. or in the parent company." To avoid these potentially significant problems, we would suggest that firms provide training and orientation not only to expatriates before they come home but also to co-workers and supervisors, in order for them to be understanding and supportive of the repatriation process.

Developing Appropriate Compensation

Most expatriates experience a significant decrease in compensation after returning from a global assignment. This decrease often reflects the "rewarding A while hoping for B" approach to compensation throughout the international assignment cycle. During global assignments, firms often reward expatriates with significant benefits and allowances, in the hope that they will successfully complete the postings. At the same time, this focus on monetary rewards as incentives often sets firms and expatriates up for failure during repatriation, since most expatriates suffer significant financial losses upon returning. While it is easy to justify increased financial support for an expatriate in a faraway land, compensation specialists can more easily gauge financial need when the expatriate returns. Perhaps most important, they often cannot see the need for extra compensation or assistance during a repatriation transition, since coming home is certainly not seen as a hardship worthy of perks.

In this awkward situation, the firm must still pay attention to the compensation of expatriates; otherwise, repatriates will either be less adjusted to work and to home after repatriation or will leave the firm and go to work where they feel that their international expertise is valued. A first step in the development of a repatriation compensation package is to compare the repatriate to cohorts of employees who stayed home and assess potential inequities. Without such comparison, problems can occur, as this American expatriate found out: "During the international assignment, I went through hell getting any recognition for my performance from my direct supervisor stationed back home. After returning to the U.S., my salary—which was not adjusted for the two years I was gone—was terrible. When I got back, I had to work my tail off to regain parity. Now the job is done, and life goes on." To avoid these types of repatriation problems and other financial dilemmas that may present themselves throughout global assignments, firms should attempt to follow the three-step approach to expatriate compensation outlined in Chapter Eight.

Facilitating Adequate Housing

Locating and acquiring adequate housing is a major challenge for many repatriates and has a major impact on spouses' adjustment after coming home. Some repatriates have had positive experiences:

> Coming back to our own home really helped. We had a place to identify with, and friends and neighbors who cared about us. It also helped being in the same school upon return, since we were in contact with teachers during the assignment, and they remembered us.
>
> —American spouse

> It is critical to keep your previous flat in your home country, especially when teenaged friends and social contacts are so important. It was terrific to have the children return to their own school and neighborhood.
>
> —Finnish spouse

Clearly, as recommended in Chapter Eight, the best-case scenario for repatriation would be one of continuity for the expatriate, the spouse, and the children. One challenge for those who do keep their homes and rent them is to repair the damage that may have been caused by tenants. Firms need to consider temporary housing, financing, and the time required to make repairs, which may be major.

People who have not kept their homes during global assignments will need assistance in locating, purchasing, and moving into new homes. House-hunting trips during the last few months of a global assignment would be helpful. If the house-selection process must occur after the expatriate returns home, the firm needs to provide adequate time for the expatriate and the spouse to make a sound decision.

Providing Support Groups

In our research, repatriates and spouses often suggested that firms should consider providing informal opportunities to meet and socialize with other repatriates and their families.[58] This would provide an opportunity to share international experiences, and, as one spouse said, "Support groups could help us answer the many questions a returning family has. A great many changes occur during the global assignment, and searching for the answers alone can be most frustrating and cause needless tension in the family unit." For a firm, this is a relatively cost-free endeavor, which may provide important benefits.

Planning for "Downtime"

The challenges of coming home to new work and home routines often require significant amounts of time, but many expatriates, like these Americans, fly home one day and go back to work the next:

> Arrived home on Saturday. Started work at 150 percent on Monday. I have worked constant seventy-hour weeks since.

> I arrived home on Tuesday and started work on Wednesday and have been working ten- to twelve-hour days since. I haven't adjusted yet to much of anything and really feel depressed.

> I worked fourteen-hour days, six days a week. There was little time to look for housing, yet the company still pressured me to move out of a hotel, in order to get me off the "expense" status.

In Japan and Finland, the situation is no less challenging. Japanese repatriates, after working five-day weeks overseas, often return to six-day weeks plus after-hours socializing until late at night, every night. In Finland, the situation is just as intense. Many expatriates suggested taking the traditional summer vacation of three to four weeks upon return, to get things in order. American expatriates recommended two weeks at the most, and some suggested that firms should force repatriates to take time off. Regardless of the amount, the important thing is that firms should allow some time to make the transition.

Appreciating Contributions to the Firm

A final aspect of repatriation adjustment focuses on appreciation. Several of the expatriates, and especially spouses, told us how much it would mean to them if firms would appreciate them for the job they have done or show a little more interest in families coming home. One spouse from Finland said, "Why can't companies take a moment to say 'thank you' to the wife and the children for the sacrifices they made to uproot, go overseas, and come back home?" We agree.

Ending with the Beginning in Mind

As the last step in a global assignment, effective repatriation provides a positive feedback loop to the next generation of expatriates. When repatriates' co-workers are offered global assignments, they may say what this Ford expatriate said: "You want to know what some of the difficulties were coming home? Were we *supposed* to have difficulties? Things went very well!" How had Ford treated this expatriate and his family after the three-year assignment in Japan? Ford provided three hours of general and culture-related training, which was seen as valuable. The company provided a job with clear work expectations and moderate levels of responsibility, as well as an excellent financial package (at least from the expatriate's perspective). The individual returned to his previous work unit (from before the global assignment), with co-workers and supervisors who placed a high value on his global experience. Finally, he had developed accurate expectations about coming home.

The bottom line is that inattention to the difficulties of repatriation hurts employees' performance and corporate performance. By contrast, small and often relatively inexpensive steps can lead to significant returns on investment and enhanced competitive position in a global marketplace.

Notes

1. Oslund, "The Overseas Experience of Expatriate Businesspeople."
2. Black and Gregersen, "When Yankee Comes Home: Factors Related to Expatriate and Spouse Repatriation Adjustment"; Napier and Peterson, "Expatriate Re-entry: What Do Repatriates Have to Say?"; Harvey, "Repatriation of Corporate Executives: An Empirical Study"; Clague and Krupp, "International Personnel: The Repatriation Problem"; Oddou and Mendenhall, "Succession Planning for the 21st Century: How Well Are We Grooming Our Future Business Leaders?"; Gomez-Mejía and Balkin, "The Determinants of Managerial Satisfaction with the Expatriation and Repatriation Process"; Adler, "Re-entry: Managing Cross-Cultural Transitions."
3. Napier and Peterson, "Expatriate Re-entry."
4. Adler, "Re-entry"; Adler, *International Dimensions of Organizational Behavior*.
5. Black and Gregersen, "When Yankee Comes Home"; Gregersen, "Commitments to a Parent Company and a Local Work Unit During Repatriation"; Gregersen and Black, "Antecedents to Commitment to a Parent Company and a Foreign Operation"; Black and Gregersen, "Antecedents to Cross-Cultural Adjustment for Expatriates in Pacific Rim Assignments"; Black, "A Tale of Three Countries."
6. Black and Gregersen, "When Yankee Comes Home"; Black, "A Tale of Three Countries"; Oddou and Mendenhall, "Succession Planning for the 21st Century"; Clague and Krupp, "International Personnel"; Adler, "Re-entry."
7. Black and Gregersen, "Functional and Dysfunctional Turnover After International Assignments."
8. Black and Stephens, "Expatriate Adjustment and Intent to Stay in Pacific Rim Overseas Assignments"; De Cieri, Dowling, and Taylor, "The Psychological Impact of Expatriate Relocation on Spouses"; Black and Gregersen, "When Yankee

Comes Home"; Black and Gregersen, "The Other Half of the Picture: Antecedents of Spouse Cross-Cultural Adjustment."

9. Black and Gregersen, "When Yankee Comes Home"; Black and Gregersen, "*O Kairinasai:* Factors Related to Japanese Repatriation Adjustment"; Gregersen, "Coming Home to the Cold: Finnish Repatriation Adjustment."

10. Clague and Krupp, "International Personnel"; Adler, "Reentry."

11. Black, "A Tale of Three Countries."

12. Black, Gregersen, and Mendenhall, "Toward a Theoretical Framework of Repatriation Adjustment"; Boyacigiller, "The Role of Expatriates in the Management of Interdependence, Complexity, and Risk in Multinational Corporations."

13. Black, Gregersen, and Mendenhall, "Toward a Theoretical Framework of Repatriation Adjustment"; Harvey, "Repatriation of Corporate Executives"; Harvey, "The Other Side of Foreign Assignments"; Oddou and Mendenhall, "Succession Planning for the 21st Century."

14. Black, Gregersen, and Mendenhall, "Toward a Theoretical Framework of Repatriation Adjustment."

15. Black, "A Tale of Three Countries."

16. Black, "A Tale of Three Countries."

17. Black, Gregersen, and Mendenhall, "Toward a Theoretical Framework of Repatriation Adjustment."

18. Black and Gregersen, "Antecedents to Cross-Cultural Adjustment."

19. Organization Resources Counselors, *1990 Survey of International Personnel and Compensation Practices.*

20. Black, Gregersen, and Mendenhall, "Toward a Theoretical Framework of Repatriation Adjustment"; Black and Mendenhall, "Cross-Cultural Training Effectiveness: A Review and Theoretical Framework for Future Research."

21. Black, "A Tale of Three Countries."

22. Black, "A Tale of Three Countries."

23. Gregersen and Black, "Antecedents to Commitment to a Parent Company and a Foreign Operation."

24. Black and Gregersen, "When Yankee Comes Home."

25. Black and Gregersen, "*O Kairinasai.*"

26. Black and Gregersen, "When Yankee Comes Home"; Black and Gregersen, "*O Kairinasai*"; Gregersen, "Coming Home to the Cold"; Black, "A Tale of Three Countries"; Oddou and Mendenhall, "Succession Planning for the 21st Century."

27. Organization Resources Counselors, *1990 Survey of International Personnel and Compensation Practices.*

28. Black, "A Tale of Three Countries."

29. Black and Gregersen, "When Yankee Comes Home"; Clague and Krupp, "International Personnel"; Oddou and Mendenhall, "Succession Planning for the 21st Century"; Adler, "Reentry"; Black, Gregersen, and Mendenhall, "Toward a Theoretical Framework of Repatriation Adjustment."

30. Black, "A Tale of Three Countries"; Oddou and Mendenhall, "Succession Planning for the 21st Century."

31. Black and Gregersen, "When Yankee Comes Home"; Black and Gregersen, "*O Kairinasai*"; Gregersen, "Coming Home to the Cold."

32. Black and Gregersen, "When Yankee Comes Home."

33. Black and Gregersen, "When Yankee Comes Home"; Gregersen, "Coming Home to the Cold."

34. Black, "A Tale of Three Countries."

35. Black, "A Tale of Three Countries."

36. Black and Gregersen, "When Yankee Comes Home"; Clague and Krupp, "International Personnel"; Gomez-Mejía and Balkin, "The Determinants of Managerial Satisfaction"; Black, "A Tale of Three Countries."

37. Black, "A Tale of Three Countries"; Clague and Krupp, "International Personnel"; Oddou and Mendenhall, "Succession Planning for the 21st Century"; Adler, "Re-entry."

38. Black, "A Tale of Three Countries."

39. Black, "A Tale of Three Countries."

40. Black and Gregersen, "When Yankee Comes Home"; Black and Gregersen, "*O Kairinasai*"; Gregersen, "Coming Home to the Cold."

41. Black, "A Tale of Three Countries."

42. Black and Gregersen, "When Yankee Comes Home"; Black and Gregersen, "*O Kairinasai.*"

43. Black and Gregersen, "When Yankee Comes Home."

44. Organization Resources Counselors, *1990 Survey of International Personnel and Compensation Practices.*

45. Black, "A Tale of Three Countries."

46. Black, "A Tale of Three Countries."

47. Black, "A Tale of Three Countries."

48. Black, "The Other Side of the Picture on the Other Side of the World: Repatriation Problems of Japanese Expatriate Spouses"; Nakane, *Japanese Society.*

49. Black, "The Other Side of the Picture on the Other Side of the World."

50. White, *The Japanese Overseas.*

51. Black and Gregersen, "When Yankee Comes Home"; Black and Gregersen, "Functional and Dysfunctional Turnover."

52. Black, "A Tale of Three Countries."

53. Black and Gregersen, "When Yankee Comes Home."

54. Black, "Coming Home: The Relationship of Expatriate Expectations with Repatriation Adjustment and Job Performance."

55. Black, "Coming Home."

56. Black, "A Tale of Three Countries."

57. Black, "A Tale of Three Countries."

58. Black, "A Tale of Three Countries."

Chapter 10

Retaining: Utilizing the Experienced Global Manager

Consider this account from a high-performing expatriate with seven years of international experience in two assignments, and sixteen years of experience with his former employer:

> After coming home, I was an "outsider" in my colleagues' eyes. The salary was lousy—a 6 percent increase after four years overseas—and they never found a "suitable" job for me. When they did locate one job, five months after I had come home, I informed them that I was leaving the firm to take a position with a 55 percent salary increase, as a technical consultant in a smaller company. After making the jump, I have used my technical skills, language skills (I learned Arabic on an earlier assignment in Saudi Arabia), and negotiation skills to benefit a competitor of my former employer. What a waste of resources!

In Chapter Nine, we discussed in detail the dynamics of adjustment and the factors that affect different aspects of adjustment for expatriates and spouses from several areas of the world. We also outlined many ways in which firms can greatly facilitate repatriation adjustment and in turn increase job performance after global assignments. In this chapter, we shift our focus to the dynamics of organizational commitment and the various factors that can affect commitment during repatriation. Organizational commitment is the critical factor for keeping high-performing repatriates in the firm after global assignments.[1]

Keeping the Best Global Managers as Strategic Assets

If a multinational firm had invested between $2 million and $4 million in a piece of critical production equipment over the past six years, it would be hard to imagine its managers' not taking serious action if the equipment were headed out the door to a competitor's production facility; yet each year, executive and managerial "assets" (in whom firms have invested literally millions of dollars) walk out the company door after returning home from global assignments. In our study of American repatriates, for example, we found that 42 percent had seriously thought of leaving their firms since returning home, 74 percent did not expect to be working for the same company one year hence, and 79 percent felt that the demand for their international skills was high and that they could find good jobs in other firms. Moreover, 26 percent of the American repatriates had been actively looking for alternate employment after coming home.[2] More specifically, we have worked with some American and European multinationals that lost between 40 percent and 55 percent of their repatriates through voluntary turnover during recent three-year periods.

Even if repatriates stay in their parent firms after coming home, they are probably underutilized in terms of overseas market knowledge, technical skills, foreign-language ability, and so on (see Chapter Nine). These sobering realities should push multinational firms to consider some strategic human resources management questions: Are we receiving an adequate return on our investment after bringing expatriates home from expensive global assignments? Are we retaining the best global managers and utilizing their unique skills after repatriation? If the answer to these questions is no, firms are probably letting valuable investments slip through their fingers as repatriates either walk out the front door to competitors or stay in the company but perform below standards.

We have found four general patterns of repatriate behavior during the repatriation process, which may or may not benefit the strategic objectives of the firm.[3] These patterns are shown in Figure 10.1. Ideally, multinational firms want repatriates to be in quadrant 1 after returning home. Essentially, *functional retention* occurs when repatriates are high performers and when they stay in the firm. Two primary factors are associated with functional retention: high repatriation adjustment and high commitment, or loyalty, to the parent company. As discussed in Chapter Nine, high repatria-

Figure 10.1. Repatriation Outcomes.

	High ORGANIZATIONAL COMMITMENT	Low ORGANIZATIONAL COMMITMENT
High REPATRIATION ADJUSTMENT	*Functional Retention* High performance High intent to stay Quadrant 1	*Dysfunctional Turnover* High performance Low intent to stay Quadrant 2
Low REPATRIATION ADJUSTMENT	*Dysfunctional Retention* Low performance High intent to stay Quadrant 3	*Functional Turnover* Low performance Low intent to stay Quadrant 4

tion adjustment leads to high job performance. Furthermore, high commitment to the organization after repatriation leads to high intentions to stay with the firm.

Firms want to achieve "functional retention" for very strategic reasons. For example, if expatriates went overseas to develop an international perspective and bring it back to headquarters, this strategic function can be accomplished only by keeping the "best." Quadrant 2 is the next most critical area of strategic concern, since *dysfunctional turnover* occurs when high-performing repatriates leave the parent company after coming home. This happens when repatriates adjust well to work, to interacting with home-country people, and to the general home-country environment but do not show a strong commitment to the parent company. When high performers leave, firms usually incur a significant loss of resources: firm-specific experience, global perspectives, international skills, and so on. As one American expatriate told us after returning from a two-year assignment in France, "Firms should be using their international managers as assets to grow and expand, instead of giving them away to competitors."

Firms not only lose their investment when high-performing repatriates quit, they also lose the chance to accomplish the strategic objectives of a global assignment. For example, an American expatriate may have been sent to a Japanese subsidiary to acquire important market information and technology innovations, but, this information and technology cannot be transferred if the expatriate quits after coming home.

Functional turnover, in quadrant 3, can actually benefit a firm, since these repatriates are those who fail to adjust and perform well after coming home. They exhibit low commitment to the firm and then leave.

Dysfunctional retention (quadrant 4) is the least desirable situation for a firm. It is represented by repatriates who are low performers but stay with the firm. These people generally have high loyalty to the parent company but fail to adjust effectively to the new work, social, and general environments after returning home.

For firms to get the best of both worlds—repatriates who exhibit high performance *and* stay with the parent company (functional retention)—firms must pay attention to two critical processes: repatriation adjustment and organizational commitment.

Factors That Affect Organizational Commitment During Repatriation

The first step toward sustaining a sufficient level of expatriate commitment during repatriation is paying close attention to commitment patterns *during* global assignments, *before* expatriates return home.[4] In Chapter Six, we discussed how expatriates can become committed not only to a parent company (which sent them out on a global assignment) but also to a foreign operation during the assignment. In addition, we presented some of the specific factors that could help a firm develop and sustain commitment throughout a global assignment. For example, American expatriates with more years of experience in the parent firm—those with clearly defined but fairly autonomous jobs—were more committed during global assignments. When expatriates return, firms need to pay attention either to redeveloping or sustaining repatriates' overall commitment to the organization.[5] The specific factors that influence this critical commitment to the parent firm are somewhat different from those that played an important role in expatriate loyalty during the global assignment. We have identified four general categories of factors that increase or decrease an expatriate's level of commitment during repatriation: Individual, job, organizational, and nonjob factors (see Figure 10.2).

Individual Factors

On the average, expatriates have significant experience in the parent firm when they embark on global assignments. In our repatriation study of U.S., Japanese, and Finnish managers, most expatriates returning home had at least twelve years of experience in the parent company.[6] This significant investment of time and energy in a particular company helps bind the expatriate to the firm. Accordingly, high levels of tenure in an organization are generally associated with high levels of commitment to an organization.[7] During global assignments, high tenure was related to

Figure 10.2. Basic Framework of Organizational Commitment During Repatriation.

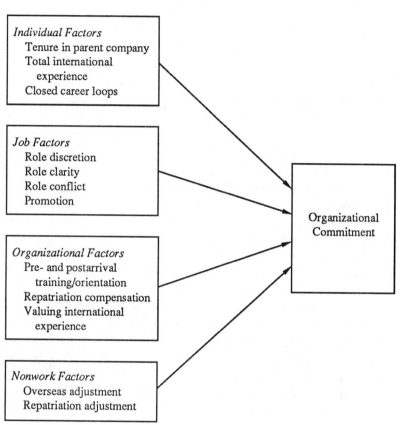

higher commitment to the parent company. During repatriation, we found that tenure in the parent company was also an important factor in sustaining American managers' commitment to the parent company.[8] In the case of Japanese and Finnish expatriates returning home, however, tenure in the parent company was unrelated to loyalty.[9] The insignificant impact of tenure on commitment for Japanese or Finnish expatriates may be partly a result of the comparatively low job mobility across companies in both countries.

Another important individual factor relevant to commitment during repatriation is the total amount of time expatriates have worked outside their home country.[10] How much total international experience do expatriates have? This is an important question because those expatriates with the highest levels of international experience (that is, career expatriates) have usually made significant investments in their international careers. Because many firms fail to utilize managers' international experience after repatriation, an obvious way for expatriates to capitalize on their international expertise is to stay out of the home country and continue utilizing their international skills and knowledge in foreign assignments. In addition, the investment expatriates make in developing a valuable set of international skills often reflects their relative level of *disinvestment* in their home country. In fact, expatriates with extensive international experience can develop an aversion, almost an "allergic" reaction, to their home country and to socializing with home-country nationals. As one American career expatriate in the banking industry explained, "There is little value placed on international experience within my company. Home nationals tend to think that the U.S. is so different that anything learned overseas is largely irrelevant to the domestic U.S. market." In Japan, career expatriates expressed similar sentiments: "When you come home, no one appreciates your international experience as much as yourself, or as much as the people you worked with overseas. In fact, overseas, the mere reality of it, does not even exist for most 'domestic' employees in this company. My suggestion for international firms? They could at least brief or work with the people at home who have never been overseas and help them to appreciate an international perspective a bit more." Reflecting these types of problems, our research has found that American expatriates with high levels of international work experience are generally less committed to the parent company after returning home. In contrast, Finnish expatriates with high levels of international experience were actually *more* committed to the parent firm.[11] This may result from the relative newness of international activity for Finnish firms, compared to the American multinationals, and from the relative importance Finnish firms place on international experience.

A final individual factor that can play an important role in sustaining commitment to the parent company during repatriation is the pattern of assignments before, during, and after an international posting.[12] Some expatriates refer to these patterns as *career loops*. A closed career loop means that expatriates work in the same division of a firm before, during, and after a global assignment. An open career loop reflects a break in this divisional continuity as expatriates are shifted from one division to the next throughout their global assignments. In our research, 30 percent of American, 42 percent of Japanese, and 36 percent of Finnish managers experienced closed career loops throughout their international assignments.[13] Creating closed career loops is important, since expatriates can more easily identify with the work units and the people with whom they are familiar throughout the assignment. The relative importance of career loops was reflected in our research, which found them important to American and Finnish expatriates' commitment during repatriation. Specifically, American and Finnish expatriates with closed career loops were more committed to the parent company than were expatriates with open career loops. In contrast, closed career loops did not affect the commitment of Japanese expatriates during repatriation.[14] This may be a result of the routine transfers that Japanese managers make across functional and divisional boundaries, which are not as common in either the United States or Finland.

Job Factors

Expatriates usually become accustomed to significant, visible jobs during global assignments. Moreover, expatriates often develop a strong action-orientation and a feeling of responsibility for making things happen during their overseas assignments in jobs with high autonomy and discretion.[15] After returning home, however, expatriates often encounter temporary low-level "holding pattern" positions, which fail to utilize their skills as a powerful strategic asset in the global expansion of a firm.[16] Unfortunately, when repatriates return to "make work" holding-pattern assignments, they often end up wanting to leave for "real work," as these comments from high-performing repatriates indicate:

> It is very important to know what the assignment will
> be after returning home. Companies will easily lose

their best expatriates if the work is not challenging and interesting enough.

—American expatriate

My current position has very little to do with what I learned overseas. What a waste for this company, to spend all the money to send me overseas and then bring me back and not even utilize what I learned while I was there.

—Japanese expatriate

My suggestions for other expatriates coming home? Update their résumés. The experience that you gain overseas is seldom valued and often discounted when you come home. Other companies will pay for what you know and can do for them. I can't understand why expatriates and companies cannot learn to plan ahead and make use of the skills and experience gained overseas. The rule seems to be that return assignments are just "landing places." What's lost is the opportunity to use an expatriate's ability to the fullest benefit of both the company and the employee.

—Finnish expatriate

Supporting these comments on the relative importance of the return assignment, our overall research found that when American, Japanese, and Finnish firms provided repatriates with clearly planned jobs, significant levels of discretion, and relatively few conflicting messages about how to do their work, repatriates exhibited higher loyalty to the parent company during repatriation.[17]

Organizational Factors

Several human resources policies and practices can enhance organizational commitment during repatriation. Each of these activities communicates to returning expatriates that the firm cares, that the firm is supportive, and, perhaps most important, that the firm can be counted on when it sends and retrieves expatriates to and from international postings.[18]

An initial step a firm can take toward being dependable and supportive in the repatriation process is providing training and orientation to expatriates and their families before and after the return home. This training not only facilitates cross-cultural adjustment during repatriation but also communicates to expatriates that they have not been completely "out of sight and out of mind" during the global assignment. In Chapter Six, we discussed the positive impacts that training had on commitment to the parent company during a global assignment, and we are convinced in principle that firms can expect similar positive outcomes during repatriation. Unfortunately, our research did not confirm this expectation, since so few firms provide adequate training and orientation during the repatriation process. In fact, 97 percent of the American, 94 percent of the Finnish, and 98 percent of the Japanese expatriates received fewer than four hours of training and orientation upon or before coming home.[19]

In addition to pre- and postreturn training, providing adequate repatriation compensation is another way firms communicate their support and dependability during repatriation. Many of the challenges of repatriation have already been outlined in Chapters Eight and Nine. We want to emphasize here that the more firms can ease the financial burdens of repatriation, the more likely repatriates are to exhibit commitment to the parent company. In our research, this was especially true for Americans returning home.[20] The most troubling aspect of repatriation compensation is the potential loss of income and associated drop in living standard. To minimize the financial loss of coming home and maximize a repatriate's organizational commitment, firms can follow the three-step approach to financial compensation outlined in Chapter Eight, which helps minimize the income shifts throughout the global assignment cycle and helps reduce feelings of financial inequity after the return home.

The final factor contributing to commitment during repatriation, and clearly the most critical of all factors in our research in all three countries, was the extent to which a firm communicates throughout the company that it truly values international experience and perspectives.[21] This is communicated through the job provided after return, the attitudes of immediate supervisors and co-workers, the formal and informal reward systems for international experience, the promotion paths, and so on. All these factors collectively create a perception that firms either really value or simply do not value international experience. For expatriates returning to the United States, Japan, and Finland, we found that developing an organizational culture that valued international experience was the most important factor in sustaining repatriates' commitment to the parent company, which kept them from leaving the parent company during repatriation. Unless firms can create this type of culture, they are likely to have repatriates who feel unappreciated and go elsewhere for the recognition they feel they deserve. In our repatriation study, we found that very few American, Japanese, and Finnish repatriates felt that their firms genuinely valued international experience.[22] Specifically, only 20 percent of American, 35 percent of Japanese, and 40 percent of Finnish managers felt this way. This low utilization rate of international experience is reflected in these expatriates' comments:

> Your own perceived increase in "value" after an international experience is just that—*perceived*. Expatriates should be prepared for the fact that few—precious few—people are interested in their international experience. Why can't firms try to take advantage of repatriates' international experience and stop treating their time overseas as out of sight and out of mind?
>
> —American expatriate

> The most challenging part of coming home was the fact that my overseas experience was not valued in my company as I had expected it to be. Keep your expectations very low when coming home. Remember that no one really cares that you spent time overseas.
>
> —Finnish expatriate

Look at your international experience as an extremely
valuable asset—but recognize that few others will fully
appreciate it.

—Japanese expatriate

If firms want to retain expatriates by developing commitment and loyalty to the parent company, they need to carefully
assess their culture and the extent to which it really communicates
global experience and perspectives throughout the organization.
While this may seem like a simple prescription, many firms are
trapped in the dilemma of "rewarding *A* while hoping for *B*," from
a repatriate's perspective. For example, American executives are
well known for giving lip service to the value of international experience, as evidenced in a recent *Wall Street Journal* article extol-
ling the virtues (and necessity) of international assignments for
CEOs of the next century.[23] The reality, however, is that fewer than
5 percent of Fortune 500 firms genuinely care about international
experience by actually paying attention to previous international
experience as a critical selection criterion in current executive promotion decisions.[24] These and other types of incongruities between
what firms say about the importance of international experience
and how they actually treat it must be examined in order for firms
to communicate more effectively and consistently that global managers with global experience are indeed valued.

Nonwork Factors

The final category of factors relevant to sustaining commitment
during repatriation concerns cross-cultural adjustment during and
after the international assignment.[25] Previous research on commitment during global assignments found that the more adjusted
American expatriates were to the foreign culture, the less committed
they were to the parent company.[26] As a result, we expected that the
more expatriates had adjusted overseas during the assignment, the
less committed they would also be to the parent company after
coming home. Nevertheless, our research found that overseas ad-

justment was not related to commitment during repatriation for American expatriates—that is, it did not affect commitment one way or the other. In contrast, our research found that Japanese and Finnish expatriates who had adjusted well during the international assignment were actually more committed to the parent company after the international assignment.[27]

This positive impact of overseas adjustment on repatriation commitment may be a function of at least three factors. First, research has found that Japanese and European firms pay more systematic attention to expatriation policies and practices than American firms do.[28] This may result in more parent-company support during the global assignment for Japanese and Finnish expatriates, which translates into more effective adjustment and more significant commitment. Second, Finnish and Japanese expatriates are simply less mobile than their American counterparts after global assignments. As a consequence, those Japanese and Finnish expatriates who adjusted well overseas are more likely to offer a positive return on that investment of time and energy by staying with the parent company, rather than attempting to change firms in relatively immobile managerial labor markets. Third, Japanese and Finnish firms in our study placed a higher overall value on global experience than the American companies did. In other words, global experience counted more, and so it paid for expatriates to adjust effectively during global assignments.

After returning home, expatriates face many significant challenges in adjusting to a new but somewhat familiar home-country culture and parent-company environment. Many details of this adjustment process were discussed in Chapter Nine. Here, we want to reinforce the importance of effective repatriation adjustment. In particular, we found that effectively adjusting to the home country after global assignments positively influenced commitment to the parent company in America, Japan, and Finland.[29] Essentially, the efforts that individuals and firms make in facilitating the repatriation process not only help repatriates adjust and perform well but also facilitate commitment to the parent company because repatriates feel the company can be counted on for support throughout the entire global assignment cycle.

Strategies for Sustaining Commitment During Repatriation

Three major issues are key in influencing commitment during the repatriation process. First, firms can increase commitment by creating a culture that genuinely values international experience, perspectives, and skills. Second, firms can keep high-performing repatriates by carefully planning appropriate return assignments. Third, firms can reduce dysfunctional turnover by paying particular attention to high-risk expatriates when they come home from international assignments.

Creating an Organization That Values Global Experience

Creating an organizational culture that communicates the positive value of global experience is the most critical factor that we have identified for developing commitment to the parent company during repatriation in America, Japan, and Finland. A global assignment demands personal and family sacrifices. Firms should ensure that those sacrifices are honored. The last thing that international firms need is repatriates like this one, who suggests that future expatriates "must realize that whatever accomplishments were made overseas, they do not count for anything back at headquarters. You have to earn your 'stripes' all over again, so look after yourself, because nobody else will back home." Firms need to pay attention to the many formal and informal activities that collectively create the perception that firms either value or do not value international experience.

Expatriates, like most other employees, carefully observe what is and is not rewarded in a multinational firm. In particular, promotions and executive advancement are critical conduits of information about what really counts. We are familiar with firms throughout the world that tout international experience as essential to global expansion, but their own boardrooms and executive ranks contain no one with international experience. Including international experience as a central criterion for the advancement and promotion process is clearly an essential first step in communicating the value of international experience.

Linked to the promotion process, compensation policies are

another significant way in which expatriates learn that firms "put their money where their mouths are" when it comes to international experience. In other words, if expatriates return home and do not experience significant financial losses, they are more likely to sense that firms value international experience. If the compensation policies outlined in Chapter Eight are used throughout the global assignment cycle, expatriates are less likely to experience feelings of inequity during repatriation. Basically, adequate compensation after coming home is another essential link in creating an international culture.

Company-provided training before and after repatriation not only facilitates adjustment to "reverse culture shock" but also shows repatriates that firms are aware of and pay attention to the challenges of coming home. When firms provide no training or orientation during repatriation, the implicit message is one of complacency ("We don't care about your problems") or ignorance ("We aren't even aware of them"). In either case, repatriates quickly learn that their international experience has little value to a firm.

An appropriate return job assignment also communicates that the firm genuinely values international experience and perspectives. In other words, if repatriates are assigned to positions that fail to utilize their international skills and knowledge, they quickly learn that such skills and knowledge are unimportant. As one American repatriate put it, "If a firm really wants to go global, it should value international experience by actually using expatriates' skills and experience gained overseas and by putting more effort into planning the reentry position and career progression within the firm." Our research agrees with this perspective.

In addition to formal mechanisms, there are a number of informal ways for firms to communicate that they genuinely value global experience. These informal mechanisms cannot be easily "legislated" through policy statements (such as repatriation training or compensation). Instead, they often result when internal human resources policy statements are put into practice. For example, if firms genuinely value global experience and promote individuals who have completed global assignments, then board meetings, executive discussions, and strategic planning processes will be permeated with international rather than just home-country perspectives. Seeing global perspectives regularly raised communicates to repatriates that global experience really does count. Another example of implicitly valued global experience can be found in the simple observation of how many foreigners are working in the home-country office, as an index of the extent to which foreigners are not really foreign to the firm. In other words, as company head-quarters becomes permanently "globalized," repatriates are more likely to feel that global experience really counts as they return, look around the headquarters, and see a global environment in their home country. Finally, the "war stories" traded among employees about the benefits and costs of global assignments are powerful indicators of how much individuals think firms truly value global experience. Essentially, as we wander about firms to observe the relative attractiveness of global assignments, we look to see whether the informal comments are more like horror stories about so-and-so losing his job, wife, and career after going overseas or more like heroic stories about expatriates accomplishing strategic objectives and returning home to a company that valued their accomplishments. These are just a few of the numerous informal ways in which repatriates are tipped off about the real value of global experience within a firm.

Strategically Planning the Return Position

Carefully planning and selecting the return position facilitates commitment by communicating that a firm values global experience and by providing repatriates with a strong sense of felt responsibility for making things happen. Essentially, commitment to the parent firm is partly a function of having a job for which one feels a strong sense of responsibility. If the positions to which repatriates return are unclear or trivial compared to what they have experienced overseas, they are less likely to feel a sense of commitment to the jobs or to the firms. Consequently, firms should identify strategic purposes that expatriates can accomplish after coming home. These might include continued executive development, coordination and control, or transfer of information and technology. The strategic purpose and how the job facilitates its accomplishment must be clearly and personally communicated to the individual. A repatriation team, consisting of an organizational sponsor and a human resources representative, should examine potential jobs within the firm. The firm should consider the level of autonomy and discretion that an expatriate has had during the international assignment. If possible, the return position should have at least an equal level of challenge and the job autonomy to meet the challenge. A well-planned and well-selected return position can be a critical key in a returned manager's feeling a sense of responsibility in the job and a sense of commitment and allegiance to the firm. If this type of position cannot be created at home, the firm should communicate in advance—before repatriation—that the return assignment may be less than desirable. It is important to remember that accurate expectations are especially critical when expectations may not be met. Finally, the firm should attempt to utilize specific international skills that the expatriate has acquired during the assignment. These might include language, negotiation, and cross-cultural communication skills or essential knowledge of the foreign market.

Identifying and Tracking High-Risk Repatriates

Firms can better manage their repatriation results by profiling and tracking high-risk repatriates. Specifically, repatriates with low tenure in the parent company or high levels of international work experience are least likely to show commitment to the parent company when returning home. Interestingly, the same profiles exist for expatriates during their global assignments.[30] Accordingly, the firm should pay special attention to expatriates with low tenure in the firm during and after global assignments, to ensure that investments are not lost through dysfunctional turnover. Furthermore, expatriates with extensive international experience are the most likely to detect incongruities between corporate talk and corporate action around the importance and relative value of international experience. This is critical to remember, since these expatriates often have international experience that could strategically benefit either corporate headquarters or a domestic operation with international linkages. Firms also need to pay special attention to selecting appropriate return assignments for high-risk expatriates, because their identity and sense of self-worth are wrapped up in their package of global skills and experience. If these are not utilized in their return assignments, these valuable human assets may very well leave.

Creating Competitive Advantage By Keeping the Best Global Managers

In the best-case scenario, multinational firms send people on global assignments to accomplish strategic objectives, such as executive development, coordination and control, or transfer of information and technology. Furthermore, these strategic objectives can be furthered when similar strategic objectives are accomplished by repatriates in their return assignments. Such strategic objectives can be accomplished only if repatriates perform well and do not leave the firm after returning home. If such functional retention occurs as repatriates effectively adjust and exhibit strong commitment, multinational firms are much more likely to create sustainable competitive advantages through the effective retention and utilization of global managers. A competitive advantage can be gained by all types of firms through keeping the best global managers after repatriation, but the advantage is even more relevant to companies at higher levels of globalization.

At the export stage of globalization, firms send relatively few expatriates overseas and thus have very few returning home. Nevertheless, the relatively large investment made in each expatriate, and the relative importance of each repatriate to the future international expansion of the firm, suggests that developing effective repatriation policies and practices to retain the best global managers is critical even for export firms with relatively few expatriates.

Firms at the multidomestic stage of globalization utilize more expatriates than export firms do. In contrast to multinational and global firms, however, multidomestic firms tend to keep expatriates on longer individual assignments or send them on multiple assignments in various countries without bringing them back home. Accordingly, compared to multinational and global firms, multidomestic firms have lower repatriation needs. When multidomestic firms do repatriate international managers, they must do it effectively, in order to accomplish current strategic functions and, more important, to accomplish future international expansion, since a multidomestic firm may develop into a multinational or global enterprise.

Multinational and global firms have the largest numbers of expatriates moving to and from the host and home countries. Accordingly, the issues addressed in this chapter and in Chapter Nine are very relevant to multinational and global firms, since these firms have the most significant investments in international managers and executive assets. One financial institution we work with invests close to $30 million per year in expatriate salaries and support, with the firm's total annual profit at roughly $150 million. Such significant costs reinforce the need of multinational and global firms to strategically and systematically plan repatriation processes that keep the best managers.

Multinational and global firms not only need people in global assignments in order to serve vital strategic functions, they also need expatriates to return and bring back international perspectives, market knowledge, technology improvements, and so on, to the home country and to the global strategic planning process. If the repatriation process is mismanaged, repatriates end up giving this type of counterproductive advice to those still out on assignment:

> Advice about coming home? Don't.
> —Japanese expatriate

> If you like your overseas position and do not have the desire to work in a bureaucratic corporate environment, stay where you are and enjoy it. If I had the choice all over again, I would go right back to Germany and live there as long as possible.
> —American expatriate

Unfortunately, the result of such advice could be that fewer and fewer expatriates would want to come home, while multinational firms need them to return. Without their return, "global sclerosis" can set in, as the following repatriates described after coming home to parent companies with few repatriates:

I was shocked at the severe lack of worldwide thinking in the executive suite.

—American expatriate

My co-workers ridiculed me for carrying and reading *Newsweek* at the office after I had spent four years in the United States. They made me feel like a traitor to my company.

—Japanese expatriate

When I returned home, I found that the home organization was totally unaware of how business is really transacted overseas.

—Finnish expatriate

The bottom line is that firms at any stage of globalization need to effectively send people overseas and effectively bring them home in order to accomplish strategic objectives. The importance of managing international assignments becomes even more crucial when firms are at the higher stages of globalization and need more expatriates to accomplish strategic objectives. Moreover, as firms make transitions between stages of globalization (for example, from an export stage to a more integrated global stage), they can make those transitions more effectively by having managed previous global assignments well, so that key decision makers have the necessary global perspective and experience, and so that other managers and employees will want to take global assignments. For these strategic reasons, firms need to keep the best international managers during repatriation by paying particular attention to their commitment, both during and after global assignments.

Notes

1. Black and Gregersen, "Functional and Dysfunctional Turnover After International Assignments."
2. Black, "A Tale of Three Countries."
3. Black and Gregersen, "Functional and Dysfunctional Turnover."

4. Gregersen and Black, "Antecedents to Commitment to a Parent Company and a Foreign Operation."
5. Gregersen, "Commitments to a Parent Company and a Local Work Unit During Repatriation"; Gregersen, "Organizational Commitment During Repatriation: The Japanese and Finnish Experience."
6. Black, "A Tale of Three Countries."
7. Mathieu and Zajac, "A Review and Meta-analysis of the Antecedents, Correlates, and Consequences of Organizational Commitment"; Mowday, Porter, and Steers, *Employee-Organization Linkages: The Psychology of Commitment, Absenteeism, and Turnover.*
8. Gregersen, "Commitments to a Parent Company and a Local Work Unit."
9. Gregersen, "Organizational Commitment During Repatriation."
10. Gregersen, "Commitments to a Parent Company and a Local Work Unit."
11. Gregersen, "Commitments to a Parent Company and a Local Work Unit"; Gregersen, "Organizational Commitment During Repatriation."
12. Gregersen, "Commitments to a Parent Company and a Local Work Unit."
13. Black, "A Tale of Three Countries."
14. Gregersen, "Organizational Commitment During Repatriation."
15. Adler, "Re-entry: Managing Cross-Cultural Transitions"; Adler, *International Dimensions of Organizational Behavior;* Black and Gregersen, "When Yankee Comes Home: Factors Related to Expatriate and Spouse Repatriation Adjustment"; Clague and Krupp, "International Personnel: The Repatriation Problem"; Harvey, "Repatriation of Corporate Executives: An Empirical Study"; Napier and Peterson, "Expatriate Re-entry: What Do Repatriates Have to Say?"; Oddou and Mendenhall, "Succession Planning for the 21st Century: How Well Are We Grooming Our Future Business Leaders?"
16. Clague and Krupp, "International Personnel"; Black, "A Tale of Three Countries."

17. Gregersen, "Commitments to a Parent Company and a Local Work Unit"; Gregersen, "Organizational Commitment During Repatriation."
18. Gregersen, "Commitments to a Parent Company and a Local Work Unit."
19. Black, "A Tale of Three Countries."
20. Gregersen, "Commitments to a Parent Company and a Local Work Unit."
21. Gregersen, "Commitments to a Parent Company and a Local Work Unit"; Gregersen, "Organizational Commitment During Repatriation."
22. Black, "A Tale of Three Countries."
23. Bennett, "The Chief Executives in the Year 2000 Will Be Experienced Abroad."
24. Korn-Ferry study cited in Oddou and Mendenhall, "Succession Planning for the 21st Century."
25. Gregersen and Black, "Antecedents to Commitment to a Parent Company and a Foreign Operation"; Gregersen, "Commitments to a Parent Company and a Local Work Unit."
26. Gregersen and Black, "Antecedents to Commitment to a Parent Company and a Foreign Operation."
27. Gregersen, "Commitments to a Parent Company and a Local Work Unit"; Gregersen, "Organizational Commitment During Repatriation."
28. Tung, "Selection and Training Procedures of U.S., European, and Japanese Multinationals"; Tung, *The New Expatriates: Managing Human Resources Abroad.*
29. Gregersen, "Commitments to a Parent Company and a Local Work Unit."
30. Gregersen, "Commitments to a Parent Company and a Local Work Unit."

Chapter 11

Managing the Entire
Global Assignment Cycle:
Establishing Best Practices

Executives do not generally receive in-depth international management training from MBA programs, from in-house executive education programs, or from their work experience within the company.[1] A recent *Business Week* survey[2] on CEOs illustrates the latter
situation. Only 13 percent of the CEOs surveyed in the poll had
done tours of duty overseas, whereas 20 percent of the CEOs who
were brand-new as of the previous year had been on overseas assignments. Of the CEOs who had worked overseas, Canada was by far
the most common foreign assignment, followed by Great Britain
and then Belgium. The study concluded that CEOs mostly gained
foreign experience in Canada or Europe; very few had lived and
worked in Latin America or the Far East. From our perspective,
spending time in Canada and Great Britain is not sufficient to give
executives enough tough cultural challenges and experiences in the
global marketplace to enhance their acuity in the thorny and complex world of international business. If a company must compete
with Japanese, South Korean, German, or Taiwanese companies,

the best way to gain a comprehensive view of how they operate is to send the best and the brightest to those countries. It is unsettling to think that of the top one thousand firms in the United States, very few have CEOs who have lived and worked in the Far East—especially Japan.

If executives are to formulate valid global strategies for their firms—both at headquarters and at subsidiaries—they need to have an international perspective. Otherwise, a "garbage in–garbage out" phenomenon occurs in strategy formulation, for strategies are only as valid as the ideas, concepts, and knowledge that strategy formulators bring to the process. Any executive would also agree that global strategy implementation is crucial to the success of multinational or international companies. Strategies do not implement themselves, however. People implement strategies. If strategies are to be implemented the way top management desires them to be implemented, the right people must be in place throughout the world to carry out the firm's worldwide strategic aims. The "right people" for global assignments are not easy to find, though, and do not automatically emerge out of the top twenty MBA programs. Instead, internationally astute people need to be developed within companies.

Expatriate executives are simply too important to the current and future financial health of a firm to relegate them to a low priority on top management's "worry list." As mentioned in Chapter One, expatriate executives and managers play important strategic roles; they coordinate between subsidiaries and headquarters, implement strategy, ensure the quality and effectiveness of organizational control systems, manage global information systems, and gain expertise in international and cross-cultural business skills that are critical to ensuring that top executive positions are filled by those with the necessary international experience and perspectives.

We contend that few large U.S. firms are effective in all the dimensions of the "people spiral" that influences expatriate productivity. In other words, these firms fail to pay systematic attention to each phase of the global assignment: selection, training, cross-cultural adjustment, dual allegiance, performance appraisal, compensation, and repatriation. This assertion is based on the research literature, our own consulting experiences, and numerous conversations with executives from many U.S. multinationals. In fact, most firms approach global assignments from a tactical and reactive perspective, rather than from a strategic and systematic perspective. These fundamental approaches are outlined and contrasted in Figure 11.1.

Fortunately, we are aware of some companies that are tackling global assignments with a strategic perspective. To do so, they have constructed some creative and competitive human resources programs to effectively manage each stage of a global assignment. We would like to flesh out Figure 11.1 by describing some of the best practices from a variety of organizations concerning various dimensions of the global assignment cycle.

Figure 11.1. Strategic-Systematic Versus Tactical-Reactive Approach to Global Assignments.

A	B
Strategic-Systematic Approach Views Global Assignment as a Long-Run Investment	*Tactical-Reactive Approach Views Global Assignment as a Short-Run Expense*
1. Develops future executives with essential global perspectives and experiences to formulate and implement competitive strategies.	1. Focuses on quick-fix approach to a short-term problem in a foreign operation.
2. Increases the effectiveness of critical coordination and control functions between the home country and international operations.	2. Randomly and haphazardly performs some functions outlined in the strategic-systematic approach to global assignments.
3. Increases the volume and efficiency of international knowledge, technology, and innovation transfers throughout a firm.	

Getting the Right People: Staffing

Our first example of excellence comes from a human relief organization, Worldvision International. It understands that its productivity is tied directly to the quality of the people it sends overseas to accomplish strategic objectives on short-term and long-term assignments. The philosophy is that the organization simply cannot afford to send the wrong people; thus, it spends significant time and energy on getting people who have the technical and cross-cultural attributes necessary for success in an international setting.

Worldvision International's staffing policies, like those of any firm, are in a constant state of change and evolution, yet one principle remains constant in any policy shifts: effective expatriates are the key to overseas success. Worldvision International's selection process has been divided into as many as nine stages, and is illustrated in Figure 11.2.

Stage 1: Identifying the Position

In the first stage, the personnel department works with the hiring manager in identifying the position. Job descriptions are developed, and a personnel requisition is submitted for approval by the division vice-president, the hiring manager, the human resources director, and the personnel director. All these individuals must be "on board" about the nature and objectives of the international assignment before the search process begins.

Stage 2: Determining Candidates' Qualifications

In tandem with the hiring manager, the personnel department determines the technical and cross-cultural qualifications required of candidates. Included in these qualifications are educational record, previous overseas background and experience, personality characteristics, and other specific qualifications that the position requires. Behavior dimensions are also determined at this stage in the process, and a list of them is developed to assess candidates in interviews.

Figure 11.2. The Hiring Process at Worldvision International.

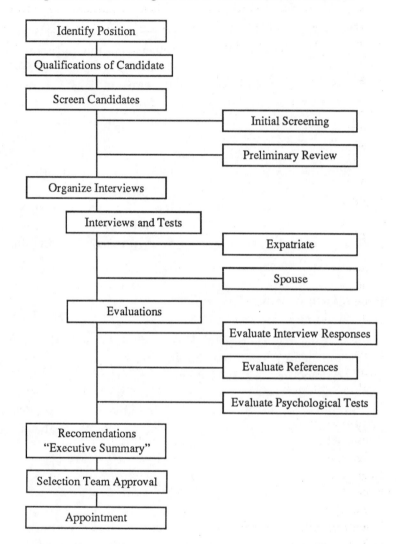

Stage 3: Screening

An initial screening of applicants is done by the personnel department, using the criteria established in stage 2. The best candidate is selected and presented to the hiring manager and the division vice-president for a preliminary review. After the preliminary review, if the decision is to proceed with the candidate, the process moves to the next stage. If the preliminary review is negative, the screening process continues.

Stage 4: Scheduling of Interviews

The personnel staff works with the hiring manager to determine who should interview the candidate. Almost always, multiple interviews are conducted. Personnel arranges the candidate's interview schedule. Interviews are generally conducted by staff from the personnel department and managers from the hiring department, along with other selected interviewers.

Stage 5: Interviews and Tests

Candidates for global assignments can be evaluated on a variety of dimensions. From the following list of twenty-eight dimensions, those most critical to a specific overseas assignment are selected for evaluation in the interview process.

Impact	Perseverance
Communication skills—written	Communication skills—verbal
Oral presentation skills	Development of subordinates
Problem analysis	Delegation
Management control	Initiative
Stress tolerance	Adaptability
Judgment	Decisiveness
Negotiation	Planning and organizing
Energy	Motivation
Leadership	Sensitivity
Listening skills	Resource utilization
Organizational sensitivity	Political sensitivity
Flexibility	Financial analytical ability
Technical translation	Independence

A single interviewer will not cover all the selected dimensions; rather, each interviewer will have specific dimensions assigned to cover in the interview. Dimensions that are not deemed relevant to a particular assignment are not covered. Interviewers are given specific questions to ask within each of their selected dimensions, although they may have some latitude to add other questions to the list. Some examples of such questions are given in Exhibits 11.1 and 11.2.

Interviewers are required to provide written evaluations of their interviews within twenty-four hours. In addition to written observations, interviewers are encouraged to express their evaluations of the candidate via two objective formats on a 1-5 scale: the degree to which each skill dimension was exhibited in the interview

Exhibit 11.1. Perseverance.

What is a big obstacle you had to overcome to get where you are today? How did you overcome it?

Have you ever submitted a good idea to your superior and he or she did not take action on it? What did you do?

Can you relate an experience in which you felt you persisted too long? How could the situation have been improved?

Can you relate an experience in which you felt you gained something because you persisted for a length of time?

I see you did not complete _____ course or activity. Why was this?

How long does it take to complete an average project? What is the longest you have ever taken? Why?

How many times do you usually call on an official before you give up?

Describe a situation where you gave your all but failed.

What is the biggest project you did not successfully conclude? What did you do?

What university course gave you the most trouble? What did you do about it?

What was the biggest problem you encountered while completing college? On your last job? How did you handle them?

The interviewer should establish the size of the problem or barrier in order to gauge the amount of perseverance required to overcome it.

Exhibit 11.2. Delegation.

Who is "minding the store" while you are here? How was he or she selected? Why? How will you know how well he or she performed?

Did you make a formal announcement to your subordinates concerning the responsibilities of the person you left in charge?

Explain your biggest mistake in delegating.

Explain your biggest mistake in not delegating.

What keeps you from delegating more?

Describe the type of decision making that you delegate to your subordinates.

Describe your criteria for delegating assignments.

If the degree of delegation varies among subordinates, explain how and why.

When did you have a major problem requiring staff help? What action did you take? Why did you ask particular people to assist you?

How much overtime do you put in per week? (Do you need to delegate more?)

How do you familiarize yourself with the current situation in your organization after being away for several days?

Can you cite an example from your own experience of having been faced with delegating authority and/or responsibility? How did it work?

> The interviewer should establish the purpose of each delegation mentioned. What did the interviewee want to achieve, and why was the particular person chosen to handle the matter?

itself; and an overall rating of the candidate as excellent, above average, average, below average, or poor.

Stage 6: Evaluations of Interviews and Tests

The personnel department evaluates the written responses of the interviewers, the candidate's references, and the results of the psychological tests that are also administered during the interview process. Although less intensively, candidates' spouses are also interviewed and given psychological tests to determine their adaptability potential.

Stage 7: Personnel's Recommendations

The personnel staff summarizes the results of the interviews, references, and psychological tests and presents a summary with recommendations to the hiring manager and the division vice-president.

Stage 8: Approval

If the recommendation is to offer the position to the candidate under consideration, it must be approved by the selection team, consisting of the division vice-president, the hiring manager, the human resources director, and the personnel director. Personnel discusses the details of compensation and benefits with the hiring manager and then submits a personnel action form, to be approved by each member of the selection team.

Stage 9: Appointment

The personnel department issues a letter of invitation, which includes the job title, starting date, salary, terms of service, specific information related to the movement of household goods, banking arrangements, travel to the field assignment, and any other essential information. While this can be a lengthy and time-consuming process, expatriates sent out under this selection process were rated as highly successful by the firm's top management. In Worldvision International's experience, the investment of time and money in effective selection has paid off in the field, with significant long-term returns for the organization and the individual.

Worldvision International directly applies many principles that were discussed in Chapter Three. Worldvision International initiated the selection process by involving more than one person. In fact, it created a team of important "stakeholders," individuals concerned with the future success of the expatriate. Then the organization decided what strategic objectives the expatriate could accomplish overseas and developed a comprehensive but focused list of the selection criteria that were most relevant to a particular global assignment. Next, multiple selection methods were used in assessing candidates against an array of selection criteria. Finally, Worldvision recognized that expatriates usually have families and involved spouses, as appropriate, in the selection process. The result is an impressive record of successful overseas assignments. Essentially, Worldvision International conforms to a strategic-systematic perspective on international staffing (versus a tactical-reactive approach). These differences are illustrated in Figure 11.3. Rather than being victimized by hasty selections based on a subsidiary's immediate need, Worldvision International carefully considers the nature and purpose of an assignment and then locates candidates who can effectively accomplish strategic purposes.

Figure 11.3. Differences in Two Approaches to Staffing.

Tactical-Reactive

Purpose
  Fix a short-term problem

Focus
  Technical skills

Process
  Single selection method
  Single selection criterion

Strategic-Proactive

Purpose
  Executive development
  Coordination
  Corporate control
  Transfer of information,
    innovation, and technology

Focus
  Technical skills
  Cross-cultural skills
  Family situation

Process
  Multiple selection methods
  Multiple selection criteria

Helping People Do the Right Thing: Training

We argued in Chapter Four that while predeparture training is important, in-country training—especially after two to six months— is very critical to expatriate productivity. After the expatriate and spouse have settled in and begun to negotiate the intricacies of the foreign culture, there is a high motivation to really understand the host culture. It is at this time that rigorous training methods can produce long-lasting results. If expatriates are not exposed to the "meat" of the host culture during this period, they can easily develop idiosyncratic "cognitive maps" that ineffectively explain the host culture. This is often when rigid stereotypes or faulty attributional tendencies are entrenched. Once these are established, it is quite un- likely that expatriates will actively seek out new and more accurate knowledge about the host culture.

To help avoid these problems, we have worked with firms like IBM–Asia Pacific and IBM–Japan, which recently offered in- country training to their senior executives and their spouses trans- ferred to Tokyo. Our intensive, week-long seminar of over sixty hours covered a variety of topics crucial to understanding the Jap- anese and Japanese business culture: ancient, medieval, and modern history, Japanese religions and philosophy, socialization within Ja- pan, psychological and sociological constructs of Japanese society, organizational behavior in the Japanese workplace, the business history of Japan, Japanese organizational design and structure, the Japanese human resources system, business negotiations in Japan, strategies for learning the Japanese language, and relationships among business groupings, the government, the education system, and the Japanese "mafia."

The three-step learning process described in Chapter Four requires expatriate managers to first *attend* to the norms of the new culture, then *retain* and understand the nature of the new norms, and then *practice* new behaviors. By doing training in-country, IBM enhanced this learning process because the executives were able to relate the concepts covered in the seminar to experiences they had just had the week or even the day before. This also allowed them to practice and validate what they were taught by implementing the knowledge immediately.

Consistent with the principles espoused in Chapter Four, IBM opted for the following methods: lecture, films, books (homework assignments), cases, survival-level language training, role plays, and field trips. Each of these methods was more effective in its delivery because the participants were studying Japan *in* Japan. Consistent with research findings and recommendations, spouses were included in this week-long training, which is not the case in most firms.

IBM's approach to the training of international executives reflects an understanding of the need to invest in such training in order to increase performance and adjustment, and to increase the likelihood that strategic objectives of the global assignment (such as executive development, coordination, corporate control, or technology transfer) will be accomplished. IBM's strategic-systematic approach to training is in direct contrast with the tactical-reactive approach outlined in Figure 11.4.

Language Training

Language training is a thorny, complex issue for companies. While many language firms claim that one can learn a foreign language in two months by listening to tapes, the reality is that it takes dedicated effort to learn a foreign language. In fact, a significant level of spoken fluency generally cannot be attained until one actually lives overseas. Nevertheless, expatriates can prepare to know the language at least at the survival or conversational level before going overseas. With that foundation, progress toward fluency can begin immediately. The danger of waiting to learn a new language until arriving in the foreign country is that fear, doubt, work responsibilities, and an overwhelming sense of how difficult it is can overcome the long, deliberate, day-to-day commitment it takes to learn a new language.

With four to six months of notice before departing on a global assignment, it is quite possible to reach the survival level in a foreign language through classes or self-instruction. Language instruction must occur *daily* during the period before departure, for at least an hour—preferably two. How much can be accomplished depends, of course, on the ability of the learner to "pick up" lan-

Figure 11.4. Differences in Two Approaches to Training.

Tactical-Reactive

Cut Costs Now . . .
  No training

Pay Later
  Low job performance
  High expatriate turnover

Strategic-Systematic

Invest Now . . .
  Job training
  Organization-business training
  Culture training
  Language training

To Achieve Later
  Executive development
  Coordination
  Corporate control
  Transfer of information,
    innovation, and technology

---

guages, how the class is taught, and the difficulty of the language itself.

In our research and consulting, we have not come across any companies that offer a strategic, rigorous, daily language program for expatriates four to six months before departure—even though language skills may be the key to accomplishing strategic objectives during the global assignment. One of the present authors did put this principle of language preparation to the test on a personal basis, however. He received an assignment to spend a semester, approximately five months, in Switzerland. Not wanting to be a tourist for this period in terms of language ability, he studied German for an hour a day for four months before departing. By the time it came to leave, he could speak beyond the survival level but not yet at the conversational level. Five months later, he was at the conversational level. The ability to converse with the average man and woman on the street increased his family's satisfaction with the overseas assignment, reduced stress, impressed the host nationals (who told him that the Americans they knew made no effort at all to learn German), and generally aided him in his ability to accomplish his assignment there.

Cross-cultural training done in-country, and language training done before departure and in-country, are indispensable to the effectiveness of expatriate executives. Each company must conduct such programs as best fit its needs, but the research literature to date shows that most companies are ignoring this very important aspect of international people management.

Determining Whether People Are Doing Things Right: Appraising

Effective performance appraisal is an important component of a successful global assignment. In Chapter Seven, we discussed several factors that result in performance appraisal systems that benefit individuals and organizations. At 3M, we found an excellent appraisal process that incorporates evaluative and developmental components.

Primarily for evaluation purposes, 3M's performance appraisal system begins with expatriates' direct functional managers (who may or may not be host-country nationals). These managers work with expatriates in order to define performance expectations for individuals and business units on an annual basis. They also jointly define the set of performance expectations that are directly related to an expatriate's own career development. After business and performance expectations have been defined consensually, these criteria are forwarded for review by the area vice-president and the reentry (or repatriation) sponsor in the home country. Each of these individuals takes the opportunity to review the strengths of the expatriate and point out potential problems in the selection of performance criteria and career or individual developmental needs. A similar "appraisal team" process occurs in assessing the accomplishment of the predefined performance expectations. Initially the year's accomplishments are reviewed by the direct functional manager and the expatriate, and then these evaluations are also examined by the area vice-president and the reentry sponsor.

3M has also developed a parallel developmental performance appraisal process, called the Human Resource Review. On an annual basis, four individuals evaluate performance and career issues during global assignments. These individuals are the executive director of human resources for the international division, the area vice-president, the area human resources manager or director, and a representative from the corporate executive resources department. These four people assess expatriates along several dimensions in Human Resource Review meetings. They examine each expatriate's performance during the past year and, more important, they consider major developmental issues for each expatriate. For example, an expatriate's career progression within the firm, in terms of current and potential positions, is often a point of discussion in the Human Resource Review meeting. The Human Resource Review meeting also provides an established forum for managers to consider specific issues, such as costs associated with each expatriate, assignment lengths, and upcoming repatriation processes.

3M's performance appraisal takes advantage of many principles discussed in Chapter Seven. For example, in both the evaluative and developmental appraisal process, 3M involves more than one person. In fact, 3M incorporates multiple perspectives in assessing an expatriate's performance and career development by including managers and executives who have a stake in the success of the expatriates they evaluate. Moreover, 3M does not just examine performance-related issues. 3M also broadens the assessment scope to career-related challenges of expatriates. In sum, 3M's approach to appraisal contains three critical elements for success: it utilizes several individuals to rate performance, incorporates a variety of assessment criteria, and focuses on evaluative and developmental aspects of the appraisal process.

Encouraging the Right Things People
Are Doing: Compensating

American Express has a well-conceived compensation program for expatriates. The approach to expatriate compensation at American Express is in principle an "equalization" approach. Specifically, American Express calculates housing and utility allowances by determining the costs of housing and utilities in the host country to which the expatriate is to be assigned and explicitly considers the job, salary level, and family size of the candidate. This housing allowance is provided in the local currency of the host country. The amount is adjusted for inflation annually or more frequently, depending on the rate of inflation in the host country. Generally, American Express discourages employees from selling their houses in the home country and from buying houses in the host country. The company provides informational as well as financial assistance in renting and managing individuals' homes while they are on assignment overseas. At the same time that a housing and utility allowance is being paid to the individual in the host country, an estimate of the housing and utility costs the employee would probably have incurred in the absence of a global assignment is deducted from the individual's home-country salary. Consequently, individuals pay approximately no more and no less for housing and utilities than they would have if they had not been sent overseas.

This approach also applies to taxes. An initial calculation of employees' home-country taxes is made at the beginning of the year, and a more detailed recalculation is made at the end of the year. This hypothetical tax is based on earned income, which includes salary and bonus. This earned income is reduced by any before-tax benefits and salary deferrals. Itemized deductions that individuals would probably claim if they were working at home are also deducted. This hypothetical tax is deducted from individuals' home-country salaries over the course of the year. Any adjustment in the taxes that should be deducted or credited, based on the year-end recalculation, is made at that time and is generally small. American Express then pays all home-country and host-country taxes actually incurred.

American Express also provides a number of other carefully considered allowances. In recognition of the difficulty of moving overseas and then back again, American Express pays part of the "mobility allowance" when individuals go overseas, and the rest when they return. The firm also pays for direct moving costs and provides a moderate sum to cover miscellaneous moving expenses. American Express also provides help with educational expenses for children, home leave, and hardship allowances for countries that have extreme and difficult conditions.

This approach allows American Express to avoid "rewarding

A while hoping for *B*"—that is, this approach affords the ability to attract capable people to global assignments but does not make financial incentives the sole or even major reason for considering or accepting a global assignment. Furthermore, paying host-country expenses in local currency while deducting expected home-country expenses reduces two potential problems. First, paying expected costs in the local currency reduces exchange-rate risks. Second, deducting expected home-country costs reduces the inequity that individuals might experience if all spendable and disposable income, as well as allowance differentials, were paid (and therefore visible) in the local currency. On top of achieving these two important objectives, these practices also reduce the overall compensation and tax costs to the firm.

Doing the Right Things for People: Repatriation

In Chapter One, we discussed GE's "people" failure in a French subsidiary. Since that experience, GE has worked hard to understand the international human resources process and in turn has created and implemented some very effective expatriate programs. One area that stands out in GE's efforts is the attention GE now pays to repatriates. For example, GE Medical Systems has initiated the Expatriate Sponsorship Program to ensure successful repatriation and contribute to expatriates' career development.[3] The program is straightforward: any long-term expatriate (one year or longer in an overseas assignment) is eligible for the program. The eligible expatriate is assigned a sponsor, who is a manager in the home country, preferably in the function where the expatriate is most likely to return. There are four elements of the Expatriate Sponsorship Program: the expatriate, the sponsor, the host manager, and the Human Resource Network.

The Expatriate

Before going overseas, expatriates are expected to take responsibility for their own professional development—that is, the company makes it clear that it will not coddle expatriates throughout the assignment; expatriates will be required to expend effort to enhance their careers. Expatriates are expected to analyze the job opportunity in terms of its potential for personal career development, assess family readiness to live and work overseas, be clear about career expectations, discuss future career opportunities with the sponsor upon completion of the assignment, and prepare for the assignment by attending language- and culture-training programs with the family.

While expatriates are overseas, they are to meet personally with the sponsors at least once a year. In this meeting, they are to discuss their own performance, career expectations, and other issues relevant to their situation in the firm. Expatriates are also expected to take advantage of company seminars, business meetings, reports, phone calls, and so on, to build and maintain a network back at the home office. While overseas, expatriates are expected to work hard and enhance their management skills. Finally, before returning to the home office, expatriates are expected to objectively reassess their career options, which is easier to do if a strong sponsor-expatriate relationship exists.

The Sponsor

The primary role of the sponsor is to ensure that a successful repatriation occurs with the sponsored expatriate. Predeparture responsibilities of the sponsor include the following:

- Participating in the expatriate selection process
- Studying the expatriate candidate's repatriation plan, to identify opportunities, roadblocks, and dead ends in terms of the expatriate's career
- Meeting the expatriate personally, to discuss the sponsor's views of the overseas assignment
- Formally communicating to the Human Resource Network the repatriation plan for the expatriate

During the assignment, the sponsor is required to monitor the expatriate's performance via phone calls to the host manager and the expatriate, as well as from copies of performance appraisals; meet annually with the expatriate and discuss the assignment; complete an evaluation of the expatriate's performance for the Human Resource Network; and encourage the expatriate's exposure to the home office, in order to maintain a personal network. Before expatriates return, sponsors should be willing and able to act as career advisers to expatriates and provide references to hiring managers on their behalf.

The Host Manager

The host manager plays an important role in the repatriation and expatriation process. Before the expatriate arrives overseas, the host manager must assess the impact of having an expatriate in the workplace, play a large role in the selection of the expatriate, prepare the organization to receive the expatriate, and assign an in-country mentor to the expatriate. During the expatriate's tenure, the host manager is required annually to complete a performance appraisal and send copies of it to the expatriate's sponsor and to the Human Resource Network. Host managers must spend more time on communication with and feedback to expatriates than with other employees. Before repatriating expatriates, host managers must activate the Human Resource Network to begin the repatriation process (this begins no later than six months before the term of the assignment is over). Host managers must also complete a performance appraisal for the overall assignment and send it to the sponsor through the Human Resource Network.

The Human Resource Network

The Human Resource Network of GE Medical Systems is required to perform the following functions before the foreign assignment:

- Organize a foreign-assignment planning review twice a year
- Coordinate expatriate candidate identification and selection
- Manage the sponsorship assignments
- Manage the repatriation plan of the expatriate that is sent by the sponsor
- Act as the focal point for all global staffing and expatriation management

- Manage the contractual aspects of the assignment
- Organize the training programs

During the expatriate's assignment, the network coordinates performance appraisal, salary planning, and reviews of the expatriate's performance. The network also monitors communications among expatriates, sponsors, and host managers and manages the terms and conditions of the assignment. Then, no later than six months before repatriation, or upon request of the host manager, the network activates the repatriation process, in order to plan for and find an appropriate position for the repatriate.

Very few companies plan for repatriation in such an organized way as GE Medical Systems does. This company understands the importance of effectively supporting expatriates in order to maintain a global competitive advantage in the future. GE remembers its expatriates by establishing several links with the home country: sponsors, frequent communication, clear repatriation processes, and planning for the return assignment. In contrast, most companies, as reflected in Figure 11.5, have an "out of sight, out of mind" approach to expatriates that stems from a tactical-reactive philosophy and results in "orphaned" expatriates during and after global assignments.

Global Assignments: A Key to Executive Success and Global Competitiveness

Throughout this book, we have traced the rationale, logic, and evidence for the necessity of constructing a comprehensive, systematic, strategically-oriented expatriate policy. In addition to the economic arguments for an integrated and well-designed international human resources system, there is another equally important consideration: a company's ethical responsibility to its employees.

One way to understand this responsibility better is to consider for a moment the preparations that go into a successful military campaign. Before going into battle, soldiers, pilots, and sailors are well trained in the use of their weapons, battle tactics, and strategies of war. In fact, they have probably undergone numerous battle simulations or training, at very high cost. Such events as Operation Desert Storm provide clear evidence of the value of such

Figure 11.5. Differences in Two Approaches to Support.

Tactical-Reactive

Out of Sight . . . Out of Mind
   No formal support

Strategic-Systematic

Out of Sight . . . With Support
   Organizational sponsor
   Communication links
   Visits to the home country
   Clear repatriation process
   Planning return assignments
   Prereturn orientation training
   Host manager involvement

---

preparation and training. Why do military and intelligence organizations spend so much time preparing their people? The obvious
answer is that without such training and preparation, performance
in the field would suffer.

There is another reason for such training and support that
is perhaps less obvious but is just as compelling: it would be un-
ethical to send people into situations where their lives could be put
at risk without also providing adequate selection, training, and
support. This logic seems clear in war, but it is not as apparent in
the case of sending individuals on global assignments for multinational companies. Nevertheless, we have seen firsthand the pain,
stress, grief, and psychological challenges that many expatriates
undergo in overseas assignments when they receive little support
and training from their organizations. The following passage summarizes some of our thoughts on this matter:

> One must wonder if it is ethical to uproot an individ-
> ual or a family, send them across the Pacific or Atlan-
> tic oceans, and expect them to make their way
> skillfully through an alien business and social culture
> on their own. Perhaps American executives reason
> that the extraordinary compensation packages expa-
> triates receive make the the exchange a fair and ethical
> one. Living and working overseas involves adjust-

ments and stresses of a high magnitude. Placing individuals in such conditions without giving them the tools to manage these conditions seems not only economically costly to the firm, and personally costly to the individuals, but simply wrong.[4]

Of course, we recognize that sending people from Chicago to Saudi Arabia is not the same as sending them off to war. Managers do not put their lives on the line in the same way a soldier does, but expatriates often put their careers, their psychological health, their marriages, their children's education, and other significant aspects of their work and nonwork lives at risk when they accept overseas assignments. This serious reality begs the question: Is it ethical for a multinational firm to send the wrong people, to inadequately train them, or to fail to understand and support them in their attempts to live and work in another culture?

We feel that companies are not only economically wise but, perhaps more important, duty-bound to offer sufficient support to expatriate employees throughout the international assignment cycle. It is time for firms to take the whole business of globalization and internationalization more seriously and invest heavily in internationalizing senior executive teams and high-potential managers who are being groomed to enter senior management circles in the future. It is also time to provide these executives and managers with the training, tools, and support to accomplish strategic objectives for firms and wage victorious campaigns against global competitors without incurring significant personal losses.

Multinational firms have strategic objectives that span the globe. Successful implementation of these objectives relies on human as well as financial assets. The strategic roles of global assignments must be valued seriously and understood deeply by top management and human resources executives before staffing, training, appraising, compensating, and developing processes can be created to support these strategic roles. Figure 11.6 illustrates a firm whose policies toward global assignments are based on the philosophy that such assignments are key to competitive advantage and future executive excellence. The figure shows an upward spiral of global competitiveness. Each stage of policy increases the potential

Figure 11.6. Upward Competitiveness Spiral.

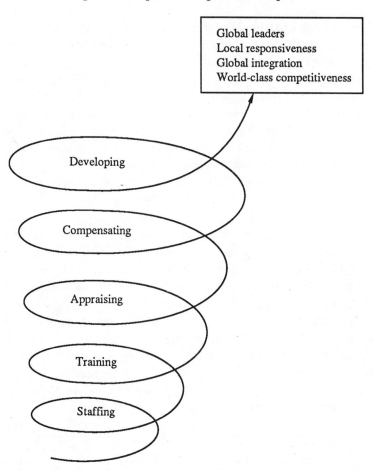

Global leaders
Local responsiveness
Global integration
World-class competitiveness

Developing

Compensating

Appraising

Training

Staffing

for success of the next stage. In many ways, this spiral of international human resources policies and practices is similar to the board game "Chutes and Ladders," where one roll of the dice can mean a serious slide and loss of the game. In an expatriate's world, one inappropriate policy can result in individual and organizational failure. By contrast, a strategic and systematic approach to global assignments helps ensure that expatriates do not slide down the policy "chutes" but rather climb up a "ladder" to accomplish strategic objectives, while overseas and after coming home. The result of systematic, coordinated international human resources policies is superior job performance overseas, along with higher cross-cultural adjustment, higher levels of performance in foreign subsidiaries, successful repatriation adjustment and performance, and future utilization of critical international experience, skills, and expertise. Successful international assignments, through successful international human resources policies, will be at the heart of successful international firms in the global marketplace of the twenty-first century.

Notes

1. Porter and McKibben, *Management Education and Development: Drift or Thrust into the 21st Century?*
2. Roman, Mims, and Jespersen, "The Corporate Elite: A Portrait of the Boss."
3. Information on this best practice comes from General Electric Medical Systems' *The Expatriate Sponsorship Program* (July 1990).
4. Black and Mendenhall, "A Practical but Theory-Based Framework for Selecting Cross-Cultural Training Methods," p. 199.

References

Abe, H., and Wiseman, R. L. "A Cross-Cultural Confirmation of Intercultural Effectiveness." *International Journal of Intercultural Relations*, 1983, 7, 53–68.

Adler, N. J. "Do MBAs Want International Careers?" *International Journal of Intercultural Relations*, 1986, *10*, 277–300.

Adler, N. J. "Expecting International Success: Female Managers Overseas." *Columbia Journal of World Business*, 1984, *19*, 79–85.

Adler, N. J. *International Dimensions of Organizational Behavior.* Boston: PWS-Kent, 1986.

Adler, N. J. *International Dimensions of Organizational Behavior* (2nd ed.). Boston: PWS-Kent, 1990.

Adler, N. J. "Pacific Basin Managers: A Gaijin, Not a Woman." *Human Resource Management*, 1987, *26*, 169–192.

Adler, N. J. "Re-entry: Managing Cross-Cultural Transitions." *Group and Organization Studies*, 1981, *6* (3), 341–356.

Adler, N. J. "Women Do Not Want International Careers: And Other Myths About International Management." *Organizational Dyamics*, 1984, *13*, 66–79.

Adler, N. J. "Women in International Management: Where Are They?" *California Management Review*, 1984, *26*, 78–89.

Adler, N. J., and Izraeli, D. N. *Women in Management Worldwide.* Armonk, N.Y.: Sharpe, 1988.

Baird, L., and Meshoulam, I. "Managing Two Fits of Strategic Human Resource Management." *Academy of Management Review*, 1988, *13*, 116–128.

Baker, J. C., and Ivancevich, J. "The Assignment of American Executives Abroad: Systematic, Haphazard, or Chaotic?" *California Management Review*, 1971, *13*, 39–44.

Bandura, A. *Social Foundations of Thought and Action.* Englewood Cliffs, N.J.: Prentice Hall, 1983.

Bandura, A. *Social Learning Theory.* Englewood Cliffs, N.J.: Prentice Hall, 1977.

Bartlett, C., and Ghoshal, S. "Organizing for Worldwide Effectiveness: The Transnational Solution." *California Management Review*, 1988, *31* (1), 54–74.

Beer, M. "Performance Appraisal: Dilemmas and Possibilities." *Organizational Dynamics*, 1981, *10*, 24–36.

Bell, N., and Staw, B. "People as Sculptors Versus People as Sculpture: The Roles of Personality and Personal Control in Organizations." In M. B. Arthur, D. T. Hall, and B. Lawrence (eds.), *Handbook of Career Theory.* Cambridge, England: Cambridge University Press, 1989.

Bennett, A. "The Chief Executives in the Year 2000 Will Be Experienced Abroad." *Wall Street Journal*, Feb. 27, 1989, pp. A1–A4.

Bennett, A. "Going Global." *Wall Street Journal*, Feb. 27, 1989, p. A1.

Björkman, I., and Gertsen, M. "Selecting and Training Scandinavian Expatriates: Determinants of Corporate Practice." *Scandinavian Journal of Management*, 1992.

Black, J. S. "Coming Home: The Relationship of Expatriate Expectations with Repatriation Adjustment and Job Performance." *Human Relations*, 1992, *45*, 177–192.

Black, J. S. "Factors Related to the Adjustment of Japanese Expatriate Managers in America." *Research in Personnel and Human Resource Management*, 1990, *5*, 109–125.

Black, J. S. "Fred Bailey: An Innocent Abroad." In M. Mendenhall and G. Oddou (eds.), *Readings and Cases in International Human Resource Management.* Boston: PWS-Kent, 1991.

Black, J. S. "Locus of Control, Social Support, Stress, and Adjustment to International Transfers." *Asia Pacific Journal of Management,* 1990, 7 (1), 1–29.

Black, J. S. "The Other Side of the Picture on the Other Side of the World: Repatriation Problems of Japanese Expatriate Spouses." Unpublished paper, Amos Tuck School of Business Administration, Dartmouth College, 1991.

Black, J. S. "Personal Dimensions and Work Role Transitions: A Study of Japanese Expatriate Managers in America." *Management International Review,* 1990, *30* (2) 119–134.

Black, J. S. "Repatriation: A Comparison of Japanese and American Practices and Results." In *Proceedings of the Eastern Academy of Management International Conference,* vol. 1. Hong Kong: Eastern Academy of Management, 1989.

Black, J. S. "A Tale of Three Countries." Paper presented at the annual meeting of the Academy of Management, Miami, 1991.

Black, J. S. "Work Role Transitions: A Study of American Expatriate Managers in Japan." *Journal of International Business Studies,* 1988, *19,* 277–294.

Black, J. S., and Gregersen, H. B. "Antecedents to Cross-Cultural Adjustment for Expatriates in Pacific Rim Assignments." *Human Relations,* 1991, *44,* 497–515.

Black, J. S., and Gregersen, H. B. "Functional and Dysfunctional Turnover After International Assignments." Unpublished paper, Amos Tuck School of Business Administration, 1992.

Black, J. S., and Gregersen, H. B. "*O Kairinasai:* Factors Related to Japanese Repatriation Adjustment." Paper presented at the annual meeting of the Academy of Management, Las Vegas, 1992.

Black, J. S., and Gregersen, H. B. "The Other Half of the Picture: Antecedents of Spouse Cross-Cultural Adjustment." *Journal of International Business Studies,* 1991, *22,* 461–467.

Black, J. S., and Gregersen, H. B. "When Yankee Comes Home." Paper presented at the Academy of International Business, Toronto, 1990.

Black, J. S., and Gregersen, H. B. "When Yankee Comes Home: Factors Related to Expatriate and Spouse Repatriation Adjustment." *Journal of International Business Studies*, 1991, *22* (4), 671–695.

Black, J. S., Gregersen, H. B., and Mendenhall, M. E. "Toward a Theoretical Framework of Repatriation Adjustment." *Journal of International Business Studies*, in press.

Black, J. S., Gregersen, H. B., and Wethli, E. "Factors Related to Expatriate Spouses' Adjustment in Overseas Assignments." Paper presented at the Western Academy of Management international conference, Shizuoka, Japan, 1990.

Black, J. S., and Mendenhall, M. E. "Cross-Cultural Training Effectiveness: A Review and Theoretical Framework for Future Research." *Academy of Management Review*, 1990, *15*, 113–136.

Black, J. S., and Mendenhall, M. E. "A Practical but Theory-Based Framework for Selecting Cross-Cultural Training Methods." In M. Mendenhall and G. Oddou (eds.), *Readings and Cases in International Human Resource Management*. Boston: PWS-Kent, 1991.

Black, J. S., and Mendenhall, M. E. "Selecting Cross-Cultural Training Methods: A Practical Yet Theory-Based Model." *Human Resource Management*, 1989, *28* (4), 511–540.

Black, J. S., Mendenhall, M. E., and Oddou, G. "Toward a Comprehensive Model of International Adjustment: An Integration of Multiple Theoretical Perspectives." *Academy of Management Review*, 1991, *16*, 291–317.

Black, J. S., and Porter, L. W. "Managerial Behaviors and Job Performance: A Successful Manager in Los Angeles May Not Succeed in Hong Kong." *Journal of International Business Studies*, 1991, *22*, 99–114.

Black, J. S., and Stephens, G. "Expatriate Adjustment and Intent to Stay in Pacific Rim Overseas Assignments." *Journal of Management*, 1989, *15*, 529–544.

Blake, R., and Mouton, J. *The Managerial Grid*. Houston: Gulf, 1964.

Bowman, E. H. "Concerns of CEOs." *Human Resource Management*, 1986, *25*, 267–285.

Boyacigiller, N. "The Role of Expatriates in the Management of Interdependence, Complexity, and Risk in Multinational Corporations." *Journal of International Business Studies*, 1990, *21*, 357-381.

Brein, M., and David, K. H. "Intercultural Communication and Adjustment of the Sojourner." *Psychology Bulletin*, 1971, *76*, 215-230.

Brewster, C. *The Management of Expatriates*. London: Kogan Page, 1991.

Casio, W. F. *Managing Human Resources*. New York: McGraw-Hill, 1986.

Church, A. T. "Sojourner Adjustment." *Psychological Bulletin*, 1982, *9*, 540-572.

Clague, L., and Krupp, N. "International Personnel: The Repatriation Problem." *Personnel Administrator*, 1978, *23*, 29-45.

Copeland, L., and Louis, G. *Going International*. New York: Random House, 1985.

Cotton, J. L., Vollrath, D. A., Froggatt, K. L., Kengnick-Hall, M. L., and Jennings, K. R. "Employee Participation: Diverse Forms and Different Outcomes." *Academy of Management Review*, 1988, *13*, 8-22.

De Cieri, H., Dowling, P. J., and Taylor, K. "The Psychological Impact of Expatriate Relocation on Spouses." Paper presented at the Academy of International Business annual meeting, Singapore, 1989.

Devanna, M. A., Fombrun, C., and Tichy, N. "A Framework for Strategic Human Resource Management." In C. Fombrun, M. A. Devanna, and N. Tichy (eds.), *Strategic Human Resource Management*. New York: Wiley, 1984.

DeYoung, G. H. "The Clash of Cultures at Tylan General." *Electronic Business*, Dec. 10, 1990, pp. 148-150.

Dowling, P., and Schuler, R. *International Dimensions of Human Resource Management*. Boston: PWS-Kent, 1990.

Doz, Y. L., and Prahalad, C. K. "Headquarters Influence and Strategic Control in MNCs." *Sloan Management Review*, 1981, 7, 15-29.

Edstrom, A., and Galbraith, J. "Transfer of Managers as a Coordination and Control Strategy in Multinational Organizations." *Administrative Science Quarterly*, 1977, *22*, 248-263.

Fuchsberg, G. "As Costs of Overseas Assignments Climb, Firms

Select Expatriates More Carefully." *Wall Street Journal*, Jan. 9, 1992, pp. B1–B4.

"GE Culture Turns Sour at French Unit." *Wall Street Journal*, July 31, 1990, p. A11.

Gertsen, M. "Expatriate Training and Selection." In R. Luostarin-en, (ed.), *Proceedings of the European International Business Association Conference*. Helsinki, Finland: European International Business Association, 1989.

Ghadar, F., and Adler, N. "Management Culture and Accelerated Product Life Cycle." *Human Resource Planning*, 1989, *12* (1), 37–42.

Glisson, C., and Durrick, M. "Predictors of Job Satisfaction and Organizational Commitment in Human Service Organizations." *Administrative Science Quarterly*, 1988, *33*, 61–81.

Gomez-Mejía, L., and Balkin, D. "Determinants of Managerial Satisfaction with the Expatriation and Repatriation Process." *Journal of Management Development*, 1987, *6*, 7–17.

Greenberger, D., and Strasser, S. "Development and Application of a Model of Personal Control in Organizations." *Academy of Management Review*, 1990, *11*, 164–177.

Gregersen, H. B. "Coming Home to the Cold: Finnish Repatriation Adjustment." Paper presented at the meeting of the Academy of International Business, Brussels, Belgium, 1992.

Gregersen, H. B. "Commitments to a Parent Company and a Local Work Unit During Repatriation." *Personnel Psychology*, 1992, *45*, 29–54.

Gregersen, H. B. "Organizational Commitment During Repatriation: The Japanese and Finnish Experience." Paper presented at the annual meeting of the Academy of Management, Las Vegas, 1992.

Gregersen, H. B., and Black, J. S. "Antecedents to Commitment to a Parent Company and a Foreign Operation." *Academy of Management Journal*, 1992, *35*, 65–90.

Gregersen, H. B., and Black, J. S. "A Multifaceted Approach to Expatriate Retention in International Assignments." *Group and Organization Studies*, 1990, *15* (4), 461–485.

Gupta, A., and Govindarajan, V. "Knowledge Flows and the Structure of Control Within Multinational Corporations." *Academy of Management Review*, 1991, *16* (4), 768-792.

Hall, D. "How Top Management and the Organization Itself Can Block Effective Executive Succession." *Human Resource Management*, 1989, *28*, 5-24.

Hall, D. T., and Goodale, J. G. *Human Resource Management.* Glenview, Ill.: Scott, Foresman, 1986.

Hammer, M. R. "Behavioral Dimensions of Intercultural Effectiveness." *International Journal of Intercultural Relations*, 1987, *11*, 65-88.

Hammer, M. R., Gudykunst, J. E., and Wiseman, R. L. "Dimensions of Intercultural Effectiveness: An Exploratory Study." *International Journal of Intercultural Relations*, 1978, *2*, 382-393.

Harris, P. R., and Moran, R. *Managing Cultural Differences.* Houston: Gulf, 1989.

Harvey, M. "The Executive Family: An Overlooked Variable in International Assignments." *Columbia Journal of World Business*, 1985, *19*, 84-93.

Harvey, M. "The Other Side of Foreign Assignments: Dealing with the Repatriation Problem." *Columbia Journal of World Business*, 1983, *17*, 53-59.

Harvey, M. "Repatriation of Corporate Executives: An Empirical Study." *Journal of International Business Studies*, 1989, *20*, 131-144.

Hawes, F., and Kealey, D. J. "An Empirical Study of Canadian Technical Assistance." *International Journal of Intercultural Relations*, 1981, *5*, 239-258.

Hofstede, G. *Culture's Consequences: International Differences in Work-Related Values.* Newbury Park, Calif.: Sage, 1980.

Jackson, S., and Schuler, R. "A Meta-analysis and Conceptual Critique of Research on Role Ambiguity and Role Conflict in Work Settings." *Organizational Behavior and Human Decision Processes*, 1985, *36*, 16-78.

Jaeger, A. "Contrasting Control Modes in the Multinational Corporation: Theory, Practice, and Implications." *International Studies of Management and Organization*, 1982, *12* (1), 59-82.

Jelenik, M., and Adler, N. J. "Women: World-Class Managers for

Global Competition." *Academy of Management Executive,* 1988, *2,* 11-19.

Kainulainen, S. "Selection and Training of Personnel for Foreign Assignments." Unpublished master's thesis, University of Vaasa, Finland, 1990.

Kendall, D. W. "Repatriation: An Ending and a Beginning." *Business Horizons,* 1981, *24,* 21-25.

Kerr, S. "On the Folly of Rewarding *A* While Hoping for *B*." *Academy of Management Journal,* 1975, *18* (4), 769-783.

Kobrin, S. "Expatriate Reduction and Strategic Control in American Multinational Corporations." *Human Resource Management,* 1988, *27,* 63-75.

Korn-Ferry International. *A Study of the Repatriation of the American International Executive.* New York: Korn-Ferry International, 1981.

Kroeber, A. L., and Kluckhohn, C. *Culture: A Critical Review of Concepts and Definitions.* Cambridge, Mass.: Harvard University Press, 1952.

Lublin, J. "Grappling with Expatriate Issues." *Wall Street Journal,* Dec. 11, 1989, p. B1.

McGregor, D. *The Human Side of Enterprise.* New York: McGraw-Hill, 1960.

Manz, C. C., and Sims, H. P. "Vicarious Learning: The Influence of Modeling on Organizational Behavior." *Academy of Management Review,* 1981, *6,* 105-113.

Mathieu, J. E., and Zajac, D. M. "A Review and Meta-analysis of the Antecedents, Correlates, and Consequences of Organizational Commitment." *Psychological Bulletin,* 1990, *108,* 171-194.

Mendenhall, M., Dunbar, E., and Oddou, G. "Expatriate Selection, Training, and Career-Pathing." *Human Resource Management,* 1987, *26* (3), 331-345.

Mendenhall, M., and Oddou, G. "Acculturation Profiles of Expatriate Managers: Implications for Cross-Cultural Training Programs." *Columbia Journal of World Business,* 1986, *21,* 73-79.

Mendenhall, M., and Oddou, G. "The Dimensions of Expatriate Acculturation: A Review." *Academy of Management Review,* 1985, *10,* 39-47.

Miller, E. "The International Selection Decision: A Study of Managerial Behavior in the Selection Decision Process." *Academy of Management Journal,* 1973, *16* (2), 239-252.

Miller, E., Beechler, S., Bhatt, B., and Nath, R. "Relationship Between Global Strategic Planning Process and the Human Resource Management Function." *Human Resource Planning,* 1986, *9* (1), 9-23.

Misa, K. F., and Fabricatore, J. "Return on Investment of Overseas Personnel." *Financial Executive,* 1979, *47,* 42-46.

Moran, Stahl, & Boyer. *International Human Resource Management.* Boulder, Colo.: Moran, Stahl, & Boyer, 1987.

Mowday, R., Porter, L., and Steers, R. *Employee-Organization Linkages: The Psychology of Commitment, Absenteeism, and Turnover.* San Diego, Calif.: Academic Press, 1982.

Nakane, C. *Japanese Society.* Berkeley: University of California Press, 1970.

Napier, N. K., and Peterson, R. B. "Expatriate Re-entry: What Do Repatriates Have to Say?" *Human Resource Planning,* 1990, *14,* 19-28.

Negandi, A. R., Eshghi, G. S., and Yuen, E. C. "The Managerial Practices of Japanese Subsidiaries Overseas." *California Management Review,* 1985, *4,* 93-105.

Oddou, G., and Mendenhall, M. "Expatriate Performance Appraisal: Problems and Solutions." In M. Mendenhall and G. Oddou (eds.), *Readings and Cases in International Human Resource Management.* Boston: PWS-Kent, 1991.

Oddou, G., and Mendenhall, M. "Person Perception in Cross-Cultural Settings: A Review of Cross-Cultural and Related Literature." *International Journal of Intercultural Relations,* 1984, *8,* 77-96.

Oddou, G., and Mendenhall, M. "Succession Planning for the 21st Century: How Well Are We Grooming Our Future Business Leaders?" *Business Horizons,* 1991, *34,* 2-10.

O'Reilly, C., and Chatman, J. "Organizational Commitment and Psychological Attachment: The Effects of Compliance, Identification, and Internalization of Prosocial Behavior." *Journal of Applied Psychology,* 1983, *71,* 492-499.

Organization Resources Counselors. *1990 Survey of International*

Personnel and Compensation Practices. New York: Organization Resources Counselors, 1990.

Oslund, J. A. "The Overseas Experience of Expatriate Businesspeople." Paper presented at the annual meeting of the Academy of Management, Miami, 1991.

Ouchi, W. G. "A Conceptual Framework for the Design of Organizational Control Mechanisms." *Management Science*, 1979, *25*, 833-848.

Ouchi, W. G. "Markets, Bureaucracies, and Clans." *Administrative Science Quarterly*, 1980, *25*, 129-141.

Ouchi, W. G. "The Relationship Between Organizational Structure and Organizational Control." *Administrative Science Quarterly*, 1977, *22*, 95-113.

Porter, L., and McKibben, L. *Management Education and Development: Drift or Thrust into the 21st Century?* New York: McGraw-Hill, 1988.

Porter, M. "Changing Patterns of International Competition." *California Management Review*, 1986, *28* (2), 9-40.

Robinson, R. *International Business Management: A Guide to Decision Making.* Chicago: Dryden Press, 1978.

Roman, M., Mims, R., and Jespersen, F. "The Corporate Elite: A Portrait of the Boss." *Business Week*, Nov. 25, 1991, p. 182.

Ruben, I., and Kealey, D. J. "Behavioral Assessment of Communication Competency and the Prediction of Cross-Cultural Adaptation." *International Journal of Intercultural Relations*, 1979, *3*, 15-17.

Schein, E. "Coming to a New Awareness of Organizational Culture." *Sloan Management Review*, 1984, *10*, 3-16.

Stening, B. "Problems of Cross-Cultural Contact: A Literature Review." *International Journal of Intercultural Relations*, 1979, *3*, 269-313.

Stening, B., Everett, J., and Longton, L. "Mutual Perception of Managerial Performance and Style in Multinational Subsidiaries." *Journal of Occupational Psychology*, 1981, *54*, 255-263.

Stephens, G., and Black, J. S. "The Impact of the Spouse's Career Orientation on Managers During International Transfers." *Journal of Management Studies*, 1991, *28*, 417-428.

Torbiörn, I. *Living Abroad.* New York: Wiley, 1982.

Triandis, H. C., Vassilou, V., and Nassiakou, M. "Three Cross-Cultural Studies of Subjective Culture. Part Two." *Journal of Personality and Social Psychology*, 1968, *8* (4), 1-42.

Tung, R. "Career Issues in International Assignments." *Academy of Management Executive*, 1988, *2* (3), 241-244.

Tung, R. *The New Expatriates: Managing Human Resources Abroad*. New York: Ballinger, 1988.

Tung, R. "Selecting and Training of Personnel for Overseas Assignments." *Columbia Journal of World Business*, 1981, *16* (1), 68-78.

Tung, R. L. "Selection and Training Procedures of U.S., European, and Japanese Multinationals." *California Management Review*, 1982, *25*, 57-71.

Walker, E. J. "Till Business Us Do Part?" *Harvard Business Review*, 1976, *54*, 94-101.

White, M. *The Japanese Overseas*. New York: Free Press, 1988.

Zeira, Y., and Banai, M. "Selection of Managers for Foreign Posts." *International Studies of Management and Organization*, 1985, *15* (1), 33-51.

Index

Jon Werner